THE COMPLETE LIVING TRUSTS PROGRAM

THE COMPLETE LIVING TRUSTS PROGRAM

Martin M. Shenkman

John Wiley & Sons, Inc.
New York • Chichester • Weinheim • Brisbane • Singapore • Toronto

This book is printed on acid-free paper. ∞

Copyright © 2000 by Martin M. Shenkman. All rights reserved.

Published by John Wiley & Sons, Inc.

Published simultaneously in Canada.

No part of this publication may be reproduced, stored in a retrieval system or transmitted in any form or by any means, electronic, mechanical, photocopying, recording, scanning or otherwise, except as permitted under Section 107 or 108 of the 1976 United States Copyright Act, without either the prior written permission of the Publisher, or authorization through payment of the appropriate per-copy fee to the Copyright Clearance Center, 222 Rosewood Drive, Danvers, MA 01923, (978) 750-8400, fax (978) 750-4744. Requests to the Publisher for permission should be addressed to the Permissions Department, John Wiley & Sons, Inc., 605 Third Avenue, New York, NY 10158-0012, (212) 850-6011, fax (212) 850-6008, E-Mail: PERMREQ@WILEY.COM.

This publication is designed to provide accurate and authoritative information in regard to the subject matter covered. It is sold with the understanding that the publisher is not engaged in rendering professional services. If professional advice or other expert assistance is required, the services of a competent professional person should be sought.

Library of Congress Cataloging-in-Publication Data:

Shenkman, Martin M.
    The complete living trusts program / Martin M. Shenkman.
      p. cm.
    Includes index.
    ISBN 0-471-36105-4 (pbk. : alk. paper)
     1. Living trusts—United States—Popular works. I. Title.

KF734.Z9 S53 2000
346.7305′2—dc21   99-049450

Printed in the United States of America.

10 9 8 7 6 5 4 3 2 1

To my three sons: Yoni, Dovi, and Dan.
In memory of Saul Gerstenfeld, a friend lost too soon.

ACKNOWLEDGMENTS

Many thanks to Michael Hamilton of John Wiley & Sons, Inc. for providing his continued encouragement and support in the creation and execution of new ideas and books. To the staff and associates of my firm: Abby S., Laura, Naomi, Abby W., Amy, Seta, Lisette, Lee, Phyllis, Margaret, Dena, and Emilie, whose efforts and diligence enable me to continue writing. To my many clients whose confidence and trust have helped me continue to learn, and who, I hope, will benefit from the many ideas developed from the preparation of this book.

CONTENTS

Part One

INTRODUCTION

1 WHAT IS THE COMPLETE LIVING TRUSTS PROGRAM?

SKIP THE PUFFERY AND SNAKE OIL

A revocable inter vivos trust (sometimes called a *living trust* or *loving trust*) can be an effective estate and financial planning tool although too much of what you read is simply baloney, puffery, and snake oil. The cover of a widely used brochure about understanding living trusts screams the following in boldface type: **"How You Can Avoid Probate, Save Taxes and More."** You can avoid probate without a living trust, and in most states and for many (certainly not all and, maybe, not even most) estates, avoiding probate is just no big deal (that doesn't mean you don't need to protect yourself—just that avoiding probate isn't how you need to protect yourself). As a consumer, you're in a tough spot. The probate process can abuse your estate. It is not an exaggeration to say that many estates are grossly overcharged and receive inferior service from professionals. Likewise, an unscrupulous living trust industry has burgeoned to capitalize on consumers' fears of the probate process. Most trusts are poorly written, the planning undertaken is inadequate, and the misinformation (often intentional) surrounding them is shocking. In addition, people often pay inflated fees for substandard work.

What can you do? Get informed. If you understand how the probate process can abuse your estate, heirs, and loved ones and how the living trust boiler shops play on these fears—if you understand what is going on—you can protect yourself. This book will help you accomplish these goals. With the information in this book, the Law Made Easy Press web site (www.laweasy.com) sample forms, and the books recommended for additional information throughout this book, you can protect your estate from avoidable problems.

Since everyone seems to like short and simple lists of key points (most how-to books are down to single-digit lists of seven to nine steps to accomplish any task!), try the following procedures.

Seven Steps to Minimize Probate Abuse

1. Never name a lawyer, accountant, or other professional (except an institution) to be executor or trustee unless you have had a long and

close trusting relationship with the person. Anyone you name can always hire an attorney, accountant, or financial planner. If the professional pushes himself, go elsewhere.

2. Never pay (nor should your heirs) any lawyer or accountant for probate work except on an hourly basis and only when you receive a detailed bill that lists who performed the work, the date it was performed, the time spent, and the price. Abuse by professionals who have detailed invoices is significantly less than by those who make up bills after the fact based on what the professionals think they can get. If the professional cannot provide itemized bills, go elsewhere.

3. You must have a comprehensive estate and personal plan. No one approach, technique, or document can solve every problem. This means for everyone a minimum of powers of attorney, living will, and will, and for many a living trust. It means reviewing the title (ownership) of your assets, insurance coverage, investment decisions, and liability risks. Any professional who takes a narrow view or claims to be able to do everything, without the involvement of other professionals, isn't for you. Go elsewhere.

4. Tell your family that they are not legally obligated to use the lawyer who wrote your will. If the lawyer who wrote your will insists on being retained, go elsewhere.

5. Much of probate work is routine for someone with backup. Hire professionals who have staff at lower billing rates, or who have either automated their work or will bill at lower rates for work performed at a simple level. If a professional cannot reasonably address these issues, go elsewhere.

6. The more administrative matters your heirs handle, the cheaper the professionals' fees should be. If they don't bill this way, don't use them. If any professional discourages you or your heirs from handling routine matters when you are capable of doing so (this doesn't mean court proceedings or complex legal and tax matters), go elsewhere.

7. There are no unexplainable mysteries. Probate is not the *Twilight Zone*. If the attorney starts the Rod Serling routine, fire him! Some of the tax and legal concepts may be complex, but you should always receive general information (via phone calls, copies of letters, etc.) about everything that happens. If you're not being informed, complain and if there is no response after a reasonable time, fire the professionals. If your professional doesn't communicate, go elsewhere.

Seven Steps to Minimize Living Trust Abuse

1. Living trusts are not the answer to every problem. Anyone who advocates them as the panacea for all your worries is selling snake oil. Go elsewhere.

2. Living trusts don't save taxes (although as explained in detail in later chapters, lots of tax planning can be included in your Comprehensive

Living Trust Plan). Any professional or salesperson who tells you they do is wrong. Go elsewhere.

3. Estate planning to avoid taxes, to protect yourself in the event of disability, and to help your heirs and loved ones is a way to achieve positive goals. These are steps to take for "life," not just for death. Do not trust anyone who plays into your fears emphasizing the evils of probate while ignoring the overall picture. Go elsewhere.

4. What is the background of the person who is telling you about living trusts? Only an attorney whose practice is largely devoted to estate planning (notice that I didn't say living trusts) and who has substantial experience in estate planning can provide the services you need. This doesn't mean that you can't save a lot of money doing much of the work on your own (which is what this book will help you do); it means that when you're buying services, buy from an expert. If the person assuring you that a living trust is critical is an insurance salesperson or a living trust company sales representative, go elsewhere.

5. There's no free lunch. You attend a free seminar, eat free doughnuts, get a free pitch on the virtues of living trusts, and then get to have a free consultation with an estate planner. How are these people making their money? They make their money on the small percentage of people who actually retain them. Do you want that to be you? There is only one way to pay for all this "free" stuff. Everyone is simply billed more than the work costs to do to cover the extra expenses. Often, the documents produced are boilerplate—virtually the same for everyone. The planning is often limited. How else could these people pay for expensive newspaper advertisements, lots of doughnuts, and a hundred free consultations? Unless this is really where you want to be, go elsewhere.

6. Anyone recommending a living trust should give you a balanced view. What are the problems with living trusts as they pertain to your personal situation? What alternatives may better achieve your goals? If the perspective isn't balanced, go elsewhere.

7. If the person recommending the living trust also wants to serve as trustee, make sure you have had a long, close, and trusting relationship with the person; otherwise, go elsewhere.

Avoiding probate is not likely to be your primary goal. Your true goals probably include assuring that most of your assets reach your intended heirs as quickly and cost-effectively as possible. Avoiding probate is only coincidentally related to accomplishing this goal.

It is not the probate process that you need to avoid, but rather the abuses that can occur.

NOTE: Too many professionals involved with estate planning and probate view your estate plan as their retirement plan. You need to understand how to protect yourself and your loved ones. This book will tell you how.

EXAMPLE: We recently investigated a probate matter handled by another lawyer, a longtime practitioner with what appeared to be a respectable reputation. The attorney had prepared a will that was an instance of complete malpractice. No contingent beneficiary was named (if the one person named to receive assets had died, the estate would have been distributed through intestacy; the will would have been worthless). No tax planning was done, which ultimately would cost the family 50 percent of the money involved (50 percent of what was left after the lawyer finished pillaging the estate, that is). This situation could have been easily avoided through a simple trust, or even by the naming of a successor beneficiary. The attorney did take great care, however, to name his nephew as executor. The nephew then appointed the uncle as attorney to represent the estate. The two of them took fees in excess of 7 percent of the estate, plus extras. The nephew then hired his wife as the broker to sell the decedent's house. All told, the lawyer's family took 12 plus percent of the estate. Their combined fees were about 20 times what the hourly cost should have been for the little work they did. Sound bad? It was worse. They did almost nothing properly. They withheld distributing estate assets for more than 1½ years. Other than increasing their fees, it was hard to identify any reason for the delay. The decedent's securities were all liquidated and the money placed in CDs at low interest rates for the entire period. During this time period, the country experienced one of the greatest bull markets in history. The family lost out on it all. Bank charges and other avoidable expenses were regularly incurred. The bills for legal services and the listing of services purportedly provided by the executor were so contrived as to be silly. Does this sound bad enough yet? Well, there's more. We went to court to object to what had been done. The court not only didn't care (gotta protect the old boy's club, ya know!), the court permitted the attorney to continue billing the estate for the time supposedly spent in court (which, mind you, was for the sole purpose of objecting to the attorney's family pillaging the decedent's estate). It was also enlightening to watch how this attorney used his time in court. The attorney sat in the court waiting for the case to be called for three hours, all of which he billed to the estate. He couldn't have brought other work to do while waiting, that would have been too fair. So he sat and did nothing while his "clock ticked" at the expense of the family. The cost of challenging these abuses is usually expensive, with no assurance that the court will be any more objective or fair than the abusive attorney, making a challenge generally fruitless. The result—unethical professionals can pillage your estate if you don't protect your loved ones.

Again, a living trust, contrary to anything living trust hucksters tell you, is absolutely not necessary to save estate taxes. A living trust provides tax savings through including a bypass (applicable exclusion) trust and a marital deduction or marital trust (QTIP or QDOT). These techniques can be more easily accomplished with less expense through your will.

This book explains how to use the living trust technique as part of a comprehensive estate plan to achieve your personal goals. It will show you how to distinguish hucksters from helpful expert advisers.

EXAMPLE: A client came to me for a consultation. Her son in California was concerned about an estate plan for his parents. In good faith and with the best of intentions, he hired a firm specializing in living trusts to help. They prepared a complex package of documents, including a lengthy "A-B" living trust. The "A-B" living trust indicates the bypass (applicable exclusion) marital trust estate planning arrangement (explained at length in Chapter 9). What were the facts in this case? The father had Alzheimer's disease. The mother was in her 80s. The entire estate was under $400,000. An "A-B" living trust was completely unnecessary. The family needed elder law planning to address their current situation. The basic estate planning documents they had before the "living trust experts" became involved probably would have sufficed. What did this package of worthless documents cost? A cool $5,000. Repeated calls for three weeks to the firm that prepared these documents failed to reach an attorney. This client was one of far too many people scammed by the living trust industry.

EXAMPLE: Another client inquired about a family limited partnership. Why? Only about 18 months before, he had purchased a living trust "plan" for about $2,500 from a firm that advertised on the radio. The fancy leatherette binder with his family name engraved in gold letters was a sure sign of problems to come. A glossy cover is usually a sign of less inside. At age 48, the client did not need a living trust (see the following discussion). What was necessary? What were the assets in this client's estate? Three rental apartment buildings. Why was the client inquiring about a family limited partnership? He had heard it would protect his assets against lawsuits. He had just lost a lawsuit over a tenant injury at one of his buildings. Since he and his wife jointly and personally owned all these properties, their buildings and assets were reachable by the tenant. Instead of having spent money on a living trust, the "lawyers" he hired should have formed a separate limited liability company for each building. This might have succeeded in insulating each property from the others and insulating all the buildings from their other assets (e.g., home, mutual funds). The living trust did no harm, but it failed to address the most important and obvious (to any skilled attorney) needs.

What's the lesson to learn from this example? Whatever you do, don't buy a living trust from anyone who sells living trusts. If you believe, after reviewing the discussions in this book, that a living trust would benefit you, as it likely may, retain a skilled estate planner. Never hire anyone who claims to be a specialist in living trusts. It makes no sense and you will never receive the quality legal work you need. Then again, don't forget the probate horror story discussed earlier. You must still protect your loved ones from abuses of unscrupulous professionals involved in the probate process. You can use the information provided here to substantially reduce the costs of legal fees and improve the quality of your planning by being an informed consumer. That is the goal of this book.

WHY I HAVE A LIVING TRUST

When someone appears to be selling you something, don't you wonder whether the person even uses it? Do those buff models on late-night cable really use those weird abdominal machines?

AUTHOR'S STRATEGY: Do I have a living trust or am I just trying to sell a book? While I've never written about my personal legal arrangements in any book before, all the hype about living trusts made me want to do it here. I hope that providing this information will give additional credibility to this book and enable you to resist overstated confidence in the advertisements, unscrupulous attorneys, living trusts salespeople, and the like. So here it is. I have a living trust, so do many members in my family. But don't jump to conclusions. My family's living trusts are used differently from most living trusts I see in my law practice.

My living trust is only one component of my estate plan. If you have or obtain a living trust—that's all it should be for you. A living trust can be the centerpiece of your estate plan, with all the other documents and planning coordinated with it. Even so, it is only one of many documents you need, and you can obtain most of the benefits you need from these other documents without a living trust. I have, as should you, a will, a durable power of attorney, and living will/health care proxy (see Chapter 7). I've prepared an emergency medical form for my children (if you have minor children you should, too). My law practice is organized as a professional corporation (although under current law I may have chosen a limited liability company, a form of entity that didn't exist when I started) (see Part Five).

To achieve the most effective and beneficial use of a revocable living trust, you should consolidate as many personal assets as you can with a single major institution. That institution is then named as successor co-trustee (i.e., to serve as trustee after you, along with a family member or close friend). This approach assures a simple, quick, efficient, and safe transition in the event of disability or death. It assures that assets will not be dissipated by a dishonest or careless family member or friend because the institutional trustee will control the finances. It assures that unethical professionals will not be able to pillage your estate since they will be subject to the oversight of the institution. It assures that you don't overly impose on the time of family and friends, all of whom are busy with their own families, lives, and careers. The institution as co-trustee can handle much of the paperwork and administrative burden.

NOTE: If your trust names an institution as a trustee, be sure to have the lawyer include a provision giving the beneficiaries or a specially appointed person (called a "trust protector") the right to change institutions periodically. This will provide the leverage to encourage the institution to act responsively. It also provides the flexibility to appoint another institution if necessary.

AUTHOR'S STRATEGY: I've used the same approach for my living trust. Almost all of my family's bank, brokerage, and other accounts have been consolidated at one institution. This assures that my family and friends can direct their time and effort where it's most important—to assure the safety and security of myself and my family, and to address the personal issues that an institution can't handle. I'd much rather have family and friends focus on personal issues than waste their limited time on administrative matters which a bank or trust company can do a better job of anyway.

You should understand what living trusts will and will not do and realize what you'll be getting. Unlike my approach, the way most people use living trusts won't achieve more than a properly planned durable power of attorney, living will, and will (all of which you need anyway). Even if you do it right, a living trust is not always worth including in your estate plan.

A living trust is an effective and useful estate planning tool. However, unless your estate is substantial or your income large enough to absorb the cost of documentation ($1,000 to $2,000) without concern, the benefits must outweigh the costs. Chapter 2 provides a comprehensive listing of the pros and cons of living trusts. To analyze the benefits, however, you need to understand the contents of this book. So what's the bottom-line answer? Living trusts are a useful estate planning tool. If the cost is not significant to you, use them. If the cost is significant, weigh the pros and cons to determine whether your personal circumstances warrant the expense. For some it will. For many, it will be better to spend the money on a vacation instead of a lawyer's fee to draft a living trust. Because hype and misinformation abound, everyone should understand what a living trust will and won't do.

AUTHOR'S STRATEGY: There is an obvious difference between my using a living trust and your family using one. I didn't have to pay a legal fee for the trust document, I did it myself. Unless you are a lawyer or someone in your family is a lawyer (but then again your relative would probably charge!), you probably will have to pay. Thus, while living trusts can be a useful part of an overall plan, the benefits need to outweigh the costs. I had no costs. What costs will you incur? I like and use living trusts to protect my own family, but I am not selling you a bill of goods: you must make your own decision. This book will give you the knowledge to do so.

THE COMPLETE LIVING TRUSTS PROGRAM

The Complete Living Trusts Program provides a comprehensive treatment of living trusts with a balanced view of the topic, not the puffery heard in the market, or the "anti-living-trust" view many planners espouse. A revocable living trust can be a useful estate, tax, financial planning, asset management, and personal planning tool. A living trust will only achieve your goals, however, if you use it as a cornerstone of a comprehensive plan, not as the sole, or even primary, solution to your needs, as so many living trust books and seminars suggest. The Complete Living Trusts Program described here integrates a complete range of tax planning, in phases, so that you need only select the level of complexity appropriate for your circumstances. The program also explains, again for circumstances of varying complexity, what additional documents you require and how to integrate them into your living trust plan. For the simplest estates, this may require a will, power, and living will. For larger estates or estates with more complicated circumstances, additional trusts for insurance and minor beneficiaries may be warranted. For extremely large and complex estates, a broad range of sophisticated tax, asset protection, business, and other documents and planning steps may have to be integrated. Again, the objective of the program is to help you select the level of sophistication that best meets your needs with the least cost and least number of documents. To better understand the phases of the Complete Living Trusts Program, an overview of living trusts is first presented.

WHY SET UP A REVOCABLE LIVING TRUST?

The reasons to set up a revocable living trust for yourself include providing for management of your assets in the event you need assistance or are disabled and avoiding probate (or at least ancillary probate in states other than the one in which you permanently reside). Estate tax benefits are generally not a primary goal when you set up a trust for yourself. This is not to say, however, that such a trust will not provide tax benefits.

EXAMPLE: You set up a living (inter vivos) revocable trust for yourself, naming yourself as the trustee during your life and prior to your disability. On your death, the first $650,000 (1999 figure, scheduled to increase to $1 million by 2006) of your assets held in your trust are transferred to an applicable exclusion trust (formerly referred to as a credit shelter trust) for the benefit of your surviving spouse and children. Where the combined estate of you and your spouse exceeds $650,000, this approach can reduce, and perhaps eliminate, any federal estate tax. However, these tax benefits do not require you to use a living trust. They can be provided under a will (see Chapter 2).

WHAT IS A REVOCABLE LIVING TRUST?

A living trust is a trust that you set up during your lifetime. Unless and until you become disabled, you retain complete control over the assets in the trust while you are alive. For tax purposes, the trust is generally ignored and all income and deductions are reported on your own Form 1040 tax return (see Chapter 20). If you become disabled or infirm, a successor (alternate) trustee takes over managing your assets (although it can be preferable to have that additional trustee serve as a co-trustee before you become disabled). On your death, provisions that serve the same purpose as a will apply to govern the disposition of your assets. Since there is no current tax benefit in setting up a living trust, you can use a flexible format to meet a broad range of personal objectives. This section will explore the benefits, as well as possible drawbacks, of using living trusts.

In the appropriate circumstances, living trusts can be an ideal vehicle to accomplish many essential planning goals. In inappropriate circumstances, they can be a waste of time and money, and may create unnecessary hassles and complications in managing your affairs. In the worst-case scenarios, you may use a revocable living trust when another technique would have been more appropriate. The results could be disastrous as one of the case studies above illustrates.

Before deciding whether to use a trust, you should be fully aware of all the benefits and costs of establishing one. The following discussion will summarize these factors and dispel the myth that a living trust can solve all your problems. It won't.

CAUTION: The most important point to remember is that no single estate planning step can solve every problem. Whatever the hot item of the day—family limited partnership, living trust, charitable remainder trust, or any other technique—no single step can possibly address all your needs. The only approach to use, no matter how much or little money you have, or how simple your situation may be, is a comprehensive estate, financial, insurance, and tax plan. Nothing less will provide you with the comfort that you have best addressed all the needs of you and your loved ones. A comprehensive plan doesn't have to be a big deal. A single consultation with a skilled estate planner may be all you need to map out your overall plan. If your means are limited, a bit of creativity and good judgment in identifying essentials can limit the costs. If your estate is large or your circumstances complex, you can use this initial meeting to outline a plan that you can then implement in phases with the necessary professionals.

REQUIREMENTS FOR A VALID TRUST

The discussion of revocable living trusts involves the use of the italicized terms in the following sentence. A trust is generally formed when a person called the *"grantor"* transfers assets, called *"trust property"* or the *"res,"* to a person who will manage the property in trust, called the *"trustee,"* to hold for the benefit of the *beneficiary,* the person for whom the income and principal of the trust is to be used, in accordance with the purpose, or *"intent,"* of the trust. These terms refer to basic requirements for such trusts that are described in the subsequent paragraphs.

Grantor

The person who transfers the trust property to the trust is the grantor, also commonly called the trustor, settlor, or donor. The grantor must generally be the owner of the property that is transferred to the trust. The grantor must also have the proper legal capacity to sign the trust agreement and to transfer assets to the trust. This means that the grantor must be of sound mind and have the intent to form a trust. This intent of the grantor to form a trust must be manifested, generally in the form of a written and signed trust agreement.

In the context of a living trust, you are almost always the grantor. Occasionally spouses may be co-grantors jointly funding one trust. Successor trustees might include your spouse (if not named as an initial co-trustee), a child or other trusted friend or family member, or institution.

AUTHOR'S STRATEGY: I've used a major financial institution as a co-trustee with a list of family members and friends.

Trust Property

This is the principal or subject matter of the trust. It is also called the trust "res." Property is transferred to the revocable living trust on formation when a funded trust is intended. A living trust, in contrast to most irrevocable trusts, is often formed without any assets and with no intent of transferring assets to it for some time. In other cases, you may establish a living trust to receive property at some future date, but none presently. This is called an *unfunded* or *standby* trust (see Chapter 6). When you set up a standby trust, you form the trust now but do not transfer the intended assets until some future date, such as your disability (via a durable power of attorney) or on death (via a pour-over will). Chapter 6 includes a discussion of funded trusts versus unfunded trusts.

AUTHOR'S STRATEGY: My living trust is funded with assets now. In the event of an emergency or disability, it is difficult to get the full benefits of a living trust unless you have consolidated your assets and funded it before the crisis occurs.

In most living trusts, a formal legal description of the trust property is attached to the end of the trust as a schedule. Merely listing the asset in a schedule attached to a trust is not really enough to transfer ownership of that asset to the trust. For real estate, a deed must be filed transferring ownership (title) of the property to the trust. For personal property, a bill of sale may be required (see Chapter 6).

Trustee

The trustee is responsible for managing and administering your trust. As the initial trustee (or co-trustee), you should make a declaration—often by signing the trust agreement—that you accept the trust property as trustee. Specify successor trustees should you become unable to serve as a trustee. The choice of trustees is not always simple and obvious and can change at different points of complexity in the trusts being used, to meet certain legal requirements, and so on. The selection of the trustee or trustees (called co-trustees when two or more persons serve simultaneously) is discussed often in this book. In some states, you might need a co-trustee (or beneficiaries other than yourself) to avoid a legal snag called a *merger* that could invalidate your trust. Consult with your estate planning attorney to address this possibility.

AUTHOR'S STRATEGY: I'm my own initial trustee. A bank and a list of family members and friends will serve as successor trustees. Thus the bank and one family member or friend will always be serving. Having someone serve as a co-trustee with you, from the beginning can, however, be a better approach for many.

Beneficiary

The beneficiary is the person, or persons, designated to receive the benefits and advantages of the property transferred to the trust. In most revocable living trusts, you are the initial beneficiary. However, you may name certain key family members or friends as additional beneficiaries in the event of your disability. This is important. If you are disabled and cannot support these important people and fail to make provisions, how will they be provided for?

Intent of Trust

Every trust has a purpose, or intent, that motivates the grantor to set it up. At minimum, you must intend to create a fiduciary relationship as to certain assets for yourself and other beneficiaries of the trust.

Apart from the obvious requirement that the intent must be legal, there are few restrictions on the grantor's intent. It can relate to:

- Benefiting a particular beneficiary (yourself, your spouse or partner, your child, a cousin, your favorite charity, or some combination of these).
- Providing for the management of certain assets (real estate, mutual funds, stock in a closely held corporation).
- Achieving certain tax benefits such as a bypass trust to preserve your $650,000 (1999) applicable exclusion amount, and a marital trust to utilize the estate tax marital deduction.

You can use a living trust to achieve all of these objectives, as well as others. The intent of the trust is usually spelled out in detail in the trust document. Where the trust document is silent, state laws and court cases may fill in some of the blanks.

Steps That Are Not Necessary to Make Your Trust Effective

A written trust document is required to transfer realty to the trust. Practically speaking, however, a written trust agreement should be used in all instances. Few of the many benefits you want will be achieved without a comprehensive written document.

Although the grantor and trustee must sign the trust, there is no requirement to deliver a copy of the trust agreement to anyone for it to become effective. Practically, however, a copy of the trust, or a memorandum of trust (explained in Chapter 6) must be delivered to those banks and other persons who will work with the trust. Another practical consideration is that if your successor trustee (the person, or persons, serving as trustee in the event of your disability or death) does not have a copy of the trust document, assuming control when necessary will be much more difficult. This lapse could defeat one of the most important benefits of a properly structured living trust, seamless management through your illness and disability. Many people prefer to have successor trustees sign the original trust document agreeing to serve.

AUTHOR'S STRATEGY: I've given organized copies of all my key documents to my bank, accountant, parents, and my closest friend. There is nothing deep, dark, and personal in any of the documents (if only life were so exciting). But I know from experience with clients that when an emergency strikes, the people you are counting on to act, often cannot find the documents and don't know their responsibilities. To avoid this, I've also reviewed with several of the previously named people what the documents do, what their responsibilities are, and so forth. It takes very little time and costs nothing, but it can make a tremendous difference.

There is no requirement to transfer any assets to your living trust. This is called an unfunded trust. However, the responsibility may then fall on a successor trustee to transfer assets in the event of your death or disability. This delay would also defeat the objective of seamless management through your illness, disability, or death (see the discussion of funding in Chapter 6).

FIVE PHASES OF LIVING TRUSTS

The following information will help you select the trust that best suits your goals and circumstances. Table 1.1 is a summary chart illustrating the levels of sophistication in the Complete Living Trusts Program. The following sections explain each phase in greater detail. The later parts of this book then expand this information by describing the steps in each phase, the tax issues to consider, the planning vehicles and entitles you may need, and so forth.

Foundation Living Trust

This is the basic living trust document. Many of the provisions and decisions in this living trust must be addressed for any estate regardless of size or complexity. The living trust agreement used as part of the Foundation Living Trust for smaller or simpler estates, as well as the ancillary documents required (power of attorney, living will/health care proxy, and pour-over will), are used as the building blocks, or foundation, for all other more comprehensive living trusts, hence the title "Foundation Living Trust." The Foundation Living Trust is intended to provide for management of assets in the event of disability, minimization of probate issues, and so forth.

Just-in-Case (Disclaimer) Living Trust

Most living trust programs and estate planning documents generally assume that if your combined estate (i.e., your estate added to that of your spouse) is less than the $650,000 (1999) applicable exclusion amount, tax planning (typically in the form of a bypass trust) is not necessary. This is a

Table 1.1 Phases of the Complete Living Trusts Program

Phase	Is this Phase of Living Trust for You?	Planning Issues Addressed	Cautions
1. Foundation	No unusual risks or issues. Estate will not be taxable.	Disability; management of assets, probate avoidance; organization.	Don't underestimate your liability risks in such a litigious society. Don't underestimate the possibility of a tax problem.
2. Just-in-Case	Your estate, or your spouse's, may be taxable. Protecting your surviving spouse's assets from claimants, a new spouse, or disability might be important.	Tax savings and asset protection if necessary.	Will your surviving spouse be willing to disclaim?
3. Family Tax Planning	Tax planning to preserve each spouse's applicable exclusion is important. Protecting assets for particular heirs from future claimants, etc. is important (QTIP/QDOT).	Mandatory tax savings; trusts to manage and protect surviving spouse's assets.	Assets must be owned in proper title to enable planning to be effective.
4. Multigeneration	Size of your estate or your unusual risks warrant asset protection and tax planning for children or other heirs.	Continue tax, legal, and other planning into the next generation, and perhaps later, generations.	GST planning is complex and generally requires the use of long-term irrevocable trusts that create costs and additional paperwork.
5. Comprehensive	Asset protection, control, addressing of complex business and legal issues, and more sophisticated tax planning are necessary.	Business, legal, tax, and related planning.	You will multiply the tax reporting requirements, the legal paperwork, and other administrative matters that must be addressed to achieve the desired benefits.

potentially costly, and often inappropriate, conclusion. Using this gauge, you might be able to ignore tax planning if your estate is estimated at about $600,000. However, what if you underestimated the value of certain assets? What if you forgot to include a particular asset? What if you inherit assets, win a lottery, or pick a hot stock? What if Congress changes the law and reduces the applicable exclusion amount to raise revenues? Will inflation alone push your estate into a taxable bracket? If your estate then exceeds the applicable exclusion amount, a tax will be due. In some cases, the solution is a disclaimer bypass trust. This distribution scheme provides that all assets are distributed to the surviving spouse outright. If your surviving spouse disclaims (files the required documents with the probate or surrogate's court within nine months of your death), then the assets disclaimed are distributed into a bypass trust. This preserves the benefit of the applicable exclusion and provides the opportunity to save estate taxes just in case it becomes necessary. Hence the title "Just-in-Case Living Trust."

The disclaimer bypass trust is important for more than estate tax planning. If the surviving spouse remarries, assets held in a bypass trust will have a significant measure of protection from the new spouse. The trust will assure that the remaining assets will ultimately be distributed to your heirs, not to the new spouse. If your surviving spouse is disabled, the assets can be managed in the structure of the bypass trust. In the event of a lawsuit or claim against your surviving spouse, the assets may be protected within the trust. For all these reasons, and because a word processor drastically reduces the time it takes to do the work, attorneys rarely, if ever, should prepare a living trust or will without at least a disclaimer bypass trust.

NOTE: If you have an existing trust without a bypass or at least a disclaimer bypass trust, call the lawyer who prepared it and ask why. If the answer isn't satisfactory, it may be a warning about the quality of the rest of your trust and plan. Consider at least having a consultation with another estate planner to determine how well you are protected.

Family Tax Planning Living Trust

If your estate is large enough to warrant estate tax planning then your living trust should be structured to provide for a bypass trust, with the balance of any asset being distributed outright to your surviving spouse or in a marital (QTIP or QDOT) trust. These two trusts (sometimes referred to as "A-B" Trusts) provide a tax plan that enables most otherwise taxable family estates to minimize, or entirely escape, federal estate taxation. Hence, this living trust is referred to as the "Family Tax Planning Living Trust."

If your estate is larger than the applicable exclusion amount, additional tax planning may be necessary. The two most common tax planning techniques are to remove the value of life insurance from the value of your taxable estate by forming a life insurance trust to own your insurance. This separate trust must be independent of your living trust. It is also an irrevocable trust, so unlike your living trust, it cannot be changed once established. The second most common step to reduce taxes is generally to make gifts using the annual gift tax exclusion. This permits you to make gifts of $10,000 (the amount to be indexed for inflation) to anyone you choose. If you plan to make significant or ongoing gifts, especially if the donee is a minor, establishing an irrevocable trust protects the donee by holding the assets. This type of trust is typically a child or minor's trust (although the donee doesn't need to be your child or even a minor).

If you are not married, or have a partner instead of a spouse, then this estate tax planning structure may not be appropriate for you. At minimum, modifications will be necessary.

The Family Tax Planning Living Trust builds on the Foundation Living Trust and the planning contained in the Just-in-Case Living Trust.

Multigenerational (GST) Living Trust

If your estate is large enough to make it likely that your heirs will face a significant estate tax on their death, it may be advisable for you to plan your estate by minimizing the overall transfer tax burden over several generations of people. The basic approach to this type of tax planning is to have assets held in trust for the life of your children or other heirs. You allocate your generation-skipping transfer (GST) tax exemption (about $1 million but scheduled to be increased for inflation) to some portion or all of these trusts. The assets so protected can then be passed by your heirs onto their heirs free of estate tax. The estate tax savings over several generations can be significant, hence the title "Multigenerational Living Trust."

This type of planning has many benefits in addition to merely saving taxes. It can provide a significant level of asset protection from your heirs' claimants and even divorcing spouses. It can control your heirs' access to assets in a manner that encourages them to become and remain productive members of society—an attribute that a large inheritance received too quickly can destroy. If an heir becomes incapacitated, the trust structure provides an ideal mechanism to protect assets for your heirs. All these benefits mean that you will be providing greater flexibility to your heirs, not necessarily restricting or controlling them. Thus, this type of planning can be appropriate even if your estate is not sufficiently large to warrant GST planning.

Comprehensive Living Trust

This is the final stage or level of living trust planning. If your estate is significantly larger than the applicable exclusion amount, more sophisticated tax planning may be necessary. Since each level or phase of living trust in the Complete Living Trusts Program builds on the prior phases, it is assumed that if life insurance and a life insurance trust, or annual gifts and possibly trusts for children, were warranted, they will have already been addressed. Thus, at this phase of planning you should evaluate additional and more complex tax planning techniques. These will almost always require the formation of entities and/or trusts independent from your living trust.

Even if your estate is not substantial in size, significant risks from malpractice, divorce, or other sources, or unusual personal or business problems may necessitate additional planning. This will often take the form of creating additional entities, such as limited liability companies or family limited partnerships to hold certain assets. These entities can limit liability, secure control, provide income and estate tax savings, and achieve other benefits.

The living trust books and seminars that have proliferated tend to supply at most a footnote to these techniques, or ignore them completely. To properly address all your personal, tax, legal, and financial goals, you must include these techniques. The Comprehensive Living Trust Program does this, and shows you how to integrate these planning measures with your overall living trust program.

SIX STAGES IN THE LIFE OF YOUR LIVING TRUST: HOW A LIVING TRUST WORKS

The best way to understand how a living trust works is to review the phases in the life cycle of a typical revocable living trust.

Phase 1. Formation

After a complete review of your tax, estate, financial, and personal goals and your current personal circumstances, you should formulate a comprehensive plan with your advisers. Where a revocable living trust is an appropriate component of this plan, you should retain a lawyer to draft the trust. The trust should be signed, witnessed, and notarized. Copies of the trust should be given to your professionals: accountant, financial planner, broker, insurance adviser, and successor trustee. These people will be helpful, if not critical, in assisting you to properly transfer assets to your trust, but remember it's your responsibility to assure assets are transferred. Assets should then be transferred to your trust, as described in detail in Chapter 6. Your accountant should receive a copy of your trust to include in your permanent file of important documents. Also, your accountant will likely be assisting your family in the event of your death or disability, and it will be helpful to have a copy of your trust on file. These scenarios are addressed in Part Three of this book and are common to all living trusts.

Phase 2. Management Prior to Your Disability

Once your living trust is formed and funded, you will continue to manage the assets in your trust as if they were your own, with one formal or technical difference—transactions affecting trust assets will be completed in the name of the trust. You will sign trust checks and buy stock in your trust's name, in your capacity as trustee (or co-trustee). These scenarios are addressed in Part Three of this book and are common to all living trusts.

NOTE: John Doe sets up the John Doe Revocable Living Trust on January 14, 2001. When John buys assets or signs checks on the trust checking account, the format should be "John Doe, Trustee, of the John Doe Revocable Living Trust dated 1/14/01." Signature lines on contracts must be signed in the following manner:

JOHN DOE REVOCABLE LIVING TRUST

By:_____

John Doe, Trustee

[You then sign on the above line. This formality is important for all trusts. If the document you are signing has only a single signature line, you should then write in the necessary information and lines using the approach shown here.]

Phase 3. You Become Disabled

If you become disabled and cannot manage your personal affairs, then your successor trustee (or successor co-trustees if you named two persons to serve) will take over the management of your trust assets. If instead you named an initial co-trustee who has served from the beginning with you, that co-trustee, and the next successor co-trustee appointed in the trust document, will then together manage the trust assets on your behalf. At this time, your agent, acting under your durable power of attorney may transfer any assets that you then own in your own name (i.e., which were not previously transferred to the trust) to your living trust. The disability provisions in your living trust will be vitally important for determining when this switch occurs, and when you may resume control of the management of your trust assets if you recover. These are important considerations since disability can frequently be temporary and short term.

Few living trusts contain detailed rules for determining when disability occurs and ends. This is ironic because one of the primary benefits of a living trust is the management of assets without court intervention if you are disabled; yet, a trust document without clear tests may require court involvement. If you have a living trust, review those sections—if they are not clear and comprehensive, contact the attorney who prepared the document and find out why. It just may be a sign you went to the wrong person.

An important part of the disability provisions of your living trust is detailed instructions for your care in the event of disability. Many "form" trusts do not provide personalized detail. Do you want to avoid placement in a nursing home as long as possible? What type of health care facility do you prefer if placement becomes necessary? If religious or geographic preferences are important to you, you should specify in your living trust that in the event of your disability you want to be placed in a facility located in a certain part of the country (perhaps near your family); if religious preferences are important, you perhaps should specify that the health care facility be near a church, mosque, or synagogue so that you can attend services, or that the facility must meet your religious dietary requirements. Do not assume that your trustees "will know." Specifying such details may be vital depending on who the trustees are. This detail can also enable them to respond to a challenge by your heirs as to the appropriateness of the trustees' decisions and expenditures. These details distinguish a living trust from simple reliance on a durable power of attorney, which almost never includes this level of personalized and detailed instruction. Thus, those who argue that living trusts are never necessary, advocating instead a durable power of attorney, miss the point.

Which of your family and loved ones can the trustee spend money to care for if you are disabled? This is another critical and typically overlooked part of a living will.

EXAMPLE: A young woman had comprehensive estate planning documents prepared by a large law firm at considerable expense. She had almost no immediate family, just herself and her aging and ill mother. Her estate was substantial, and her two primary concerns were care for herself and her mother. In the event of illness, a durable power of attorney enabled her nephew to act as her agent. Would the nephew really do what was best for her, or would he perhaps spend less money on her to preserve his eventual inheritance? Even if the nephew was willing to spend every last penny to care for the mother, consistent with the woman's wishes, could he? The power of attorney did not authorize any expenditures for the mother! The solution is a living trust with an institution to serve as co-trustee with the nephew. Explicit provisions should be included in the trust specifying that the best medical and other care should be provided to both daughter and mother. This approach fills in the gap in the existing documents assuring care for her and her mother if she became disabled.

These scenarios are addressed in the "Foundation Living Trust" in Part Three of this book and are common to all living trusts.

Phase 4. After Your Death

Your trust will no longer be revocable once you die. On your death, the provisions of your living trust will be implemented by the successor trustee named in your trust. These provisions could include the outright distribution of property to intended beneficiaries (such as adult children), or the establishment (or continuation) of one or several trusts, as provided in your revocable living trust. For example, the Family Tax Planning Living Trust will typically include a bypass trust to preserve the tax benefits of the applicable exclusion amount, a marital trust to qualify for the unlimited marital deduction while still protecting and controlling the assets involved, and one or more children or grandchildren trusts. Several of the other types of trust described throughout this book can be incorporated into your living trust to take effect following your death.

EXAMPLE: The only way to know which types of trust are appropriate for inclusion in your living trust is to complete a comprehensive analysis of your overall estate, financial, insurance, and personal planning. The diversity of trusts, and combinations of different trusts, is why it can be so dangerous to rely on "self-help" trust books. No single form that purports to be adaptable by all readers of a book could possibly give everyone the optimal combination of trust arrangements to meet their unique goals. Consider the many planning techniques discussed in Parts Four and Five as examples.

At this point, any assets that were not already transferred to your trust (either by you when you formed the trust, at a later date by you or by someone making a gift to you, or by your agent under your durable power of attorney after your disability) can be transferred under what is known as a pour-over will. The key provision of this will is that any assets you may have owned at your death which were not already in your trust should be transferred (or poured over into) your trust. Most pour-over wills are inadequate to protect your heirs. They are a few pages long and provide little more than a few statements appointing an executor and guardian (if you have minor children) and pouring assets into your trust. If all goes as planned, this simplistic approach may work. But you wouldn't be reading this book or going through the trouble of planning your estate for contingencies, or buying insurance, if you knew everything would go as planned. You're taking precautions because you know that often life's events unfold in unexpected ways. The "Safe-Keeper Will" recommended in this book includes a pour-over provision similar to those included in most pour-over wills. However, it has a complete listing of all the dispositive provisions in your living trust (the statements as to how your assets are to be distributed). This is essential if for any reason your living trust is found to be invalid or you revoke it (see Chapter 7). The Safe-Keeper Will also includes a full range of powers granted to your executor. If there are any issues facing your estate, these powers may be important. For example, significant or unusual assets, claims, or litigation may affect your estate. Your executor will be helped by having a broad and detailed list of powers. The simplistic pour-over wills most people use with living trusts will not suffice. These scenarios are addressed in the "Foundation Living Trust" in Part Two of this book.

If your estate is large enough, on your death assets from your Foundation Living Trust will be distributed further into a bypass trust and perhaps a marital QTIP trust. These scenarios are addressed in the "Family Tax Planning Living Trust" in Part Three of this book and are common to many living trusts.

If asset protection, divorce protection, asset management, or other goals warrant further planning, the techniques described in Part Four of this book for the "Comprehensive Living Trust Program" should be considered.

Phase 5. After Your Spouse's Death

If you are married, assets will typically be distributed to children or other residuary (secondary) heirs after the death of your spouse. If your estate was large enough to warrant the use of a bypass trust and a marital (QTIP) trust (both explained in detail in Chapter 9, these trusts may terminate. In many estates, on the death of the last of you and your spouse, the trust assets are distributed from the bypass and marital trusts outright to the children, free of any further trust. If the children are too young, the assets may stay in trust until the children (or grandchildren, or other minor heirs) attain a specified age, say 35. Thereupon, the assets would be distributed to the beneficiary outright. These scenarios are addressed in the "Family Tax Planning Living Trust" in Part Three of this book.

Phase 6. After Your Children's Deaths

In larger estates, or for those opting for more sophisticated estate plans (to secure better asset protection benefits), the assets may be held in trust for the lives of your children (or other secondary beneficiaries) or even for the lives of your grandchildren, or longer (i.e., forever, in a dynasty trust). If you have decided that providing further asset protection for your children and future heirs, and that saving your children and perhaps later heirs their estate taxes is worthwhile, assets will continue in trust for the lives of your children, and perhaps longer. The tax and legal benefits of this approach are substantial, but the planning is more complex and costly. This type of planning is discussed in the "Multigenerational Living Trust" discussed in Part Four of this book.

BUILDING BLOCKS OF THE COMPLETE LIVING TRUSTS PROGRAM OVER TIME

Table 1.2 illustrates how the different ancillary documents and subsidiary trusts of the Complete Living Trusts Program relate, when they become effective.

SUMMARY

Living trusts are an important and flexible estate and financial planning tool that can provide substantial benefits. Much of what you read and hear about living trusts is simply inaccurate. The "experts" love lining up on one side of the fence or the other: living trusts are either the answer to all your problems or a waste of money. Neither extreme is correct. As explained in this chapter, living trusts—if properly drafted, implemented, and managed (which most are not)—are a powerful estate planning tool.

However, if you want to use a living trust, you should carefully consider whether the benefits to you now outweigh the costs and bother of setting one up. For many people, they will not. Further, if you use a living trust, it should only be one part of an overall estate plan that includes a durable

Table 1.2 Component Relationships of the Complete Living Trusts Program

Coverage of the Complete Living Trusts Program versus Other Living Trusts	Provisions at Formation of Your Living Trust	Other Entities/ Trusts Created at Formation of Your Living Trust	Successive Trusts Formed over Time:		
			After Your Death	After Your Spouse's/ Partner's Death	After Your Children's/ Heir's Death
Included in most living trusts, although disability and dispositive provisions often too simplistic and pour-over will often too limited to address executor's needs or failure of living trust.	**Foundation Living Trust.** Goals: Avoid probate; minimize publicity; manage assets if disabled. Provisions: Pour-over will; disability clauses; dispositive provisions.	None.	None.	None.	None.
Included in the Complete Living Trusts Program but in few others.	**Just-in-Case Living Trust.** Goals: Permit tax or legal planning only if necessary. Provisions: Comprehensive gift provisions; Disclaimer bypass trust.	None.	Disclaimer Bypass Trust.	None; possibly minor's trust.	None.
Included in all but the most basic living trusts.	**Family Tax Planning Living Trust.** Goals: Minimize estate taxes and protect survivors assets with by-pass and QTIP/ QDOT trusts. Provisions: Bypass trust, QTIP/QDOT.	Insurance trust. Minor's trust.	Bypass trust. QTIP/ QDOT trust.	Children's/ minor's trust.	None.

(continued)

Table 1.2 *(Continued)*

Coverage of the Complete Living Trusts Program versus Other Living Trusts	Provisions at Formation of Your Living Trust	Other Entities/ Trusts Created at Formation of Your Living Trust	Successive Trusts Formed over Time:		
			After Your Death	After Your Spouse's/ Partner's Death	After Your Children's/ Heir's Death
Included in the Complete Living Trusts Program; included in few if any other living trusts.	**Multigeneration Living Trust.** Goals: Estate tax savings and legal protection for heirs and future generations. Provisions: GST planning; grand-children or other trusts; possible dynasty provisions.	Insurance Trust with GST exemption allocated. Grand-children Trust qualifying for GST annual exclusion.	Bypass Trust, possibly with GST allocation. QTIP with GST portion.	Children's Trusts for life with GST allocated.	Grand-children Trust protected by GST. Dynasty Trust.
Included only in the Complete Living Trusts Program.	**Comprehensive Living Trust.** Goals: Asset protection; suc-cession planning; control. Provisions: QSST; business powers; trust protector; investment directions.	Limited Liability Company ("LLC"). Trusts for Children. Inter Vivos QTIP. Alaska/ Delaware Trust.	QSST or ESBT Trust.	Nothing additional.	Nothing additional.

power of attorney with authority to make gifts and transfer assets to the living trust, a living will/health care proxy with guardian appointment, and a Safe-Keeper Will. This plan should also address any other tax and asset protection techniques discussed in Parts Four and Five of this book that are appropriate to your situation. Anything less will not give you the peace of mind that a proper plan should provide.

2 PROS AND CONS OF REVOCABLE LIVING TRUSTS

THE PROBLEM WITH THE "PROS AND CONS" OF LIVING TRUSTS

A living trust is primarily touted for its use as a method of avoiding probate. A living trust can also enable you to avoid having your assets disclosed to the public, which a will cannot. Reality, however, can be different.

Probate is not usually the evil and expensive process many people fear; when it is, there are often other causes, such as unscrupulous professionals, or children suing each other, that a living trust cannot address.

A living trust, if properly done, is not the simple and inexpensive document many people expect. To achieve the real benefits offered by a living trust requires planning and increases the legal and other fees you will incur. In the appropriate circumstances, a living trust is an outstanding planning tool. In other situations, a living trust can be at best an unnecessary expenditure of time and money, and at worst a nuisance and a costly mistake.

A living trust can provide a benefit that is far more important than privacy and avoidance of probate—the management of assets in the event of advanced age or disability.

The proper approach is to evaluate the costs, benefits, and objectives of using a living trust in the context of a review of your overall financial, estate, and tax planning. To complete this analysis, consider the pros and cons discussed in this chapter before deciding whether a living trust is appropriate for you, and if it is, how to implement it.

ARGUMENTS AGAINST USING REVOCABLE LIVING TRUSTS

Setting Up the Trust Can Be Expensive

To properly set up a living trust, you must retain a lawyer. A typical trust document, if properly done, is somewhat complex. It should address your personal goals and objectives, estate taxes, and other needs. Be certain that the attorney coordinates the tax allocation clause in your will with the tax clause in the trust. This is not easy or simple to do. Make sure the trust addresses the phases in a living trust as they pertain to you.

The trust document, however, is only the first step. You must then arrange to transfer assets to the trust. For real estate, you will need to execute a deed, and depending on where you live, complete various tax and other forms. If the property has a mortgage, you will have to review the mortgage for a due on sale clause and most likely notify your bank. Fire and casualty insurance policies on real estate and art will have to be changed to the name of the trust to be effective. The title insurance company that insured any real estate you want to transfer to the living trust should be asked whether a new policy in the name of the trust is required. The transfer of personal property will require a bill of sale. These steps can be time consuming, can require the assistance of an attorney, and can create additional fees and charges, none of which would be incurred if you didn't set up the living trust. New bank accounts may have to be opened (see Chapter 6). A separate tax identification number may have to be obtained and tax and other filings may be required (see Chapter 20). You should assume there will be a minimum of $1,000 to $2,000 (or more) in additional cost over the cost of obtaining the will, durable power of attorney, and living will you need in any event. Be wary of quotes that are lower—how can the sophisticated work discussed in this book be completed, and tailored to your personal situation, for less?

Living Trusts Can Cause You to Incur Unnecessary Costs

To fund your revocable living trust, you have to transfer assets to the trust. If you later sell the asset prior to death, the cost of transferring the assets to the trust will have been a waste. You will have paid twice for the same transfer tax costs. Consider also local transfer fees, recording fees, additional accounting costs, and so forth.

Living Trust Costs Are Incurred Now, Probate Costs Are Incurred in the Future

If all the costs of a living trust are actually cheaper than probate costs, it still doesn't mean that setting up the trust is the low-cost option. Remember, the costs of setting up your living trust will be incurred now, where as the probate costs may not be incurred for 10, 20, or more years in the future. There is a time value to money. The money you spend today on all these costs is not available to invest as it would have been if you had not set up the living trust. If you instead invest the money it would have cost to set up a living trust, the value at the date of your death may exceed the cost of probate. Thus, while the actual dollar cost of setting up a living trust and having your trustees transfer assets after your death under the trust may be less than the cost of a probate (assuming that with a living trust you avoid probate completely), on a present-value basis the cost of probate may easily be less.

EXAMPLE: Your estate consists of one house and sixteen securities or mutual funds. You heed the advice discussed in this book and consolidate all your financial assets in one account. You live in New Jersey where the probate process is efficient and simple, and the court personnel exceedingly cooperative. The aggregate costs of probate, having your will admitted, is at most a few hundred dollars. Your executor has a one-hour consultation with an estate planner to understand what he or she as executor must do. The costs of probate are well under $1,000, considerably less than the cost of a properly drafted living trust. The fact that your executor may hire a real estate lawyer to complete the sale of your house, an accountant to complete a final tax return, and a lawyer to complete a state inheritance tax return is not relevant to the analysis since these same expenses will be incurred if you have a living trust. These latter costs are often considered part of "probate" but are not part of the costs of having a will probated.

To better understand the distinction, see Martin Shenkman, *The Complete Guide to Probate* (New York: John Wiley & Sons, 1999).

Laws Affecting Revocable Living Trusts Are Less Settled

Most of the case law involves wills and not revocable living trusts. Antilapse, abatement, and other statutory provisions, and the cases interpreting them, are primarily or entirely focused on wills, not living trusts. Why do you care? If there is a challenge or suit against your estate, it may be easier for your estate's lawyers to apply rules-based on cases that are similar.

You Need a Will Even if You Have a Living Trust

Using a living trust is not a substitute for a will. You should always have a will because there is no assurance that every asset of yours will be owned by your living trust at your death. This could occur because of the improper or incomplete transfer of assets, acquisitions for which there was inadequate time to complete a transfer to your trust, assets that could not be assigned, and finally assets that you may not be aware of. Your will should not be the typical overly simple pour-over will many people use. This type of will provides that all assets under the will are simply to be transferred to (poured-over into) your living trust. The will should go on to state how your estate assets should be distributed if for any reason the trust is invalid or unable to accept property. If you're concerned enough to minimize legal and other problems by having a living trust, you should be concerned enough to insist on a complete Safe-Keeper will. If for some reason your trust is not valid, using a pour-over will with a nonexisting trust will be like dying without a will or any document. It will be as if all your planning didn't occur.

So by using a living trust, you won't eliminate the cost of a will; in fact, you've increased your legal costs by needing two documents where one might have sufficed. A will is often necessary to designate a guardian if you have minor children. A complete will is necessary to authorize your executor to take the actions that might be necessary if circumstances change.

You May Not Legally Be Able to Sign a Living Trust, But You Could Sign a Will

In unusual instances, a person may possess the testamentary capacity to sign a will, but lack the required legal capacity to sign a living trust. Because a trust is a type of contract, the person establishing the trust must have the comprehension, understanding, and state of mind required to create a binding legal contract (see Chapter 21).

Avoiding Probate through a Living Trust May Not Protect Confidentiality

You may not realize the confidentiality you hope to obtain through the use of a revocable living trust. Although the living trust generally does not have to be recorded in public records, there are many exceptions and special circumstances. If your will contains a pour-over provision, the will in many situations may have to be probated. If the will pours over into your living trust, the probate court may require that your living trust be recorded in the public record in a manner similar to the will.

If there are any legal disputes between beneficiaries or other persons claiming an interest in your assets, or if your living trust is contested, these events might easily wind up in court records that are open to the public. The result is that a living trust may offer little additional secrecy. Once your estate becomes so contentious that litigation develops, any of the contesting heirs may seek revenge by intentionally leaking private information. And it may be impossible to prevent or prove such leaks.

If your successor trustee is uncertain how to properly interpret a provision in your living trust, the trustee may petition the court to interpret your trust agreement and advise the trustee of the appropriate action. This will obviously defeat any confidentiality your living trust may have provided. Similarly, where any beneficiaries, or persons who believe they should be beneficiaries, challenge the disposition of your assets, the ensuing litigation and court proceedings could make the terms of your living trust public information.

If you transfer real estate to your living trust, depending on the customs in your area, you may have to record the trust, or a summary (called a Memorandum of Trust) in the public records to transfer the deed. Again, anonymity could be defeated (see Chapter 6).

Unless you're a well-known public figure, it is unlikely that the media would have any interest in your will even if it is probated and thus available to the public records. Even if someone sees your will, do you care?

AUTHOR'S STRATEGY: My will provides that all my assets are transferred to a bypass trust for my wife and children. Big deal! Does that tell you anything confidential? I've also included a few modest charitable bequests, to demonstrate to my children the importance of making a contribution back to society. Should I be worried that the public may find out that I'm trying to inculcate good values in my children? Few wills contain many details more personal than that. So who should care about confidentiality? This issue is mostly a sales gimmick used by living trust hucksters. It rarely matters, and if it does, a typical living trust estate plan won't be the answer. For those few people—movie stars, politicians, sports figures (authors of estate planning books?)—who are really concerned about publicity, a web of irrevocable trusts, limited liability companies or limited partnerships, and other techniques will be used.

Jury Trials Are Available for Wills, But Not Always for Revocable Living Trusts

Depending on the jurisdiction, a jury trial may be available in the case of a will contest, but not for the challenge of a revocable living trust. This dichotomy is inappropriate since most revocable living trusts are used to accomplish identical objectives of a will. Which result is better will depend on the circumstances. A living trust, however, may provide some benefit in this area in giving you the flexibility to select which state law applies (or to have your successor trustee move the trust to another jurisdiction). This would, in theory, enable you to select the best jurisdiction and the best laws. In reality, however, this type of sophisticated planning is rarely done.

NOTE: The best approach is to plan your estate in a way that avoids problems that could lead to court proceedings. See Martin Shenkman, *The Complete Book of Trusts* (2nd ed.) (New York: John Wiley & Sons, 1998) for planning ideas.

A Revocable Living Trust Increases Risks of Inconsistency

No matter how well drafted, a revocable living trust will invariably increase the likelihood of inconsistencies in the estate plan. It is more difficult to coordinate the disposition of assets when probate and nonprobate assets are involved, and when two documents (will and living trust) apply. Coordinating the payment of expenses and taxes is always troublesome.

Having two documents (typically the pour-over will and the living trust) creates greater risks when the estate plan is amended. If one of the documents is changed, but the other is either not changed or changed inconsistently, problems can occur. Perhaps the worst scenario is that a revocable living trust is revoked, and the pour-over is not amended to reflect this. The result is a will pouring assets into a nonexistent trust. In such instances, all planning might be for naught since it will be the equivalent of dying intestate unless the will includes complete dispositive provisions in the event of such a problem.

Two documents naming different fiduciaries (i.e., the executor and the trustee are different people) can create considerable problems if all the fiduciaries don't coordinate and agree on what tax elections should be made for the taxable (as contrasted with probate) estate. The elections are numerous and include electing qualified terminable interest property (QTIP) treatment for a trust for a surviving spouse to qualify for the unlimited estate tax marital deduction; the special valuation rules under Code Section 2032A for farms and real estate and 2057 for closely held business deductions; and the generation skipping transfer (GST) tax exemption.

Estate Litigation Is Not Avoided with a Revocable Living Trust

Some people mistakenly believe that using a revocable living trust will somehow avoid will contests and other litigation triggered by using a will. A disgruntled potential heir who challenges a will, also will challenge a revocable living trust. Issues such as undue influence, insufficient capacity, or no independent advice of an attorney that might be argued against a will can be argued against the revocable living trust as well. In fact, the arguments may be harder to fend off for a revocable living trust than for a will because the standard of competency for a trust is higher (see Chapter 21).

NOTE: See the web site "www.laweasy.com" for more details on will challenges.

Deductibility of Expenses May Be Jeopardized

For taxable estates, the deduction of estate expenses and executor fees can provide important tax benefits. Trustee commissions paid to the successor trustees of a living trust may not provide a deduction for federal estate tax purposes as would executor commissions. Similar issues may arise with respect to deducting other administration expenses incurred by the living trust. The general rule is that for a decedent who is a citizen or resident of the United States a deduction is allowed for amounts in two categories:

First Category. Funeral expenses, administration expenses, claims against the estate and unpaid mortgages or any indebtedness in respect of property the value of which is included in the decedent's gross estate.

Second Category. Amounts representing expenses incurred in administering property that is included in the gross estate but which is not subject to claims and which would be allowed as deductions in the first category if the property being administered were subject to claims; and were paid before the expiration of the period of limitation for assessment provided in the tax laws.

Except to the extent that a trustee is in fact performing services with respect to property subject to claims that would normally be performed by an executor, amounts paid as trustee's commissions do not constitute expense of administration under the first category and are only deductible as expenses of the second category to the extent provided in the tax regulations.

Trustee Is Liable for Payment of Federal Estate Taxes

One of the oft-cited advantages of using revocable living trusts rather than a will subject to probate is the speed at which the decedent's assets can be distributed. This purported benefit is often not realized. One reason for this is the personal liability that the trustee of the now irrevocable (i.e., your revocable living trust becomes irrevocable on your death) trust will have for federal estate taxes. This risk is potentially significant and should not be taken lightly. For smaller estates, the risk may become negligible as the applicable exclusion amount increases toward $1 million, and widens the margin of safety (estimated taxable estate compared to the applicable exclusion amount).

In other situations, trustees will have to proceed with care since the trustee can be held personally liable for taxes due if distributions are made. A trustee may be able to avoid personal liability by first obtaining a release from the Internal Revenue Service. To obtain this, the trustee would apply for a prompt determination of the estate tax. The result is to limit the personal liability of the trustee for the tax. The trustee would then be discharged from liability by the payment of the tax and the provision of a bond for taxes for which payment has been extended. This request requires that the estate tax be determined within eighteen months of the decedent's death. Again, the quick distribution most living trust books and plans tout will probably never be realized by anyone with a taxable estate.

This also doesn't mean that distributions will be quick if your estate is not taxable. The trustee will still have to address planning issues, marshal assets, notify creditors, and so forth.

Probate Court Filing and Other Fees

Probate fees, depending on the jurisdiction, can be based on the size of the estate. In such cases, there might be some modest savings from using a revocable living trust. As a percentage of the assets and estate involved, however, the amount is usually negligible. In many states, the fees are modest, so any savings in those states is meaningless.

Legal Fees Will Be Incurred on Death Whether a Will or Living Trust Is Used

If legal fees are to be paid based on a percentage of estate assets as provided under state law, the use of a revocable living trust may affect overall legal fees. However, if the fees are paid based on hours worked, always a fairer and more realistic approach (if the hours are honestly billed), the costs should be approximately the same for an estate regardless of whether a living trust was used. There simply is no significant legal cost savings through transferring assets at death from a revocable living trust compared with transferring assets from a will.

When a person with a living trust dies, the assets in that trust must still be transferred to the designated beneficiaries. Thus, whether assets pass through probate or under a living trust, steps still must be taken to transfer those assets. Where the property is real estate, stocks, or other assets, the paperwork may not be that different. Also, probate sometimes costs far less than suggested in many popular books and articles in financial publications. Numbers like 5 percent of total assets are frequently mentioned as typical legal fees for probating an estate. In many instances, this is a gross exaggeration. The size of the estate often has little to do with the cost of the necessary work so long as the estate attorney is billing hourly and not basing a fee on a percentage of the estate. The nature of the assets, cooperation of family members, and organization of necessary financial and personal records are important factors in determining the legal work involved. In all events, however, you have to monitor the lawyer and other professionals involved to minimize the likelihood of abuse. To do this, request and review detailed periodic bills from all professionals. Use unrelated professionals. If you hire the accountant, appraiser, and broker that the attorney recommends will they be loyal to your heirs or to the referring attorney? If you have independent professionals and encourage them to overview the steps taken by other professionals, you can achieve an important check-and-balance system.

Also, the particular probate court that will handle the estate can have a significant effect on the overall cost of a probate. Probate courts that are efficient, helpful, and professional can drastically reduce cost and time delays. You cannot be assured of this positive environment.

If your estate is taxable, a federal estate tax return will have to be filed. It is a complex return which typically costs many thousands of dollars. For complex estates, the costs can be far greater. Using a living trust does nothing to reduce the costs of this filing.

The real issue is the misunderstanding of what probate is. The technical process of probate merely involves having the will accepted for filing by the court and a form, often called "letters testamentary," issued authorizing the executor to act. Once this is done, the executor, like your successor trustee under your revocable living trust, must deal with assets, heirs, tax filings. The duties are usually much the same.

NOTE: For a detailed explanation, see Martin Shenkman, *The Complete Guide to Probate* (New York: John Wiley & Sons, 1999).

Court Costs Are Not Always Significantly Less with a Living Trust

Even with a living trust, it may not be possible to completely avoid probate. Many of the forms and court filing fees are about the same even if your probate estate (your assets that go through probate in the event of your death) has been reduced through the use of a living trust. Also, the court costs are modest in many jurisdictions, and for most estates.

Third Parties May React More Favorably to
Letters Testamentary

Some third parties may favor the legal certainty and familiarity of the formal document (letters testamentary) issued by the court authorizing an executor to act on behalf of your estate. These same people or institutions may be somewhat reluctant to accept the authority of a trustee under a revocable living trust.

Executor and Trustee Commissions

State law provides for a maximum amount that can generally be charged by persons serving as executors under your will and trustees under your trusts. In some instances, however, additional fees and administrative costs may be permitted. On the other hand, in many situations, close family or friends serve as executor or guardian for no fee. So will fiduciary (i.e., executor and trustee) fees be lower by using a living trust instead of relying wholly on a will and the probate process? It depends on who is serving and the work involved. Even if trustee fees are lower over several years, the savings may be reduced if the administration of the trust continues after the grantor's death.

If an institutional trustee or co-trustee is named on the revocable living trust, it may charge a settlement fee for winding up an estate through a living trust, in addition to the trustee fee. This would be appropriate since the institution would be performing double services. Often the best, cheapest, and easiest way to minimize fees (and delays) is to simplify and consolidate asset holdings.

AUTHOR'S STRATEGY: I am not incurring any fees on my living trust since I am the sole initial trustee. If I am disabled or die, the institutional successor co-trustee that steps in will charge a fee. The family member who is the successor co-trustee may waive fees unless there is a tax or other reason not to. Am I concerned about incurring the fees? No. I believe that the institution's fees will be well earned taking care of my family. If not, I would have used a different approach.

You Can Take Simple and Inexpensive Steps to
Reduce Probate Expenses

A significant cost in administering many estates is the time and effort necessary to ascertain exactly what assets and liabilities the decedent has. By maintaining accurate and complete records during your lifetime, you can substantially reduce professional fees later. The majority of people ignore this simple step. When your heirs hire a lawyer or accountant to handle the probate of your estate, they should insist on hourly billing and detailed bills itemizing all steps taken. They need to obtain estimates in advance and request regular billing and quick notification if actual costs may exceed any budgeted costs. They shouldn't be shy about questioning a bill, retainer agreement, or budget that doesn't makes sense.

CAUTION: When an attorney you hardly know suggests or insists that he or his firm be named executor or trustee, quickly head for the door! When an attorney is the sole executor or trustee, and hires himself or his firm to manage the estate, double fees may be earned with no independent oversight over what is being done or charged. This is especially true when the heirs are elderly or quite young and unable to monitor the attorney. These abuses can occur whether a will or living trust approach is used. Diligence is always necessary.

Durable Powers of Attorney May Be a Lower Cost Solution

If you're young and healthy, the cost of a living trust to provide for disability may be excessive when compared with the use of a durable power of attorney, which is simple and inexpensive to complete. The preparation of a living trust to avoid probate, even if warranted based on an analysis of the other considerations listed here, would be a premature expenditure at such a young age. However, for older or infirm taxpayers, depending on the laws and customs in your area, a revocable living trust may help avoid the need for a guardianship proceeding in the event of disability.

A Living Trust Does Not Save Taxes

For income tax purposes, there is no tax impact from funding a revocable living trust. The trust is taxable to you as the grantor because it is revocable by you. For gift tax purposes, the funding of a revocable living trust should have no tax consequences. This is because the property is a transfer that remains revocable by you as the grantor so no tax will be assessed on formation. For estate tax purposes, the revocable living trust provides no savings. The assets included in the trust are taxable in your estate as the grantor of the trust because you retain a life estate in the trust and the trust remains revocable. Estate tax benefits are possible only where the other planning techniques and trusts discussed in this book are incorporated into the living trust (see Part Three). The trust itself does not provide any tax benefit. This purported benefit is mere fiction used to scare consumers into purchasing expensive legal documents.

NOTE: You establish a living trust that helps you avoid probate on your $1 million estate entirely. On your death, your living trust provides that your entire $1 million estate passes outright to your children. Although you've avoided probate, your living trust will do absolutely nothing to save estate taxes.

EXAMPLE: Assume the same facts as earlier, except your living trust provides that the first $650,000 of your assets will be transferred to a bypass, or applicable exclusion (credit shelter), trust. The remaining assets are transferred to a QTIP trust for the benefit of your wife qualifying for the unlimited estate tax marital deduction. A revocable trust can be used to create a QTIP trust providing an income interest to a surviving spouse. Your living trust, with these provisions, may have enabled you to entirely avoid any estate tax (see Chapter 9). However, these same benefits could have been obtained at less cost under your will.

Anyone or any book suggesting that a living trust saves you taxes is wrong. It provides no advantage over a will. Get a new lawyer and a new book!

NOTE: The opposite is thus also true. Congress has often spoken about repealing or scaling back the estate tax. Even if this happened, it would not change most of the important benefits of a living trust. As an aside, the estate tax only affects about the wealthiest 2 percent of families. A recent survey by a national finance magazine determined that if your net worth is about $275,000 you'd be in the wealthiest 11 percent of the nation. Consider that the applicable exclusion amount (i.e., what you can pass on without incurring tax) is scheduled to increase to $1,000,000 by 2006. The amount you can pass tax-free is about four times what it takes to be in the wealthiest 11 percent of the country! Repealing the estate tax will only serve to accelerate the already dangerous concentration of wealth in this country. Is that really in anyone's long-term best interest?

Transferring Assets to a Revocable Living Trust Will Create Additional Work and May Create Additional Costs

To transfer certain assets to your living trust (e.g., real estate), you will incur additional hassles and possibly additional costs. For example, to transfer a house to a living trust, you will have to complete and file a deed, which requires legal fees and filing costs. You will have to update the insurance coverage to reflect the trust. This should not add to your costs but will require some modest effort. Real estate transfer taxes and property transfer costs should not be incurred in most situations because most laws will treat the transfer to a living trust as a mere change in identity not requiring any taxes. However, this should be carefully reviewed in advance because every jurisdiction may not take this view.

If you transfer stock in a closely held business, you may have to sign a new shareholders' agreement or partnership agreement. This will trigger additional legal fees.

Other Probate Avoidance Techniques Are Available

If avoiding (minimizing is a more realistic goal) probate is an important goal, a living trust is not the only approach to accomplishing your objective. For example, if you own property as a joint tenant with the right of survivorship (often abbreviated "JTWROS"), this form of ownership will pass the asset to the surviving co-owner without probate. This simplistic approach, however, may not permit implementation of some of the estate, legal, and other planning discussed in this book (see Chapter 3).

Trustee Actions May Be Subject to Less Scrutiny Than Executor Actions

The successor trustee under your living trust may not operate under any court supervision. There may be no reporting requirements. While this might appear advantageous when the trustee is honest and careful, it doesn't take much imagination to consider what an unscrupulous trustee can do.

Use of Revocable Living Trusts Could Affect S Corporation Status

The most common form of ownership for closely held businesses remains the S corporation. S corporations have considerable restrictions on the types of trust that can be shareholders. While there should be no problem with a revocable living trust serving as a shareholder during the grantor's lifetime (since the trust will be taxed as a grantor trust) problems can arise following the grantor's death if proper planning is not addressed (see Chapter 16).

Living Trusts Don't Afford Asset Protection Benefits

Since you can revoke your revocable living trust at your whim, it cannot afford you any protection from creditors. Although not a legal advantage vis-à-vis creditors, a revocable living trust may provide a modest tactical advantage. On your death as the grantor, the trustee may be able to distribute assets to beneficiaries quickly (but see the caveats noted above). Creditors would then have to pursue the beneficiaries for the funds. This might be somewhat more costly and time consuming than pursuing an estate and hence present some modest barrier. If asset protection is a concern, you must take additional steps (see Chapter 17).

In Terrorem Clause

An "in terrorem" clause is designed to discourage will challenges. Such a clause provides that if any beneficiary of a will challenges it, that beneficiary's interests in the estate will lapse. The use of a similar clause in a revocable living trust may provide a similar result. However, most of the case law relates to wills, so depending on the jurisdiction involved, there may not be as much certainty as with a will.

Outright Gifts or Irrevocable Trusts May Be Better Options Than Either a Living Trust or a Will for Certain Assets

Probate and a will, or a living trust and avoidance of probate, are not the only choices. Again, a thorough review of all estate, financial, insurance, and other goals and status is essential. If your estate is large enough, it may be better to give away certain assets as gifts to your adult children, to remove them from your estate, rather than transferring into a living trust that won't remove them from your estate.

EXAMPLE: Your estate is valued at over $2,000,000; $600,000 of your estate is stock in a closely held business. If the value of the stock exceeds 35 percent of your adjusted gross estate, your estate will qualify for favorable estate tax deferral provisions. These can permit your estate to pay out any estate tax on an installment basis over about 14 years. This can be a tremendous benefit and perhaps minimize the need for expensive insurance coverage. However, for your estate to qualify, the stock must exceed the percentage threshold of 35 percent. If you transfer your assets to a living trust or retain your assets in your estate (to pass under your will), this valuable estate tax deferral will not be available. Alternatively if you gave away assets to your adult children, or transferred to trusts for the benefit of your minor children and grandchildren $285,715 [$2,000,000 – ($600,000/35%)] of assets other than the stock in the business, your estate will qualify for this favorable tax benefit. If you have five married children, each with four of their own children, you and your spouse could give away $300,000 in a single year using your $10,000 annual gift exclusions. If your family is smaller, the same gifts could be completed on a tax-free basis over several years. In this situation, limiting your decision to probate versus living trust could miss an important point, reducing and deferring the potential federal estate tax cost.

If your estate is modest in size, and your liquid savings inadequate, a living trust may not be worth the expense, particularly if you and your spouse are relative young and in good health. A preferable approach may be simply to sign durable powers of attorney, living wills, and simple wills. When your ages and assets increase, a living trust may become more worthwhile.

BENEFITS OF USING A REVOCABLE LIVING TRUST

With all the preceding caveats, is there any reason left to use a revocable living trust? Absolutely. It remains a vitally important and useful estate planning technique for many people.

EXAMPLE: You're a widower age 78 and have few family other than your children and minor grandchildren. They all live several hundred miles away. A living trust is likely to make sense unless the other facts and circumstances are very persuasive against using such a trust. Considering the age and scarcity of those who can help in a financial emergency, the living trust may be ideal to provide protection against disability. If you have no people to name as successor trustees in whom you have total confidence, you could name an institution to serve as a co-trustee with friends or family members. The institution is subject to substantial regulatory scrutiny and safeguards and thus gives comfort that your assets will be looked after for your benefit. Institutions will not generally serve as agents under a durable power of attorney, so a living trust may be necessary.

EXAMPLE: You're in your mid-70s and have a substantial estate. Other than your house and some bank accounts, your entire estate comprises a diversified securities portfolio located in three major brokerage firms. A living trust to avoid probate (considering the size of your estate), and to provide for disability is almost certainly to be the appropriate decision. For probate avoidance alone, a living trust is perhaps going to be the desired option. The estate is substantial and the assets are so easy to transfer to the trust's name—simply advise your broker what is necessary.

A review of the many real benefits that a living trust can provide, however, will help you better understand how it should be used and what provisions it can contain.

A Living Trust Facilitates Organized Management

You can use a living trust to establish a range of procedures to govern the management of your assets. Unlike other methods, such as a durable power of attorney or court-designated guardian, a living trust can provide an ideal tool to test your procedures before death. If you are not satisfied with how things are working, you can always modify the provisions governing management. This ability to assist in managing assets in the event of illness, disability or merely advanced age, is perhaps the most important and best use of the revocable living trust.

The revocable living trust can be a powerful tool for asset management for several reasons:

- You can specify in great detail (far more so than is ever included in a durable power of attorney) how you should be cared for, where you should live, and how your money should be invested and distributed.
- You can specify the people or institutions to be in charge of your assets. A common approach is to consolidate investment assets in a particular bank or trust company and name that institution as successor trustee. This kind of consolidation makes for a much easier and smoother transition.
- Use of a funded revocable living trust, if you also have a comprehensive living will/health care proxy, may avoid the need for a guardianship proceeding.

You Won't Do What You Should without It

Consolidation and simplification of your financial picture will help you achieve important estate planning goals while minimizing probate expenses and delays. Consolidation will protect you in the event of disability, advanced age, or other emergencies. Finally, it will often enable you to achieve better investment returns with lower investment risk. Over the years, people tend to accumulate a proliferation of bank accounts, brokerage accounts, mutual funds, and stocks and bonds held in individual names and kept in a safe deposit box, and so forth. In the event of disability, it becomes extremely burdensome for an agent to identify and track dividend and interest payments, to marshal assets to assure proper cash flow, and so forth. Attorney fees magnify probate costs dramatically. Time delays are exacerbated as executors and lawyers attempt to identify and gain control over these assets. Finally, from an investment perspective, it's nearly impossible to properly determine your asset allocation when investment assets are held in so many forms and accounts.

It can be tremendously beneficial for you to consolidate all of your stocks, bonds, and other brokerage account assets into a single (or a few, depending on the size of your portfolio and any legal requirements, e.g., pension or independent entities) account with one brokerage bank or trust company. By having all your assets in a single account (one for each spouse or partner is often necessary to assure assets to fund a credit shelter trust, as will be explained), one monthly statement could conceivably reflect almost all your assets, except for your house, pension, and insurance. Does it require a revocable living trust to consolidate. Absolutely not. But the fact is that most people never get around to it. When they set up a revocable living trust, however, this serves as a point of focus, and an encouragement, to undertake and complete the consolidation process. Silly, but it works.

Living Trusts Are the Best Vehicle to Plan for Disability

A power of attorney is a simple approach to enable someone to act in your behalf in the event of your disability. However, a living trust can be a far more effective vehicle. A living trust can provide far more detailed provisions and contingency plans for dealing with disability than does the typical durable power of attorney. The authority of an agent under a durable power of attorney could be less certain than that of a successor trustee under a revocable living trust. The successor trustee (the trustee that takes over as trustee when you become disabled) has legal ownership (title) to the assets in the trust, so the line of authority of the trustee is perhaps stronger than that of an agent under a power. Banks and other financial institutions may more readily accept the authority of your trustee than your agent. The agent under a power of attorney may not be subject to the same requirements of maintaining books and records as would a trustee.

NOTE: The two documents, a living trust and durable power of attorney are not mutually exclusive. A durable power of attorney should always be signed as part of any estate plan. There are few exceptions. When a living trust is determined to be an appropriate tool for your estate and financial goals, you still could consider signing a durable power of attorney that gives your agent the right to make gifts (this must coordinate with your trustee's right) and most importantly, that has an express provision giving your agent the authority to transfer assets to your living trust. Rarely does anyone transfer every asset they own to their living trust when they set it up. A checking account, gifts received after the trust was formed, personal property acquired after the trust was formed, and assets which are costly or difficult to transfer (perhaps a car) are often not in your trust. If you become disabled the only mechanism to get these assets into your trust is for your agent, acting under a durable power of attorney, transfer these assets.

A living trust is an excellent vehicle for a single person who can't rely on immediate family to handle financial matters in the event of disability. You should also compare it with another option for providing for financial management of a disabled or incompetent person, having a court appoint a guardian, conservator, or committee. The definitions and functions of each differ under each state's laws.

In the event of disability, a power of attorney to facilitate the funding of a revocable living trust, and a health care proxy/living will to govern health care decisions may avoid the need for a conservatorship or guardianship. Many people are best served by a living trust since if properly handled it not only obviates the need for a guardian, but it can be convenient, and largely private. Thus the appointment of successor trustees under a funded revocable living trust (or one which can be funded via the durable power of attorney) may preempt guardianship. Even if a guardian is appointed, it will probably only be to supplement the trust (a "gap" filler). Don't forget, however, the power and living will (see Chapter 7).

You Have Greater Flexibility in Designating Fiduciaries

Some jurisdictions place restrictions on who can serve as an executor or trustee. For example, relatives or in-state institutions may be favored. By using a revocable living trust in such jurisdictions, you may name the fiduciaries you prefer.

Revocable Trusts Are Not Always Subject to the Same Formalities of Signing (Execution)

Generally, the requirements to formally sign a will are more stringent than the requirements for signing a revocable living trust. This can be positive in that it may be more difficult for a person challenging the validity of the trust to argue that the requisite formalities of execution were not followed. However, this can also be detrimental if the result is lax execution proceedings. The execution proceedings for wills are designed, in part, to confirm the testator's understanding and identification of the document being signed as well as knowledge of his or her assets and natural bounty. If these same matters are not addressed during the execution of a living trust, it could create greater difficulties in fending off a challenge to the documents based on fraud or incompetence.

In other jurisdictions, the formalities are the same. For example, Florida law requires that a revocable living trust be executed with the same formalities as a will if the testamentary provisions of the living trust are to be valid. Florida, however, will not apply this statute to revocable living trusts created by nonresidents if the trust is valid in the state where the grantor executed the trust.

Is less formality really a benefit? If the will or trust is challenged, one argument would say that the less formality the more difficult to challenge for having not complied with a formality. However, complying with formalities may actually make the document more secure against a challenge.

A Living Trust Minimizes Difficulties in Transferring Assets

Many people are concerned about the difficulties their heirs will have transferring assets following the grantor's death. A revocable living trust on the surface may change little since the trustee will have to transfer assets just as would an executor under a will. In both cases, a deed will have to be completed and filed to transfer real estate. In fact, a revocable living trust appears at first to be worse since two transfers are required—one transfer into the trust during your lifetime, and a second transfer out of the trust by the successor trustee following your death. However, the revocable living trust may actually prove easier and cheaper in the long run. In many instances, title to assets is not properly held, some documents haven't been properly completed, others may be lost. In the case of a revocable living trust, the initial transfer will enable you to identify and resolve these issues while you are alive and able to handle them. Then, after your death, the transfer process could be simple. This may favorably contrast with the difficulties an executor may have after your death dealing with third parties and having to ferret out facts you knew instantly to complete transfers.

You Can Avoid Probate

Probate can be time consuming. Thus, unless your family has sufficient assets of their own to sustain them during the probate process (or at least until interim distributions can be made), a living trust can prove (but won't always) a simpler and quicker method for getting needed cash and other assets to your heirs. While this doesn't always work, it can. But remember the legal horror stories described in Chapter 1. You have to do more than just sign a living trust to minimize the likelihood of problems.

You Can Avoid Publicity

Subject to the many caveats discussed in this book, a revocable living trust can minimize the publicity and public availability of information concerning your assets and bequests. Is the margin of privacy obtained from using a living trust worthwhile? It will depend on personal preferences, the circumstances involved, and how you use the living trust.

NOTE: If you are part of a relationship with a nonmarried partner that your family members may not approve of, a living trust may minimize scrutiny, interference, and potential challenge. Your revocable living trust may have a degree of confidentiality that a will does not. If you transfer only a portion of your assets into the trust, retaining the remaining assets in your estate, family members adverse to your relationship may not even realize that a trust governing some portion of your estate exists. This can be an effective planning technique. If you use this approach, don't use a "pour over" provision in your will.

In most cases, however, the degree of privacy obtained is less than that ballyhooed by living trust proponents. Litigation can make the document public. If real estate is held in the trust, the trust (or at least a Memorandum of Trust; see Chapter 6) may have to be recorded thus making it public. If the will involved is a pour-over will, the surrogate's court may require a copy of the revocable living trust in order to probate the will. This copy may or may not become public record. If the approach recommended in this book (see Chapter 7) to have a comprehensive "Safe-Keeper Will" (not merely a two page pour-over) is used, then the will admitted to probate may have all the dispositive provisions reflected and thus everything in the living trust will become public record via recording of the will.

It May Be Easier to Relocate a Trust Than an Estate

There can be many reasons to consider changing the state where a trust has its location (situs) and the state law that governs the particular trust. For example, the prudent investor act defining the investment objectives and procedures that fiduciaries (including executors under wills and trustees under trusts) must follow can differ significantly. The rule against perpetuities (which governs how long assets can be held in trust) varies considerably in different states. Thus, there might be a legal incentive to relocate the trust to another state. Income tax laws vary considerably from state to state. Changes in state tax laws may create an incentive to move the trust or estate to another jurisdiction. It may prove simpler and easier to relocate a trust to another state than an estate.

Avoid Continuing Involvement of Court

If a trust (e.g., for a minor child) is formed under your will, the surrogate's court may continue to have involvement with that trust after its formation, even after the conclusion of probate; for example, the trust may be subject to periodic reporting. In some jurisdictions, forming these testamentary trusts under a revocable living trust which is not subject to the surrogate's influence, may avoid this continued involvement. This isn't always a benefit. If the family, professionals, or others involved have less than ideal ethics, the independent oversight of a court could be vitally important.

SUMMARY

Checklists of pros and cons of living trusts are useful for understanding whether you should use a revocable living trust as part of your overall estate plan. However, a simple weighing of pros and cons to come up with an answer is at best misleading. In most cases, a revocable living trust will be a beneficial document or tool to add to anyone's estate plan if done properly in the context of the circumstances involved. The next question for most people, is whether the additional cost of a living trust is worthwhile. In many cases, the answer will be that it is not.

3 PROBATE AVOIDANCE WITHOUT LIVING TRUSTS

OTHER METHODS TO AVOID PROBATE

The most commonly cited reason for using a revocable living trust is to avoid probate. As this book makes clear, merely avoiding probate is only one, and in most circumstances not an important, benefit of a living trust. If probate avoidance is an important goal to you, consider the many alternative methods of avoiding probate set forth in this chapter before incurring the cost of a living trust to accomplish the same thing.

It should also be noted that successful use of the estate tax planning, structure of business entities, and other planning techniques discussed in Part Five of this Book will often depend on the title-to-asset issues discussed in this chapter.

IMPORTANCE OF HOW ASSETS ARE OWNED (TITLED) AND BENEFICIARY DESIGNATIONS

Title to assets can affect the ultimate beneficiary, asset protection benefits, tax planning implications, and asset management issues. Beneficiary designations (i.e., the indication of who receives insurance, pension, or other assets on your death) can avoid probate and affect taxes and distributions. These seemingly mundane decisions as to ownership and beneficiary designations can affect virtually every key aspect of an estate plan. The following discussion will review many of the common ways that you can own (title) your assets and designate beneficiaries. Ownership and beneficiary designation issues, like living trusts, have been dangerously oversimplified in the popular media. They can easily be used to avoid probate, but the consequences of doing so, legally, economically, and from a tax perspective, can be undesirable. This chapter will help you understand not only how to avoid probate, but the real consequences of doing so.

JOINTLY HELD PROPERTY

Jointly held property provides a simple and inexpensive means of avoiding probate because on death of one joint owner, the ownership of the entire property transfers automatically to the surviving owner. No probate is necessary. However, joint ownership is usually not the best way to own an asset.

Common-Law Definition

Joint tenancy is a possessory interest in the same property where all co-tenants own a whole or unified interest in the entire property. Each joint tenant has the right, subject to the rights only of the other joint tenants, to possess the entire property interest. The traditional common-law definition of a joint tenancy requires four conditions, referred to as "unities": unity of interest (each joint tenant must have an identical interest); unity of title (the same will, deed, or other document must confer title to all joint tenants); unity of possession (each has the right to possess the entire property interest); and unity of time (the rights of each joint tenant must vest at the same time).

Joint Title as a Will Substitute

Jointly held property is often advocated as a will substitute. No living trust is necessary to avoid probate if you simply own everything jointly. While a will won't be necessary to transfer ownership of jointly held property, this approach is never a substitute for a will for the same reason that a living trust isn't, you can never be sure you've dealt with every asset. A living trust, however, affords greater flexibility, and can be an excellent substitute for joint ownership where the size of the asset justifies the costs involved. More importantly, joint ownership can impede proper tax planning in a larger estate since you and your estate planners won't be able to control the disposition of the assets held in joint title unless they first eliminate the joint ownership status of the property involved.

Jointly held property may be an imperfect will substitute for yet another reason. If the two joint tenants die simultaneously, the Uniform Simultaneous Death Act presumes that the property should be distributed as if it were tenants in common, one-half to the heirs of each joint owner. This may not be what you would wish to have happen. This rule, however, is not binding on the IRS so that the IRS could argue that some portion or all of the property is included in the estate of each joint tenant thus resulting in a more unfavorable taxation of the jointly held property.

Estate Planning Considerations of Joint Property

Where an account is taken in title of joint tenants with rights of survivorship (JTWROS), the account title itself states who receives the property on death (i.e., it serves as the beneficiary designation). When an account is opened as "John Doe, payable on death to Nephew Doe," or "John Doe, ITF (in trust for) Nephew Doe," the beneficiary designation is accomplished by the account title. From an estate planning perspective, this type of arrangement determines the beneficiary and avoids probate. However, you must consider three issues:

1. Does this simple approach really assure the dispositive scheme you want? In many cases, it will not. People mistakenly believe that if they designate, for example, half their accounts in joint name for each of their two children that each child will receive one-half of the estate. Often, you are far more likely to accomplish this distribution scheme through holding all assets in your name alone (or in the name of your living trust) with distribution of equal shares to your two heirs after your death. Grantors often overlook that accounts may grow at different rates, or funds may be spent from one, but not all, accounts to meet your living expenses.

2. How should taxes be allocated under your will or revocable living trust? Taxes due on, or attributable to, property passing outside your will or living trust will have to be paid. Who pays it?

3. Do you have control over your assets? You must consider the tax consequences of joint property.

Where asset protection planning is important, you should exercise caution to assure that the interest created is in fact a joint tenancy.

In some states, for example, one owner cannot convey joint tenancy to himself and a second person. Instead a third person or intermediary must accept conveyance and reconvey back to the two joint owners to establish the four unities.

Joint Property—What Language to Use

Where you own property jointly, "Sam Smith and Joe Jones, as joint tenants with right of survivorship" on the death of the first joint tenant the asset will automatically become owned by the second. Even where the account is simply listed as "Sam Smith and Susan Smith" a presumption may exist under your state that the tenancy is a joint tenancy with right of survivorship. An issue with respect to joint tenancy is the determination of the ownership interest where the title is unclear. Therefore, the preferable approach is to play it safe. If joint ownership with right of survivorship is desired, the account title should so specify. This is especially important where one purpose of establishing the joint ownership is to protect the property from the creditors of one of the joint owners.

Distinguishing Joint Property from Other Forms of Ownership

Joint tenancy should be distinguished from tenancy in common, where each person owns an undivided interest in the property. Although in both types of ownership you and a second person can own equal interests in property, the legal consequences are substantially different. On the death of a joint tenant, the survivor obtains ownership of the entire property.

On the death of a tenant in common, the deceased person's will (or living trust) determines to whom the property is distributed.

When a husband and wife own property jointly, it can become a special form of joint ownership called "tenancy by the entirety." Joint ownership should be distinguished from tenants by the entirety where asset protection planning is an important goal. Tenants by the entirety cannot convey or encumber (i.e., put a debt or mortgage on) their interest in property held as tenants by the entirety without all owners consenting. However, a mere joint tenant can encumber his or her interest in the joint property. The key asset protection aspect of this form of ownership is that having a joint tenant makes the property less valuable, and hence less desirable, to the creditor/claimant.

Income Tax Consequences of Joint Ownership

Where property is transferred to joint ownership the income earned on that property can be divided between the joint owners. Where the donor/depositor joint owner is in a higher tax bracket than the donee joint owner, a tax savings may be realized (assuming the Kiddie Tax doesn't apply because the child/joint owner is above the age of 14). If property subject to joint ownership is sold, the profits on the sale may be allocated to the joint owners in proportion to their interests.

If the property transferred to joint ownership has a mortgage or other liability in excess of the donor's tax basis, the transfer could be characterized as a part-sale (to the extent that the liability exceeds basis) and part-gift (for the balance) to the extent of the interest given up. This can be a costly and unexpected trap.

EXAMPLE: You, as parent, transfer as a gift a $10,000 asset to your child and yourself as joint owners. Your tax basis (cost less depreciation) in the asset is $10,000. But the asset has a debt, secured by a mortgage, of $40,000. A taxable gain would be realized by you of $15,000 [$1/2 \times (\$40,000 - \$10,000)$].

The preceding rules do not apply to savings bonds and joint bank accounts.

Estate and Gift Tax Consequences of Joint Ownership

Joint ownership can create significant tax consequences that you need to be aware of before changing the ownership of any assets to joint name. The general tax rule is that on the death of a joint tenant the entire value of the joint property is included in the estate of the first joint tenant to die. If, however, the executor can prove that the surviving joint tenant contributed some portion to the property, then some portion of the value can be excluded from the estate of the first joint tenant. The consideration furnished by the surviving joint tenant will not be counted where it was provided to the surviving joint tenant by the deceased joint tenant. Where contribution is demonstrated, it is not only the amount contributed that is removed from the gross estate of the decedent (first joint tenant to die), but a proportionate amount of any appreciation in the property could be argued to be included in determining the contribution by the surviving joint tenant. Income earned on the property given to the joint asset counts toward contribution.

EXAMPLE: Jim Doe and Steve Smith purchased a rental condominium several years ago for $96,000, as joint tenants with the right of survivorship. On Jim's death, the entire $500,000 fair value of the condominium will presumptively be included in his estate. However, if Jim's executor (or the trustee of Jim's living trust if the condominium were owned by his trust) can demonstrate that Steve contributed $48,000 of the original purchase price a proportional amount of the value of the condominium won't be taxed in Jim's estate. If the executor is successful, then $250,000 will be excluded from Jim's estate [$48,000/$96,000 × $500,000].

Where the joint tenants are husband and wife, the presumption is that one-half of the value of the jointly held property is included in the estate of the first to die.

Creating a joint tenancy can also have important gift tax consequences. If each joint tenant owns half of the property, but only one joint tenant contributed to the purchase of the property, then the creation of the joint tenancy will create a gift equal to one-half of the value of the property from the contributing joint tenant to the noncontributing joint tenant. The unlimited marital deduction, the $10,000 (indexed for inflation) annual gift tax exclusion (indexed), or the $650,000 (1999) applicable exclusion amount may eliminate any tax. Joint owners will generally report equal amounts of income on their respective tax returns. However, if one joint is a minor under age 14, the Kiddie Tax may apply.

You might decide after reviewing the concepts in this chapter with your estate planner that it would be preferable to terminate one or more joint tenancies. There could be a gift tax consequences to this if you and the other joint tenant receive interests in the joint property that differ from the percentage interests each of you own. For example, if you and a friend owned real estate equally, but on the division of the joint tenancy you let her take a 75 percent ownership interest, this could constitute a gift by you to her equal to 25 percent of the value of the property. A similar result could occur where the joint tenants have very different ages. For example, if you're 85 and your joint tenant is 25, there could be gift tax consequences to an equal division of the property since your life expectancy is so much less. This is because according to actuarial calculations you would be entitled to much less than a 50 percent share.

It is important to review the laws of the state where you are domiciled (permanent resident) to ascertain whether there are any special rules affecting joint ownership. If you own real estate in another state, you should also consult that state's laws. The rules differ for community property states: Arizona, California, Idaho, Nevada, New Mexico, Texas, Washington, and Wisconsin.

The tax consequences to the surviving joint tenant are also significant. The surviving joint tenant should receive a stepped-up tax basis of that portion of the property passing to the surviving joint tenant from the deceased joint tenant. Thus, it may be advantageous to include the joint property in the estate of the deceased joint tenant. This could occur where the estate is not large enough to be taxable because the applicable exclusion eliminates the estate tax cost.

If the deceased joint tenant received his or her interest in the joint property from the surviving joint tenant, within one year of death, there is no tax basis step-up. This restriction makes it more difficult to make a gift to a terminally ill patient to obtain a tax benefit. Similarly, to realize the stepped-up basis, the property must be included in the estate of the first joint tenant to die. If the property was purchased entirely with the money of the surviving joint tenant, it cannot be included in the first-to-die joint tenant's estate. Therefore the property will not receive a stepped-up tax basis.

Gifts made within three years of death are no longer included automatically in the decedent's gross estate. However, if you retitle property, as a gift, into a joint tenancy within three years of death, those gift transfers will be pulled back into your gross estate for purposes of calculating the amount of estate tax which can be deferred (an approximately 14-year deferral), stock that can qualify for tax-favored redemption benefits; and special use valuation of certain property. When property is included, in whole or part, in the estate of the first joint tenant to die, the surviving joint tenant could be liable for the estate tax attributable to the property.

Types of Property That Can Be Held as Joint Tenants

Joint tenancy can be used for real and personal property. A common example of nonreal property held in joint title is a bank account. Care must be exercised, however, to review the terms of the underlying bank application agreement to properly ascertain what exact type of legal title/relationship has been created (see "Beneficiary Designations for Bank Accounts").

Some "property" transfers may affect a joint tenancy and create an unexpected gift tax cost. For example, if you have given property to your child by creating a joint tenancy, there may be a current gift tax cost based on the concepts already discussed. However, if you later unilaterally make payments on a mortgage on the jointly held property, each payment could be construed as an additional gift to your child/joint tenant.

COMMUNITY PROPERTY CONSIDERATION

Generally all property acquired by a husband and wife during their marriage, while they are domiciled in one of the community property states such as Wisconsin or Texas, belongs to each of the marriage partners, share and share alike. They share not only in the physical property acquired but also in the income from the property and their salaries, wages, and other compensation for services. At the same time, each may have separate property. They may also hold property between them in joint tenancy and generally may adjust their community and separate property between themselves (i.e., use a transmutation agreement).

Couples can state prior to marriage via a prenuptial agreement that they will not be bound by the community property laws of their state of domicile. Generally, community property assets retain that character even after the parties have moved to a non-community-property state, unless the parties themselves are able to adjust their rights between themselves.

Real estate will generally retain the form of ownership assigned to it. Real estate in a community property state acquired by either spouse while married may be treated as community property without regard to the domicile or residence of the spouses. The law of the state where the real estate is located determines whether the income is community property.

Property acquired before marriage retains the form of ownership it had when acquired—separate, joint, or other. Property acquired during the marriage by gift or inheritance by one of the parties, such as perhaps gifts received by one spouse from his or her parent, retains the character in which it was acquired. Property purchased with community property is community property, and property purchased with separate property is separate property. Property purchased with commingled community and separate property, so that the two cannot be separated, is community property.

Community property is included in the estate of the first to die only to the extent of the decedent's interest, generally half of its value, and that half will be subject to probate. Transfers of community property between spouses qualify for the marital deduction.

On the death of one spouse, all property belonging to the community estate of the husband and wife vests in the surviving spouse if there are no children of the deceased spouse or descendants of the children. If there are children or children of the deceased spouse or descendants of these children, then the surviving spouse is entitled to one-half of the community property and the other one-half of the community property vests in the children or their descendants.

If you're hoping to avoid probate and may have any community property, be certain to review the consequences with an attorney expert in these rules.

TENANCY BY THE ENTIRETY

This is a special type of tenancy available only to husband and wife. Tenancy by the entirety can be distinguished from joint tenancy, discussed earlier, in that the methods for terminating a joint tenancy do not apply to end the tenancy by the entirety. The spouses however, can terminate a joint tenancy by agreement or divorce. Thus, neither tenant alone can force the termination of the tenancy by the entirety or the division (partition) of the property. This form of ownership can be used to avoid probate on the death of one spouse. Exercise caution, however, because it can also make it difficult for the estate of the first spouse to die to take advantage of the applicable exclusion amount. A disclaimer may be required and state law and your actions will be important to determining the effectiveness.

TENANCY IN COMMON

In tenancy in common, two or more persons share ownership in a property at the same time; but each party has a separate undivided interest in the property (as contrasted with joint tenancy where each has an equal interest in the whole). A key consequence of this difference is a tenant in common can bequeath property anywhere he or she wishes, whereas the joint tenant property passes to the surviving tenant by operation of law. This is critical from an estate planning perspective. Where a major asset, for example, is the house, it is typically owned as joint tenants thus defeating the ability to use a one-half interest in the house to fund an applicable exclusion trust under the will of the first spouse to die. Converting the ownership interest to tenants in common (by deeding the house from "John Doe and Jane Doe, his wife" or "John Doe and Jane Doe, as joint tenants with right of survivorship" to "John Doe and Jane Doe, as tenants in common") is sufficient to permit the spouse to fund the bypass (credit shelter) trust.

NOTE: While converting a house owned as tenants by the entirety into a tenants in common arrangement, the parties will be able to fund an applicable exclusion trust using that asset under the will of the first spouse to die, the change in title may also expose the property and make it vulnerable to attack by the creditors of either spouse. While a creditor of one tenant by the entirety can generally not attach that spouse's one-half interest in the property, a creditor of a tenant in common can attach the tenant/creditor's interest in the property.

Using tenants in common, however, will require that the estate be probated to transfer title. This form of ownership will not avoid probate unless held in a living trust.

NOT ALL JOINT OWNERSHIP AVOIDS PROBATE

There are many other types of joint ownership. For example, where an asset is owned by a corporation, limited liability company, or partnership, the principals (shareholder, members, or partners, respectively) are joint owners of the property. Time shares are another form of joint ownership. These types of ownership don't guarantee, however, that you will avoid probate. Unless a stock certificate, limited liability company membership interest, or partnership interest is owned jointly with another, a probate proceeding will be necessary to authorize your executor to carry out the terms of the shareholders, operating, or partnership agreement. A living trust can avoid the need for probate in these situations.

Life estates can provide a means of having more than one person own an interest in property, although they generally are created under a will, which means probate if a living trust isn't used. Trust arrangements can provide many types of joint ownership. In a charitable remainder trust (CRT), the donor may own a current income interest, and the charity the remainder interest, resulting in joint ownership of the same asset. On death, the charity will succeed to the assets without probate.

BENEFICIARY DESIGNATIONS FOR BANK ACCOUNTS

The title of your bank accounts can be used to avoid probate. However, the consequences are almost always more complex, and often different, than anticipated. Many people, especially senior citizens, may establish a joint account for purpose of facilitating management of that asset (e.g., to enable a younger family member to assist by paying bills). Unaware of the use of a revocable living trust or durable power of attorney, they often opt for the method suggested by a bank clerk. In other instances, the intent of such an account is to pass assets on the death of the transferror (i.e., for the account to serve as a will substitute). In still other situations, the intent of establishing a joint account is to make a gift (e.g., parent wants to give child money but finds it advisable to keep parent's name on the account to facilitate making future gifts or helping the child make investments). Difficulties arise because the person establishing the account (only sometimes really being a donor) could have such a broad range of intents, and those advising them often do not understand the legal and tax implications of the various available account titles.

For the following discussion, assume that Parent Taxpayer is the person establishing the account and placing funds in the account. Junior Taxpayer is the child (or other heir) of Parent Taxpayer.

Junior Taxpayer

Where Parent Taxpayer opens an account solely in the name of Junior Taxpayer, the funding of the account should constitute a completed gift for gift tax purposes. Junior owns and controls the account. There is no probate of the account on Parent's death, but Parent has lost control of the funds immediately.

Parent Taxpayer in Trust for Junior Taxpayer

Parent Taxpayer may want the funds transferred to Junior's control only on Parent's death. Thus, Parent Taxpayer likely has the right to revoke, in whole or part, the account at any time simply by withdrawing funds from the account. This type of account should likely not constitute a completed gift until such time as funds are spent on Junior Taxpayer's benefit, or Parent Taxpayer dies resulting in a transfer to Junior Taxpayer of the balance of the account. Unlike the joint account to be discussed, a completed gift should not occur where Junior Taxpayer withdraws funds because this account should not permit Junior the powers to withdraw without Parent's approval or act. In almost all situations, Parent possesses the exclusive right to control or withdraw funds. While this type of account should not constitute a completed gift on formation, cases have arisen where the beneficiary attempted to demonstrate that the depositor intended a completed gift.

This type of account is often called a "Totten Trust." This name derives from a landmark case which held that the depositor's right to withdraw funds at any time, thereby revoking the gift, did not serve to revoke the arrangement and thereby deny the survivor (Junior Taxpayer) from receiving the balance on Parent Taxpayer's death.

This type of account title can therefore be used to avoid probate while preserving for Parent control over the money while alive. However, things rarely work that smoothly. Invariably, if you have more than one heir, it becomes impossible to monitor the balances in the accounts you establish. The result is typically an unequal distribution of assets on death.

Parent Taxpayer and Junior Taxpayer, Jointly, with Right of Survivorship

In this type of account, funds can generally be withdrawn by either joint tenant. This is perhaps the most common structure for a joint bank account. Parent Taxpayer likely has the right to revoke, in whole or part, the account at any time simply by withdrawing funds from it. This type of account should likely not constitute a completed gift until such time as Junior Taxpayer withdraws funds, funds are spent for Junior Taxpayer's benefit, or Parent Taxpayer dies resulting in a transfer to Junior Taxpayer of the balance of the account.

The Uniform Probate Code provides that while both joint tenants are alive the account balance is presumed to be owned in the proportion of the contributions of each joint tenant to the account. In the preceding examples, this would result in Parent Taxpayer owning the entire balance of the account until death.

On death of Parent Taxpayer, Junior Taxpayer succeeds to the entire property interest. The deceased Parent Tenant has no right to transfer the joint account by will or otherwise. Thus, this type of ownership has been used as a will substitute.

This account can also be used to avoid probate, but presents two problems. First, Junior could walk off with the money while Parent is still alive and wants access to the funds. Second, the assets with these types of accounts, if there is more than one heir, rarely get distributed as intended.

Often some accounts are spent down, while others grow. Equality among heirs is impossible to maintain.

Parent Taxpayer and Junior Taxpayer

This account could be an attempt to establish the type of account referred to above, namely, a joint account with right of survivorship: Parent Taxpayer and Junior Taxpayer, Jointly, with Right of Survivorship. Courts have held that the depositor/Parent's control of the right of withdrawal from the account did not invalidate the intended survivorship feature. Thus, probate avoidance is possible.

Parent Taxpayer, Payable on Death to Junior Taxpayer

This type of account, often called a POD for short, is not a completed gift. The account balance should be included on Parent's estate tax return and should be transferred outside probate directly to Junior at such time. This avoids probate, but not estate tax consequences.

Issues Affecting Various Types of Bank Accounts

Controversies can arise where on the death of the depositor, Parent Taxpayer, both the estate of Parent and the survivor (Junior Taxpayer) claim the funds. The fact that an account is a type of joint account (e.g., Parent Taxpayer and Junior Taxpayer) is not always conclusive that Junior Taxpayer should inherit the balance existing in the account on Parent Taxpayer's death. For example, as discussed earlier, Parent may have set up the account merely as an administrative convenience, and not with the donative intent necessary to make a gift or even an ultimate transfer on death, to Junior Taxpayer. Overcoming the presumption of Junior's inheritance, however, is likely to be a difficult task.

Where a creditor of one but not both joint account holders seeks to reach the assets, the question arises as to what protection exists. Where one tenant, such as Parent, has the exclusive and complete right to withdraw funds from the account, the funds in that account are more likely to be reached by a creditor of Parent. Where the two tenants own the property as joint tenants, a creditor of one joint tenant often does not have rights against the interest of the other joint tenant. If the joint tenant who owes the debt dies first, the surviving joint tenant may be able to take the entire asset free and clear of any creditor claims.

Where the IRS exerts a lien over an account, they will levy on the entire account even if only one of the joint owners is liable.

Similar concepts have been applied to assets other than bank accounts, such as securities.

BENEFICIARY DESIGNATIONS ON LIFE INSURANCE POLICIES

Life insurance is often the largest asset in an estate, and even where not the largest asset, it may still be one of the most important by providing liquidity to pay estate taxes and other death costs. Careful planning of the beneficiary designations is critical to properly implementing your estate plan, including avoiding probate if that is one of your goals. However, probate avoidance is not always consistent with minimizing estate taxes and other important goals.

The Insured

If the insured spouse (i.e., the husband where the wife is the intended beneficiary) owns the policy, it will be included in the husband's estate on his death. However, by virtue of the unlimited marital deduction, the policy proceeds can escape taxation if payable to the wife outright or in the form of a marital trust. The proceeds that remain in the surviving wife's estate will, however, be subject to taxation on her later death. If the husband survives the wife (then presumably the children or other designated secondary beneficiaries will benefit from the policy), the policy proceeds will be included in the husband's estate because of the husband's incidence of ownership in the policy. Unless payable to a charity as the secondary beneficiary, the proceeds will be taxable in the husband's estate.

If the insured does not have a spouse and does not designate a charitable beneficiary, the policy proceeds will be taxed on the insured's death if the insured's combined estate, inclusive of the insurance, exceeds the insured's remaining applicable exclusion amount ($650,000 maximum in 1999 if no prior use).

CAUTION: In alternative relationships, where the partner is not legally classified as a spouse and thus the marital deduction is not available, the insurance proceeds will be taxed. This trap is often overlooked because most insureds assume erroneously that insurance is not taxed.

The Spouse of the Insured

Prior to the enactment of the unlimited marital deduction, a common estate tax planning technique was to have the beneficiary spouse (e.g., the wife when the husband was the insured) own the policy. This prevented any tax on the first death. Since the enactment of the unlimited marital deduction, there is no estate tax significance to which spouse owns the insurance: the insured spouse or beneficiary spouse. Caution must be exercised because:

1. Many insurance agents continue to structure insurance policies with the beneficiary spouse as owner "as if" this is adequate tax planning, which in most situations it is not.

2. Ownership of a valuable policy with a significant potential cash value should be determined with consideration to creditor/asset protection planning. If one spouse has greater exposure to creditors, the less vulnerable spouse should be the owner of the policy.

3. Divorce implications can be significant. If the noninsured spouse (or an irrevocable trust that does not address the issue of divorce) is the owner of the policy, the insured spouse's options could be severely limited in the event of a divorce.

NOTE: For more information on insurance trusts, see Martin Shenkman, *The Complete Book of Trusts* (2nd ed.) (New York: John Wiley & Sons, 1998).

---

4. On the death of the second spouse (i.e., the spouse intended to be the beneficiary of the policy) the insurance proceeds will be subject to estate taxation in the estate of the second spouse. This is the primary reason an irrevocable life insurance trust is often the best choice as the owner of the policy. The benefit of having the insurance trust rather than the beneficiary spouse own the policy includes the possibility that the insurance proceeds be removed from the surviving spouse's taxable estate as well as any growth in the invested proceeds.

The Children/Heirs of the Insured

In some cases, insurance agents structure the ownership of an insurance policy with the children or other heirs of the insured (i.e., any heir other than the spouse) as owner. This approach can be effective to remove the insurance proceeds from the insured's estate (and the estate of the insured's spouse, if applicable). The premiums are typically paid using annual exclusion gifts. However, there are potential problems with this approach (which generally result in the insurance trust being a better option). The children/heirs may not use the proceeds as desired. They may not make the proceeds, for example, available via immediate loan (or to purchase assets from the insured's estate) thus strapping the estate for cash to pay taxes or expenses. If the children are divorced, the insurance could be deemed an asset in their marital estate. If the children are sued, the insurance cash value could be an asset attached by creditors.

Thus, insurance can easily avoid probate on the death of the insured by being paid to the named beneficiary. However, the proceeds of the policy may be subject to tax on the insured's death, or in the estate of the named beneficiary. While an insurance trust can avoid probate and possibly estate taxes, it is complex and will require additional legal fees and formalities.

U.S. SAVINGS BONDS

U.S. savings bonds are commonly held in joint name. The ownership will pass to the surviving joint owner by operation of law. Where the bond is issued "Parent payable on death to Child," the government will only pay Parent during Parent's lifetime. There is no completed gift at the time of the purchase of a bond by Parent in the joint name of "Parent and Child" because Parent can cash in the bond and reclaim all monies. However, where the bond is redeemed by Child or the bond is reissued solely in Child's name, a completed gift will occur. The value of the bond where a gift tax is due is based on the redemption value of the bonds. So to avoid losing control, exercise caution when adding any heir's name to a bond. Pick the title that gives you the rights you want. Also, as noted for much of this discussion, if your estate could be taxable, joint ownership to avoid probate could be counterproductive.

DETERMINING HOW YOUR ASSETS SHOULD BE OWNED

Now that you have reviewed the various forms of ownership and understand how you can use ownership to avoid probate, the important decision remains—how should each of your assets be owned? To make this complex decision, you must address legal, tax, and other issues. Avoiding probate should not be the only criterion.

How Are Your Assets Owned Now?

In determining how you should own a particular asset, you must first identify how your assets are presently owned. This task is almost always far more difficult than it sounds because few people understand the basic legal concepts or know the correct ownership of many of their assets. Review all relevant ownership documents. This includes deeds (for your house, vacation home, and rental property), stock certificates (for interests in closely held and other businesses), brokerage account statements (for mutual funds and other securities), and so on to determine the exact ownership of the assets involved.

What Is Your Tax Basis in Each Asset?

Determine your tax basis in the property. For an asset you purchased, this is the purchase price (acquisition cost) plus the cost of improvements and less any depreciation (such as that claimed on a rental property). If you received the property as a gift (e.g., your parents gave you 100 shares of XYZ stock), your tax basis is the same as what your parents had. In tax jargon, this is called *carryover basis*. If you received the property as an inheritance, your tax basis is usually the value of the property at the date of death of the person who gave it to you. In tax jargon, this is called a *stepped-up basis*. Sometimes the executor or trustee may have chosen to value all assets 6 months after death. This is called the alternate valuation date. If so, then the value at that date will be your tax basis. There are adjustments in tax basis that can occur after you receive property. For example, you have to adjust your tax basis for stock dividends or new purchases.

Tax basis is important because low-basis assets are generally better to hold until death so that they receive a stepped-up tax basis for your heirs. Assets without much appreciation (but that will likely appreciate after you've made the gifts to remove that incremental growth from your estate) are better to gift. Tax basis is also important for deciding which assets to sell. All of this affects how you decide to own assets.

Does Anyone Else Own the Asset with You?

Where there are co-owners, determine the contribution of each co-owner. Where the contributions were made at different times, this should also be identified. The timing could be critical for properly allocating the contributions and appreciation to determine tax benefits. Also, timing is critical where a husband and wife acquired property while married and in a community property state. The contributions of co-owners is important when determining the consequences of accounts you own jointly with your heirs. For example, if you have a joint bank account with a child and the child has contributed nothing, that account will be included full in your taxable estate. That asset will also be reachable by your creditors as well as the child's creditors or divorcing spouse. So while you can avoid probate with a joint account with a child, what of tax and liability consequences?

How Do the Legal Documents Affect Title?

Determine the legal consequences of ownership interest. This could include a review of applicable local law as well as the application or contract documents for the bank, brokerage firm, or other legal entity involved with the establishing of the asset. Many people misunderstand the legal structure of their bank accounts until they read the documents used to open the account.

How Does Your Financial Position Affect How You Should Own Assets?

Analyze your overall personal, tax, investment, liquidity, and other status with your tax or financial adviser. Determine the optimal, or at least a preferable, methods of ownership for each asset. If your spouse is not a United States citizen, the more limited gift tax marital deduction for noncitizen spouses, as well as the QDOT requirements for a bequest to a noncitizen spouse, should be considered.

How Much Cost and Bother Is There in Changing an Asset's Ownership?

Consider the costs and difficulties of restructuring each ownership interest that should be changed. For example, if real estate is involved, transfer and recording fees may be incurred. Environmental review may be necessary to approve a transfer. Changing title may require a consent of tenants who have leases, mortgagees on any loans you've taken on the property, and your title insurance company. For a small rental property, it may generally not be worth the bother. For a small rental property in another state, which will require ancillary probate to transfer after death, it may well be worth the bother.

Changing Ownership Can Affect Control

Transferring an asset from your name alone to your spouse, or to joint title with your spouse or another person, will cause a loss of some control. Are you willing to give up any control? This issue must be carefully considered in evaluating how your assets should be owned.

SUMMARY

This chapter has provided an overview of other common probate avoidance techniques. While probate avoidance may be an important goal, don't become so focused on avoiding probate that you overlook far more significant planning issues. Also, consider the advantages of using a revocable living trust over the probate avoidance techniques in this chapter.

Part Two

FOUNDATION LIVING TRUST

4 ORGANIZE YOUR FINANCES TO PLAN AND IMPLEMENT YOUR LIVING TRUST

YOU NEED A FINANCIAL SNAPSHOT TO CHOOSE THE LIVING TRUST APPROPRIATE FOR YOU

One of the most important steps in analyzing your personal financial status and your estate so that you can determine what business, tax, legal, and other steps you should take, is to prepare a summary balance sheet highlighting your financial picture.

Basic financial information is critical to your planning. At least once every several years, or following any significant event, you should analyze your assets to verify your plan will accomplish your objectives and to identify changes you must make to keep your planning on track.

If you are married, you may want to take advantage of the $650,000 unified credit (this is the 1999 figure, which is scheduled to increase to $1 million by 2006) available to each of you and your spouse. Ownership of assets will have to be divided between you and your spouse so that each estate can fund a credit shelter trust (because it uses the unified credit to shelter assets from estate tax). This trust is also called a bypass trust since the assets bypass taxation in the survivor's estate. After the 1997 Tax Act, it is also sometimes called an applicable exclusion trust in light of the new name given to the credit. The surviving spouse is generally provided for by this trust but the trust assets will not be taxed in the survivor's estate. Joint ownership of assets can defeat this planning (see Chapter 3). If you want to leave assets of more than $650,000 (1999) to anyone other than a spouse, special tax planning may be necessary. IRA and pension assets raise special issues. You will have to coordinate complex income and estate tax rules to best name the beneficiary of retirement assets and choose the optimal payout period. For larger estates, financial information may be necessary to plan for the generation-skipping transfer (GST) tax and the $1 million (indexed) GST exemption (see Part Four).

Joint ownership can also obstruct the distributions provided in your revocable living trust since joint assets pass automatically to the joint owner on death, and not as your revocable living trust directs. You have to coordinate the ownership of assets with your documents and plan.

Form 4.1 Assets and How They Are Owned

Asset Description*	Yourself	Spouse/ Partner	Joint Owned	Pension Assets	Total by Category
Cash/CDs Marketable securities Money market accounts	$	$	$	$	$
Mutual funds					
House (net) Vacation/second home (net) Real estate investments					
IRA/401(k)/KEOGH/pension					
Closely held business					
Other investments Insurance (at death value)					
Totals	$	$	$	$	$

* All values should be listed net of mortgages and loans. Identify loans, partners, and other important points in the margin.

Insurance

Insurance Company	Type of Coverage and Amount	Value/ Annual Cost	Owner/ Covered Person	Beneficiary

Partnerships, LLCs, Other Investments

Name of investment	Type of Investment	Current Value	Ownership*

*H = Husband; W = Wife; P = Partner; JT = Joint Tenants; TC = Tenants in Common

Form 4.1 (Continued)

Retirement Accounts

Type of Account	Tax Basis	Current Value	Ownership*

*H = Husband; W = Wife; P = Partner; JT = Joint Tenants; TC = Tenants in common

Liabilities

Creditor	Amount	Property Secured

Form 4.1 shows a sample balance sheet and supplemental schedules. When you fill in the balance sheet, don't try for too much detail. Save it for the supplemental schedules following the main balance sheet. The purpose is to look at the big picture. Focusing on detailed asset allocations, the specific stocks you own, and so forth is important, but it can obscure larger, more important issues. Once you've completed the process, review the balance sheet with your professional advisers periodically to obtain their input and confirmation of the steps you plan.

SIMPLIFY AND CONSOLIDATE YOUR ASSETS TO ASSURE THE SUCCESS OF YOUR LIVING TRUST

Even the best living trust estate plan will be of limited value if you haven't organized, simplified, and obtained control over your assets. The key to this for most people is to consolidate asset holdings. This can help you achieve better investment returns and lower risk since you can better identify your asset allocation mix. You will minimize probate expenses and delays since there will be less paperwork to handle. It will also help you protect yourself in the event of disability, advanced age, or other emergencies.

Make a list of each separate asset or account that you have. For every asset, ask yourself: Is there a reason I own it? If not, consolidate or divest.

For example, small bank accounts at a local branch in your old neighborhood, can be closed out. A small $5,000 real estate investment in another state can create substantial liability exposure and ancillary probate. Is it really worth keeping? Do you really need CDs in four banks? Can't you consolidate them at one brokerage firm where the insurance limits provide adequate protection? If you have nominal holdings in several small stocks or bonds, do you really need them? Remember, when simple works, simple is better.

Over the years, people tend to accumulate bank accounts, brokerage accounts, mutual funds, and stocks and bonds, the reasons for which have long ago been forgotten. In the event of your disability, it will be burdensome for your agent or trustee under your living trust to identify and track dividend and interest payments, to marshal assets to assure proper cash flow, and so forth. In the event of your death, attorney fees dramatically magnify probate costs. Time delays are exacerbated as trustees and lawyers attempt to identify and gain control over these assets. Using a living trust will not avoid this since assets will still have to be valued for tax purposes, distributed to heirs, and so on. Simplifying your financial picture will help assure that your Living Trust Program will do everything you want.

SIMPLIFYING FINANCES PROTECTS YOU DURING DISABILITY

If you're disabled, think of what you're going to do to manage your investments, pay bills, handle daily affairs. If something happens to you (and your spouse or partner), on whom would you rely to help care for financial matters? Your children? Friends? A distant cousin with whom you have almost no contact? If you are ill or disabled, you will have to rely on someone to help you. If you've implemented a revocable living trust, you will have taken an important step toward organizing and controlling your legal, tax, and financial affairs in the event of disability. However, without consolidating and simplifying (to the extent feasible) your assets, you won't have the best protection. Almost any person you have appointed to serve as your trustee to manage your living trust if necessary, will have their own families, jobs, other personal responsibilities. For someone to take the time from their own busy lives to handle all your financial responsibilities is probably unlikely. Therefore, you want to make it as easy and simple as possible for the persons you've named as trustees to help you (and anyone else dependent on you). One of the most important ways to do this is by consolidating your financial assets and simplifying your financial and legal affairs.

There are added bonuses of consolidating assets into one or few financial institutions. By consolidating most of your liquid assets into a single brokerage account, you will generally obtain a higher level of service from the institution and truly make your broker part of your estate planning team.

BE CAREFUL OF COSTS AND ISSUES
CREATED BY CONSOLIDATION

Although consolidation should be a cornerstone of every Complete Living Trust Program, you must carefully choose the institution or institutions to which you are transferring your assets. Consider the risk of default, early withdrawal penalties on certificates of deposit, and tax costs of liquidating a mutual fund. For example, the institution you have decided to be the one in which you will keep all your assets may not sponsor a particular mutual fund you own. If you want to simplify, you may have little choice other than to sell the funds and reinvest with a comparable fund in the new brokerage firm. Obviously, this will raise tax, investment, and other considerations. Also, if you are married, one account should be set up for yourself and one for your spouse in approximate equal amounts to preserve tax-planning benefits.

DON'T CONSOLIDATE EVERYTHING

Don't consolidate any asset without first verifying that there will not be adverse consequences to doing so. If there are adverse consequences, evaluate whether it is worth the cost or problem before acting. You will never consolidate or combine IRA or other qualified pension assets with other nonqualified assets. You must carefully avoid any transactions with pension or IRA money that could trigger an income or other tax problem. However, if you have four IRA accounts at different institutions and there is no tax or legal impediment to consolidation, it may just be advantageous to consolidate them to one institution.

If you have substantial assets (but check your bank and brokerage firm to confirm their insurance and other limits) you should be careful because many of the brokerage firms cap their insurance coverage. Inquire and verify that you will not be transferring assets to an institution that exceed the institution's insurance coverage. Increased financial risk is not the objective of consolidation.

Finally, if you are married, it may be advisable to divide assets approximately one-half in each spouse's name to enable each of you and your spouse to fund an applicable exclusion trust. Asset protection, ancillary probate, and other considerations may all affect these decisions.

HOW TO ORGANIZE AND MANAGE YOUR
FINANCIAL AFFAIRS

Form 4.1 is at most only a starting point for getting your financial, legal, and estate matters organized. More work is advisable. Consider whether you should purchase any of the many data organizers, computer software programs, or other systems available in bookstores.

See Martin Shenkman, *The Beneficiary Workbook* (New York: John Wiley & Sons, 1998) for more details on how to organize legal, tax, and other papers.

Deeds (e.g., for your house or an investment property), contracts (with your employer, for property you sold on the installment method), corporate records (stock certificates, partnership agreements, shareholder agreements, buy/sell agreements), and so forth are essential components of any estate plan and it is critical to keep track of these to organize your records.

Originals of important documents should always be kept in a locked fireproof location such as a safe-deposit box. Be certain to make photocopies of these documents to keep with your other financial and estate papers so you have easy access to them when needed (such as for a meeting with an estate planning attorney).

Copies can be organized by category in looseleaf binders or files. If you do decide to meet with an estate or financial planner, be certain to bring copies to your initial meeting. These documents are essential for ascertaining the actual title (ownership) to assets. This information is necessary to plan for taxes, to determine who will inherit the assets and to collect the information your agents, executors, and others will need.

Consider giving copies of all key summaries and documents to a trusted friend or family member. This will facilitate their acting on your behalf in the event of an emergency.

SUMMARY

You must organize and evaluate your legal, tax, and financial data to identify the appropriate planning steps, implement the plan once made, and assure your heirs the information necessary to carry out their roles as fiduciaries.

5 DRAFTING THE FOUNDATION LIVING TRUST

The Foundation Living Trust is the basic living trust document. It is the foundation for building all living trust documents discussed in this book. Many of the provisions and decisions in the Foundation Living Trust must be addressed no matter the size of your estate or the issues you face.

For smaller or simpler estates, the living trust agreement used as part of the Foundation Living Trust as well as the ancillary documents required (power of attorney, living will/health care proxy, and pour-over will) may be all that you need. For larger, or more complex situations, the Foundation Living Trust and the ancillary documents are used as the building blocks, or foundation, for the more comprehensive planning you will need, as well as for the more comprehensive living trusts documents discussed in later chapters.

The Foundation Living Trust provides for management of assets in the event of disability, minimizes probate problems, and serves as a vehicle to encourage and assist you in consolidating and simplifying your assets. It is to apply when your estate (when combined with your spouse or partner's estate) does not presently, and will unlikely in the future, create an estate tax cost. If a tax cost is even possible, you should consider more advanced planning discussed in later chapters. The Foundation Living Trust and the ancillary documents discussed in this part of the book also assume that you do not have any unusual liability risks (e.g., threats of lawsuits) and don't own any rental real estate or business assets. If you do, consider the additional planning discussed in Part Five.

ASK THE IMPORTANT "WHAT IF" QUESTIONS

You must address the key question—"what if?"—in evaluating your plan. Consider some of the following: What if the person you named as successor trustee of your Living Trust (i.e., to serve when you can't serve) is unable or unwilling to serve as trustee, who's next? How many "next" or successor trustees should you have? Enough so that a court won't have to step in to name a successor. What if the person who is to inherit your property is under age? Ill? Deceased? Who should be next? And after that? If you name your good friend, Joe, as your successor trustee of your living trust, what if Joe dies? What if Joe cannot serve? You had better name someone else as a further successor trustee to Joe. So you name your good friend, Joan. But what if Joan is not around? You might respond: "They are both younger than me and healthy, I am not worried." But you have to ask "what if" because there are no guarantees as to what may happen.

One of the most common mistakes is naming insufficient successors (alternates) for trustees under your living trust. Another common mistake is naming insufficient persons to serve as guardians for minor children under your will. If you have a living trust that lists two people as successor trustees, what happens if they are not alive? You name somebody else, especially if you put a contingent trust in for children or grandchildren. For a child four years of age, a trust could be in place for 30+ years! So you have to name several alternates.

Most people do not name enough alternates. It does not cost any more money to prepare a living trust with three or four alternates instead of only one. But do you know what happens when not enough are named? Your family and estate end up in a court proceeding where the court will look at the trust document and state law to determine who will be named the next successor trustee. It is expensive, time consuming, and not what you want to happen. All that can be avoided by putting in a few more names.

What about the contingency of protecting the money for your child or other heirs? When a child receives money, most wills usually hold it in trust until ages 25, 30, and 35; the heir would receive a mandatory distribution of one-third of all trust monies at age 25, another one-third at age 30, and the final balance at age 35. This restrictive approach does not mean the heir cannot benefit from the money at an earlier time. It simply means that distributions prior to those ages are at the discretion of the trustee. The trustee can give the heir any portion of the money to maintain the heir's standard of living, health, education, maintenance, and welfare. But typically trusts require a distribution of, roughly, equal amounts at various ages. A common approach is one-third at ages 25, 30, and 35.

This chapter will help you understand the concepts you need to build flexibility into your Complete Living Trust Program. This is essential because too often wills are not revised as frequently as they should be and often the unexpected occurs. This chapter explains many of the concepts, which you can then apply when you hire an attorney to draft a will for yourself.

Don't Overlook the Personal Aspects of Your Living Trust and Plan

---

NOTE: You must not overlook the emotional issues of your estate plan. You can often achieve your goals in both a formal legal manner or in a way that reflects sensitivity and concern for the people involved. Wherever possible, do the latter.

Your living trust should not be a sterile legal document. Most people tend to focus on saving taxes, naming executors, and dealing with legal technicalities raised by their lawyer. These are all important, but a will should always reflect your emotional and personal concerns as well as those of the family, heirs, and others involved. For example, you name your youngest child as the first successor trustee because she is an accountant and has the skills you believe the other children lack. If your will simply reflects the sterile language of appointing one child over the others, one or more of the children could be insulted. Consider departing from merely using cold, formal, legal terms and instead express why you've named the younger child first: "I appoint my daughter, Jane, as Trustee because I believe that her background as an actuary ideally suits her for carrying out these duties and because of the substantial personal and professional demands on my other children. It is my hope that my other children are not insulted by the order selected." Often the brief explanation or personal comment can prevent hurt feelings that might last for many years.

To Whom Should You Distribute Your Assets?

Some of the most basic decisions in drafting any living trust and estate plan involve the distribution of assets. For most people, it's fairly obvious. Their wealth goes to their immediate family and loved ones (spouse, children, partner, siblings), and perhaps a few select friends or others who have a relationship you might want to recognize. The order and amounts are important matters that you must resolve.

Always name additional alternates. While it may be unlikely that your first choices as beneficiaries won't be alive to receive the assets, it is always best to consider several layers of alternates. In the unlikely event your primary heirs cannot receive your estate, the last thing you want is for court and legal fees to consume a substantial portion of your estate in determining who should receive what's left. When naming people to receive assets under your will, you must be careful with the wording you use. If you have two children and name them, what if there are future children? What about children adopted by you? Should they be treated the same as natural children? If you name a class or group of people (e.g., all my first cousins) make absolutely clear who is included and not included in that group.

A family listing of all the people important to your plan (and also family members whom you may not wish to involve) is essential to assure that your goals are carried out. A family tree is just as important when you wish to leave assets to nonfamily members. This is because your will should mention the family members to whom you are not leaving assets so that those family members will have difficulty challenging your will by stating that you simply overlooked them when drafting your will.

CAUTION: The difficulty of properly and carefully delineating who should receive assets as part of a group or class is a good example of why fill-in-the-blank forms, although cheap, are not best. This type of wording can be critical to carrying out your wishes and heading off a battle or will challenge. Don't be penny-wise and pound-foolish. If your distribution arrangements start getting complex, hire an estate planning professional.

There are many ways to structure assets given to the people you've designated. For minor heirs (children, grandchildren, nieces, nephews, or anyone under age), a trust is often the best way to provide for management of assets when they are too young to do so. The age and ability of the recipient are critical in making this decision. The younger and less able the recipient, the more important it is that some mechanism of formal control, namely a trust, should be used. If the amounts are not large enough to warrant a trust, a Uniform Gifts to Minors Act account may suffice. A typical will may provide that money is held in trust for any beneficiary who receives an inheritance before age 35. The trustees have considerable flexibility to make distributions to the child before the ages at which distributions are required (25, 30, and 35).

A special needs trust may be important for a beneficiary who is aged or ill to prevent the funds from being used for basic care expenses that state or federal government programs would otherwise cover.

The best approach will depend on the people involved, the amount of money, and your goals.

A primary purpose for a child or other minor's trust is that the minor may not be mature enough to handle money. Even if the minor is more than sufficiently sophisticated and mature, the 50 percent divorce rate should concern you enough to have the inheritance held in trust for a period of time. Also, you want to protect the assets in the event of a lawsuit, which is always a concern. Another important reason for using a trust is to permit the minor to "be a kid." If the child is 18 years old with $150,000 in the bank and has friends who are scrounging for money to buy a used car while he or she goes out and buys an expensive imported sports car, you are not giving the minor a chance to grow up by being a kid like everybody else. Does the minor have the freedom to make the mistakes others can in their carefree and youthful days? If the minor has to worry about having so much money, he or she may be stifled. The minor may be too fearful to make the same mistakes that most of us had the chance to make in business and personal endeavors. If you put everything in the child's name and the child makes an investment or starts a business that fails, not only has the child lost what he or she invested, everything you have given the minor could be at risk. Thus, a trust is not an implication that you don't trust your child or other heir; it is a protection you provide because you care.

SHOULD THE GRANTOR BE THE SOLE INITIAL TRUSTEE?

If the Grantor, Trustee, and Beneficiary are the same person, the legal doctrine of "merger" has applied in some states to make the trust void, but has generally been eliminated. The laws of some states, however, require that one or more other persons hold a beneficiary interest therein, whether such interest be vested or contingent, present or future. Even in states where this is not an issue, consideration should be given to whether it is appropriate for the Grantor to be the sole Trustee. If the Grantor has failing health or doesn't have the time or inclination to manage assets, it may be prudent to have the Grantor serve as a co-trustee with another person. An institutional trustee can be used, with the funds invested by the institution.

In the context of a living trust, you are almost always the grantor. Occasionally, spouses may be co-grantors jointly funding one trust. For many people, it may be safer to name someone other than a spouse as an immediate co-trustee. If it is difficult for you to manage your financial and related affairs, an institutional co-trustee may be named. If not, you may name a child or family member. The purpose of this is to provide a measure of protection in an emergency. If you and your spouse travel together, for example, you can name a child or other person as initial co-trustee (you would just reserve control for yourself). This way, in an emergency or accident, someone other than your spouse, who is with you, can act on your behalf. Your spouse would then be the successor to you and you to your spouse. Thus, a person likely not to be in the car, or on the vacation, will be a co-trustee.

If your assets include a substantial securities portfolio, the institutional money manager handling the account may be a natural to serve as co-trustee. There may be little additional cost over the asset management fee for the institution to serve as co-trustee.

If your assets include closely held business interests, especially businesses that require active management, you must consider these needs in selecting a co-trustee and successor trustee. You should evaluate whether the trustees can hire professional help to manage the business, what expertise they will require to supervise the professionals, and what the cost of both trustees and hired professionals will have on your earnings.

If your trust is to include multigenerational living trust planning at some point, you may have to name as co-trustee an institution with its principal place of business in a state that has laws permitting a dynasty trust (see Part Four).

SUMMARY

The Foundation Living Trust is the basic document on which all living trusts are to be organized and drafted. The decisions discussed in this chapter are thus important for you no matter which living trust you select.

6 OPERATING YOUR FOUNDATION LIVING TRUST

SHOULD YOU FUND YOUR REVOCABLE LIVING TRUST?

Funding means actually transferring assets to the ownership of the trust. This is not an all-or-nothing decision.

Fully Funded Revocable Living Trust

You can fund a trust with every asset you own. This would be the appropriate course of action if you've decided that you want to entirely avoid probate. If every asset you own is held by your revocable living trust, there may in fact be no need to engage in a probate proceeding since letters testamentary authorizing the executor to transfer assets will not be necessary. Avoiding having assets in the probate estate, however, does not resolve the problems with the revocable living trust approach discussed in Chapter 2.

NOTE: Rarely is the fully funded revocable living trust completely successful. Inevitably, some asset somewhere, sometime, surfaces that requires letters testamentary, and hence a probate proceeding. It may be a bank account that was overlooked, or a car which was mistakenly assumed to be in another's name, or even a last-minute court award or lottery winning.

If your target goal is total probate avoidance, you must transfer title to every asset you own to either the trust or to a form of ownership that achieves probate avoidance. These are discussed in Chapter 3. Your checking account for daily check writing must be either in the name of your living trust or in joint name with another person. Your household and personal property must be transferred to the name of the trust (see Chapter 8).

Partially or Substantially Funded Revocable Living Trust

In many situations, the preferable course of action is to partially, not fully, fund your revocable living trust. Again, as with any estate planning, the approach used should be designed to meet your personal goals and objectives.

If you are establishing a revocable living trust to provide a mechanism to protect you in the event of illness or disability, you should transfer significant financial assets to your trust so that it will be easier for a co-trustee or successor trustee to immediately use and manage those assets for your benefit in an emergency. How much should you transfer? Anything from just enough money to carry you through the transition period until your successor trustee obtains the rest of your assets, to all of your assets which are convenient to transfer. If you have a durable power of attorney, your agent under the power of attorney can transfer assets from your name to the name of your revocable living trust so that your successor trustee can use those assets for your benefit. Thus, as soon as this transfer is completed, your trustee will have adequate assets. Rather than risking underestimating how much should be held initially in the trust, transfer extra assets. Perhaps the most common approach is to include all assets whose transfer don't present costs or complications.

Occasionally, people use a revocable living trust to provide for a particular distribution that they do not want to attract the attention of their other heirs.

EXAMPLE: Father wants to provide an extra $200,000 distribution to a particular child who has certain health issues making it more difficult for that child to earn a living than for her siblings. The father does not want the other children to feel insulted because this one child received more. So the father funds $200,000 into a revocable living trust to provide for this distribution. A joint or POD account could have also been considered.

Unfunded or Standby Revocable Living Trust

In some situations, you may prefer not to fund your revocable living trust at all. You may simply sign the trust document. This approach may be appropriate in many circumstances.

For example, your primary purpose for having a revocable living trust is to provide for the management of your assets in the event of disability. You may, because of your current young age or good health, prefer to have the trust document signed and "ready to go," but not bother setting up the accounts. When your health begins to fail, you may then transfer assets to the trust. If an emergency strikes, you needn't worry that the trust is unfunded because the agent under your durable power of attorney can then fund the trust for you by transferring your personal assets to the successor trustee of your revocable living trust. If you name an institution, such as a bank or trust company, as a successor trustee, consolidating assets into accounts at that institution before you become disabled will make the transition of assets to your living trust safer, quicker, and easier. It also gives you a chance to "test drive" working with that institution.

On your death, for example, you may prefer to have assets distributed according to your trust since you don't want to make certain details about your distributions known. This might be because you are a celebrity and want to avoid attention, or perhaps you just have some rather strange wishes for what should be done with your money when you die. You might execute a pour-over will that would then distribute all estate assets to your trust following your death for distribution from the trust. Your personal and confidential distribution provisions will be contained in your trust, not your will. But don't count on the confidentiality being absolute (see Chapter 2). The court may require that the trust be filed if you have a pour-over will, litigation could bring the trust into public records, or other contingencies could occur.

Finally, you may set up a revocable living trust today for use in distributing assets in the event of your death, but you may not have any significant assets to fund it with presently. The trust will instead be funded on your death by insurance and other assets payable to the trust at that time.

GENERAL INSTRUCTIONS FOR FUNDING AND IMPLEMENTING YOUR FOUNDATION LIVING TRUST

It is strongly recommended, if not essential, for the success of your living trust, and the related planning objectives, that you carefully implement the steps outlined. These include addressing tax reporting requirements, properly transferring assets to the trust, and following other steps. Failure to do so will likely have adverse consequences.

Who Should Complete the Legwork to Implement Your Trust?

Generally, to the extent you can properly handle the implementation of your trust (funding, tax identification number, coordination with your accountant, etc.), it will be advantageous for you to do so on your own (i.e., limiting the assistance of your attorney and accountant), thus minimizing professional cost. If you cannot complete the necessary administrative tasks, be certain that your estate planner, accountant, financial adviser, and other professionals know which matters you expect them to handle for you. Don't assume that they automatically undertake such work. Most don't.

Obtaining a Tax Identification Number

Once you have signed the trust document you should usually fund the trust and apprise your accountant so that he or she can advise you concerning any necessary income tax returns. You should determine whether your trust needs its own tax identification number or whether instead it should operate using your Social Security number (see Chapter 20).

If you are to obtain a tax identification number, it can be done by your calling the Internal Revenue Service or you can fill in IRS Form SS-4 and mail it to the IRS. It is pretty easy.

In preparing this form, consider the following:

- The mailing address should be a convenient address to receive IRS correspondence. If you are getting on in years, anticipate moving frequently, or are relying on co-trustee to help you out, consider whether an address other than yours may be best to use (e.g., a P.O. Box).
- The grantor is you, the person setting up the trust.
- The trust will use a December 31 fiscal year-end.
- The trust will not have any employees or to engage in any manufacturing activities, so indicate "0" and "N/A."
- The trustee or grantor should sign the form. You'll be both (even if you have a co-trustee).
- Mail one signed copy to the IRS. If you obtain the tax identification number by telephone, write the number in the upper-right-hand corner of the form first.

The tax identification number should be used on all Living Trust transactions, bank, and brokerage accounts.

Funding Your Revocable Living Trust—Generally

Merely signing a trust document will not enable you to realize the most important benefits your living trust can offer. You should fund the trust by transferring assets to it. The nature and amount of assets will depend on your goals and objectives. Although the courts have recognized living trusts as valid that have simply listed in an attached schedule assets intended to fund the trust, this should not be relied on. Too often, the "Schedule A" lists attached to many revocable living trusts have incomplete or inaccurate information. Importantly, the third parties you need to recognize the transfers will not be swayed by a mere schedule. Banks, brokerage firms, and others will want to have the assets properly transferred on their records. In some states, merely listing assets on a schedule attached to the revocable living trust will not suffice to legally transfer those assets to the trust.

You will have to transfer assets to the trust for it to provide you and your loved ones with the benefits of (1) managing of your assets in the event of disability; (2) minimizing or avoiding probate; and (3) consolidating assets to facilitate investment objectives. You must also consider which trust assets should be transferred to your living trust and which to your spouse's living trust to enable your respective estates to both take advantage of the applicable exclusion amount ($650,000 in 1999), protect assets from one spouse's creditors (i.e. assets in your trust can be reached by your creditors, but assets in your spouse's trust may be safe from your creditors), and so forth. For example, if one spouse owns all assets, or all assets are owned jointly, in most states you will not be able to maximize your estate tax savings. Sometimes it is advantageous, even at the risk of forgoing possible tax benefits, to have the spouse who faces the least risk of lawsuits own most assets.

How to Transfer Specific Assets to Your Trust

Real Estate

You should consider retaining a real estate attorney to assist in the proper transfer of any real estate to your trust. Local governments or agencies may have reporting requirements. Environmental compliance requirements concerning the transfer of real estate may have to be addressed. You should also address the consequences of transferring real estate from its present form of ownership to that of a trust. Real estate owned by you and your spouse as tenants-by-the-entirety may have certain advantages over real estate held in the name of your trust. You or your real estate attorney should verify with your title insurer whether such transfer of ownership would create any title problems. "Title insurance" protects you if someone makes a claim that they have ownership rights in the property. A new title insurance policy in the name of the trust may be required.

If the title is transferred, an adverse estate tax consequence may also follow with respect to obtaining a step-up in tax basis.

Real estate can be transferred to your trust by completing and filing a deed from you to the trust. For a cooperative apartment, you should first obtain the written consent of the cooperative board of directors as to any requirements that you must comply with to make the transfer. If the house to be transferred is in a homeowners association or subject to any special restrictions, be certain to obtain any necessary approvals before making the transfer. Liability and fire insurance policies should be amended to reflect the name of the trust. The trustees and others perhaps should be named as insured persons. Permission of your lender may be required. If the property is rented, the leases may have to be amended.

Review all of the preceding issues before transferring the real estate to your trust.

Bank Accounts

Bank accounts can be transferred by completing the necessary bank forms so that the account will be in the name of the trust, not in your name. New checks and bankbooks should be obtained. The trust's tax identification number should be given to the bank (the bank will probably request this on Form W-9). All interest income following the date of transfer should be under the trust's tax identification number if you're using one.

Marketable Securities

Marketable securities (those traded on an exchange and not equity interests in a closely held business or investment) are generally transferred by contacting the transfer agent for the security and obtaining the necessary transfer forms, such as a stock power. Complete the forms and return them with the original stock or bond certificates in accordance with the transfer agent's instructions. You may have to provide a guaranteed signature. This is generally done by your signing at a bank that can guarantee your signature. The transfer agent will reissue the securities in the name of the trust.

Carefully consider the advantages of having marketable securities held in a trust brokerage account (called "street name") rather than retitling individual securities to the trust. This means the brokerage firm would give you a monthly statement listing the securities they are holding for you, instead of you actually having direct ownership of the actual certificates. If you have many different securities, this can save you a lot of time and effort. Even more importantly, using a street name account can save tremendous administrative problems in the event of your disability or death. If you retain actual stock certificates, just in the name of your living trust, where do you keep them? If you safeguard them in a safe-deposit box, probate may be necessary for your heirs to open the safe-deposit box to get stock certificates owned by your trust!

If you retitle securities to the trust, use the following format: "Your Name, as Trustee of the Your Name Revocable Living Trust [the name you've given the trust], dated January 4, 2001 [the date the trust was signed, or the date of the most recent amendment]."

Equity in Closely Held Business

For stock in a closely held business, review the shareholders' agreement for any specific requirements or restrictions. Minutes for the corporation should be signed and new stock certificates issued in the name of the trust on surrender of the old stock certificates bearing your name. The tax identification number for the trust should be given to the corporation, and all dividend income following the date of transfer should be under the trust's tax identification number.

Limited liability company (LLC) interests are transferred by signing an assignment of LLC membership interest form. Carefully review the LLC's operating agreement prior to making any transfer. A certificate of LLC membership interests may be issued to your trust, and the old certificate in your name would be canceled. Many LLCs don't issue certificates (like those of companies), and signing the operating agreement will be all that is done. The Certificate of Formation or Articles of Organization (the formal documents filed with your state to form the LLC) may have to be amended. The LLC should report your trust's share of income or loss following the transfer on a new Form K-1 under the trust's federal tax identification number.

Partnership interests are transferred by signing an assignment of partnership form. Carefully review the partnership agreement prior to making any transfer. A certificate of amendment of the partnership's limited partnership certificate may have to be filed. The partnership should report your trust's share of income or loss following the transfer on a new Form K-1 under the trust's federal tax identification number.

In all cases involving closely held business interests, carefully consider the advantages of having the transaction reviewed by an attorney. Apparently simple matters often have complexities and potentially costly traps you may not realize. This is especially important if unrelated persons own any of the businesses involved or if you will be making gifts to reduce your taxable estate.

Personal Property

You will transfer furniture, art, jewelry, and other personal property through a signed and notarized a bill of sale. Be certain to check with your accountant to confirm whether there will be any sales or other tax filing or reporting requirement.

If you want to retitle an automobile to a trust, consult with the department of motor vehicles first. If the trust is a revocable living trust, you may have to title and insure the vehicle in both the name of the trust and the grantor/settlor of the trust. While this might be a hassle, consider the costs and time of having to undertake a probate proceeding when the only probate asset is the one old car you didn't transfer to your trust.

Retirement Assets

Retirement assets should not be retitled to your revocable living trust. Also, the improper designation of a retirement account beneficiary (or the improper transfer of a retirement account) could have substantial adverse tax consequences.

Information to Provide When You Retitle Assets to Your Living Trust

In most cases, the following items should be provided to your broker, banker, or other person transferring assets to the name of the trust:

- Copy of the entire trust. Most firms will require an original signed trust. However, some will accept a certified true copy, or perhaps even a mere photocopy. Many will accept a memorandum of trust. This is a formal summary of key provisions of your living trust. Some will only require a copy of the first page and signature page of your living trust. Generally, you should try to give them as little of the document as possible to preserve confidentiality.
- A letter of instruction authorizing the transfer signed by the trustees in a manner that complies with the terms of the trust.
- The trust's tax identification number. You can send a copy of the form you receive from the IRS assigning the number.

Form 6.1 Sample Letter

YOUR NAME, Grantor
CO-TRUSTEE NAME, Trustee
TRUST-NAME
YOUR ADDRESS

August 26, 1999
CERTIFIED MAIL RETURN RECEIPT
Big Brokerage Firm, Inc.
123 Main Street
Bull Run, Somestate

NOTE: Different terminology is used by different institutions. Be certain to confirm the appropriate terminology (e.g., to avoid an unintended liquidation and reinvestment that could trigger a tax cost).

RE: *Change in Registration of Existing Account*

Dear Sirs:

I want to change the registration (sometimes referred to as "transfer the ownership") on the current account indicated below to a new account. I understand that this change in registration will *NOT* result in any sale of the current interests so that there will be no tax consequences of the change. I understand that a new account number will be issued.

The current account is:

CURRENT-ACCOUNTNAME
CURRENT-ACCOUNTADDRESS
Customer No. ACCOUNT-NO.

I am not holding the certificate shares on the account in my possession.
Information on the new account is as follows:

New account name:

Big Brokerage Firm, Inc.
Trustees: CO-TRUSTEENAME

NOTE: Confirm per trust document.

Either co-trustee has the authority to sign individually. Two signatures (i.e., signatures of both co-trustees are not required).

Tax Identification No. 00-000000.

Trust Date: 00/00/00

The new registration/account should have check-writing privileges and fund exchanges by telephone.

NOTE: Amend and modify the following language to address whether check-drawing privileges, credit card services, margin, and so forth should be attached to the new trust account.

Form 6.1 (Continued)

Please send new checks as soon as possible.

As required, a copy of a memorandum of the Trust Agreement is enclosed.

If there are *ANY* questions, you may also feel free to contact my lawyer/accountant:

NOTE: Use the title of the professional adviser the bank or brokerage firm should contact and add the full name, firm name, address, telephone number, and facsimile machine number here.

Sincerely,

_____ Date:11/____ /02   SIGNATURE GUARANTEE
Your Name, Current Co-Owner and Co-Trustee of Trust

_____ Date:11/____ /02   SIGNATURE GUARANTEE
Co-Owner, Current Co-Owner

_____ Date:11/____ /02   SIGNATURE GUARANTEE
Co-Trustee, Co-Trustee of Trust

enc.
cc:

- The date the trust was signed by the grantor (person forming the trust). If you provide a copy of the trust or a memorandum of trust that may suffice.
- The names of the trustees.
- A copy of the current brokerage, bank, or other statement being transferred.

How to Transfer Brokerage or Bank Accounts to Your Living Trust

To benefit from your revocable living trust, you should transfer at least meaningful liquid assets to the trust since in an emergency, these funds will quickly be available to a co-trustee or successor trustee to use to protect you and your loved ones. To transfer existing brokerage or bank accounts to your living trust, call each bank and brokerage firm to ascertain any special requirements they have, obtain transfer forms, and clarify what (if any) costs or charges may be involved. Consider confirming the instructions in writing to avoid any confusion. Form 6.1 is a sample letter that can be modified for these purposes.

Bill of Sale to Transfer Personal Property to Revocable Living Trust

If you want to transfer personal property to your living trust, the most common step is to attach a list of property (usually referred to as a "Schedule") to your trust document listing all of the property you are transferring. You have to be careful when you transfer personal property. If you later sell, give away, or otherwise lose the property, the trust schedule should periodically be amended. Also, it is not clear that under all state laws simply listing "All personal property" on a schedule attached to your living trust will suffice to transfer the ownership of that property to your trust. A more assured method of accomplishing this is by signing the type of legal document that is used in business settings to transfer ownership of personal property, a "Bill of Sale." A bill of sale is to personal property (furniture, equipment, etc.), what a deed is to real estate.

If you're going to transfer personal property to your living trust, be sure to follow up with your property insurance company. If your house is in your trust, your personal property can also be listed as owned by the trust. Since personal property is generally insured as part of your homeowner's policy, this should be relatively straightforward. If your house is owned by a different trust or your spouse, assuring that your coverage is in order might be more complex.

Finally, there may be an issue of state sales tax due on the transfer, or an impact on local or state property taxes. Be sure to review these with your accountant.

Form 6.2 illustrates how to transfer personal property to your trust.

YOUR FOUNDATION LIVING TRUST WHILE YOU ARE ALIVE AND WELL

While you are alive and well, your living trust should be practically invisible. But for a bit longer title (i.e., "John Doe Living Trust" instead of just your name "John Doe"), there should be few formalities once you've signed the document and retitled your assets to the trust and addressed other formation steps (but that does not mean you can ignore these formalities).

Memorandum of Trust

To open some types of accounts or to transfer real estate to your living trust, the trust document may have to be provided to the institution with which you are dealing or the trust may have to be recorded. Because the living trust documents are so lengthy and may be quite personal, a summary or memorandum of your living trust may be provided instead. The memorandum of trust should be tailored to address the needs involved without unduly disclosing personal affairs. For example, if you were required to record a memorandum of living trust in the public records of

Form 6.2 Sample Bill of Sale

KNOW ALL MEN BY THESE PRESENT, that Your Name, Grantor, an individual who resides at 123 Main Street, Anytown, USA (the "Donor") for and in consideration of the sum of $1.00 and as a gift to Your Name Revocable Living Trust, dated 01/22/02, c/o John Smith, co-trustee, an individual who resides at 456 Big Street, Sometown, USA (the "Donee"), has granted, transferred, and conveyed and by these presents does grant, transfer, and convey unto the said Donee, and said Donee's successors and assigns, all ownership in the property hereinafter described ("Asset"):

1. Painting of "Girl and Horse" by John Artist, dated 1/1/89.
2. Ceramic Vase by Pauline Pottery, dated 2/4/89.
3. Sonic Boom stereo system.
4. Assets listed in the "Home Inventory" attached hereto as Schedule A, including all Donor's right, title, and interests in the Asset.

Donor hereby represents and warrants that donor has good and marketable title to the Asset named hereinabove, subject to no liens, mortgages, security interests, encumbrances, or charges of any nature.

This Bill of Sale has been executed to complete the gift contemplated herein. Nothing herein contained shall be deemed or construed to confer upon any person or entity other than Donee any rights or remedies by reason of this instrument.

TO HAVE AND TO HOLD the same unto the said Donee and the Donee's successors and assigns forever; and the Donor covenants and agrees to and with the said Donee to warrant and defend the said described Asset against all and every person or persons whomsoever.

IN WITNESS WHEREOF, the Donor has set her hand and seal to be hereto affixed this January 3, 2003.

Signed, Sealed, and Delivered by:

Your Name

_____

in the Presence of:

_____

Witness

State of Somestate   )

                          :ss.:

County of Anycounty   )

On January 3, 2003, before me personally came, Your Name, to me known and known to me, by presentation of a driver's license of Somestate, to be the individual described in and who executed the foregoing instrument, and such donor duly acknowledged to me that such donor understood the meaning of the instrument and that such donor executed the same for the purposes expressed therein and with due authority and powers to do so.

_____

Notary Public

(continued)

Form 6.2 (Continued)

Your Name
123 Main Street, Anytown USA
SCHEDULE A, ATTACHMENT TO BILL OF SALE
HOUSEHOLD INVENTORY

Room: _____   Date: _____

Item—Description	Quantity	Photo	Purchase Date	Bill Enclosed	Payment Reference	Purchase Price	Current Value

your county to transfer your house to the trust, the Memorandum of Trust would have to include the name of the trust, the name of the trustees, and specific excerpts or summaries of the provisions of the trust document that authorize the trustees to acquire real estate. You want to include all the information that the persons relying on the Memorandum of Trust will need to know, but disclose the least amount of extra personal information. Form 6.3 is a sample memorandum of trust.

YOUR FOUNDATION LIVING TRUST ON YOUR DISABILITY

One of the most important uses of your Foundation Living Trust is to protect you and your loved ones should you become disabled. While an overall plan to address disability is necessary, your trust, if properly structured, can be the cornerstone of such a plan. In the event of your disability, the

Form 6.3 Sample Memorandum of Trust

Prepared By:

_____

Your Attorney Name

MEMORANDUM OF TRUST
YOUR NAME REVOCABLE LIVING TRUST

1. A revocable living trust for the benefit of Your Name [there may be other current beneficiaries whose names you will list] was executed on January 3, 2003.

2. Your Name was the grantor of the "Your Name Revocable Living Trust," which was signed and executed on the above date.

3. Your Name and Cindy Cotrustee were named as the co-Trustees of said trust pursuant to Article Two. If either of such co-Trustees are unable or unwilling to serve, then Sandy Successor shall serve as co-trustee of said trust Article One.

4. Each of the parties to the trust are authorized to act independently and individually of the other, without any requirement for joint action, with respect to banking and real estate transactions. Article Five.

5. The trust provisions provide that the trustees shall have authority to transact all business in regard to purchase and sale of real property included in the trust estate. Article Four says: "To invest and reinvest any assets comprising the Trust Estate in any . . . property, whether real or personal . . . " Article Eight also includes additional rights and powers, including: "To sell at public or private sale . . . assets constituting the Trust Estate at the time, price, and terms as the Trustee deems advisable." Article Nine includes the following powers: "To sell, exchange, partition, convey and mortgage, and to modify, extend renew or replace any mortgage which may be on all, or any part, of any interest in real property included in the Trust Estate."

6. Said trust is still in full force and effect and has not been amended since the date noted above [if amended, list all dates and state clearly that the preceding information is consistent with the current version of this trust].

In Witness Whereof, I have set my hand this October 12, 2004.

Co-Trustee:

_____

Your Name

State of Somestate   )

  :ss.:

County of Anycounty   )

On October 12, 2004, before me personally came, Your Name, to me known and known to me, by presentation of a driver's license of Somestate, to be the Trustee described in and who executed the foregoing instrument, and such donor duly acknowledged to me that such Trustee understood the meaning of the instrument and that such Trustee executed the same for the purposes expressed therein and with due authority and powers to do so.

_____

Notary Public

successor trustee or successor trustees will become empowered to act on behalf of the trust. The provisions determining when you become disabled, and even more importantly when you recover and can resume control over your trust, are critical. Most living trust documents give little if any attention to this vital issue. If you have a living trust in place, review the provisions governing disability. Do they make sense? Are they complete? Can anyone reading the document understand how to determine whether you are disabled? Whether you have recovered? What happens in both situations?

YOUR FOUNDATION LIVING TRUST FOLLOWING YOUR DEATH

Following death, your successor trustees will assume control, organize a balance sheet listing all assets and other rights you had at death, and determine what assets to collect, bills to pay, tax or other filings to make, and so forth. Since the Foundation Living Trust does not include any tax planning (the more comprehensive versions provided later in this book will), no tax-oriented trusts, such as a bypass trust, will be funded following death. However, if any of your heirs are minors, trusts for minors may be funded.

NOTE: For additional information on these types of trusts and their use in planning, see Martin Shenkman, *The Complete Guide To Probate* (New York: John Wiley & Sons, 1999).

SUMMARY

This chapter has provided an overview of the Foundation Living Trust. Many of the issues discussed, steps involved, and points raised, will be similar for any living trust you use. Thus, this foundation trust will be the base for developing all the living trust planning in this book. Whatever your financial situation, you can benefit from the provisions of the Foundation Living Trust.

7 ADDITIONAL DOCUMENTS ESSENTIAL TO EVERY PLAN

A revocable living trust is merely one of many documents and techniques to be used as part of your overall Foundation Living Trust estate and financial plan. The following discussion provides an overview of what this plan, at minimum, should entail.

NOTE: For more information on many of these documents see Martin Shenkman, *The Complete Book of Trusts* (New York: John Wiley & Sons, 1998). Also see the web site: www.laweasy.com for sample forms and current planning tips.

RELATIONSHIP OF YOUR LIVING TRUST TO YOUR WILL, POWER, AND LIVING WILL

The following chart summarizes the relationship of your key estate planning documents. Each of the basic estate planning documents only protects you for the time, and concerning the matters, in the box in which it appears. The shaded area illustrates matters addressed by the Comprehensive Living Trust document. A properly drafted living trust can avoid gaps in other documents and be used to bring order to your overall estate plan. It can provide you more comprehensive protection.

Time/Event	Financial Issues	Health Issues
Alive and well	Nonspringing power of attorney	
Alive but disabled	Springing durable power of attorney	Living will/Health care proxy
After your death	Will	

USE REVOCABLE LIVING TRUSTS AS PART OF AN OVERALL ESTATE PLAN

Estate planning can best be explained by viewing it from several perspectives. Each approach will help you achieve different goals and objectives.

Documents

Every estate plan will require basic documents to implement your planning, save taxes, and protect you and your loved ones. The three most basic documents that everyone should have are a durable power of attorney (authorizes someone to handle financial and legal matters if you can't), a living will or health care proxy (authorizes someone to handle health care issues if you can't), and a will (governs distribution of your probate estate).

Beyond these core documents, a host of other documents may be essential, or perhaps merely helpful, for you to achieve your estate planning goals. If you have significant insurance, you should consider the benefits of having an insurance trust own it. If you have a family business, corporations, limited liability companies, and family limited partnerships may be useful. Also, a shareholder, partnership, buyout, or other agreements may be essential for your business. If you own real estate, leases and other documentation may be necessary.

Charitable lead trusts, charitable remainder trusts, qualified personal residence trusts, grantor-retained annuity trusts, and other documents and techniques may be helpful in reducing your estate tax costs. These documents are almost purely tax motivated.

Tax Planning

A revocable living trust and other documents alone aren't enough to achieve most estate planning goals. You must have a comprehensive plan to address estate taxes. Don't be lulled into relying on the increasing applicable exclusion amount (the amount you can give away or bequeath free of estate tax), without taking action. You may have to change the ownership (title) of assets. Insurance to fund part or all of the estate tax may be appropriate. If it is, you must select the optimal characteristics for the policy (term, variable, which insurer, etc.). A gift program can be a key planning step to reduce your estate and take maximum advantage of the annual gift tax exclusion. To implement a gift program, you may have to restructure assets, obtain an appraisal, obtain new legal documents, and more.

What if the Estate Tax Is Repealed?

Congress has frequently mentioned the possible repeal of the estate tax. This is rather an amazing proposition considering the extreme concentration of wealth in this country, a situation that the repeal of the estate tax will only exacerbate. Statistics from the IRS show that only about 1.8 percent of the people dying had to file estate tax returns. As the amount that can be given away tax-free increases toward $1 million, this percentage will fall further. According to a recent survey, a net worth of about $275,000 puts you in the top 11 percent of the country's wealthiest! The estate tax will, by 2006, permit you to give away $1 million free of tax. So who pays the tax?

How does the possible repeal affect your planning? As is clear from the preceding statistics, only a very small percentage of people ever did worry about the estate tax. So, if a living trust made sense for you, the odds are that the repeal of estate tax won't affect your decision to use a living trust. If your living trust includes estate tax planning and the tax is repealed, simply update your trust. All the nontax reasons for using it will remain.

If you're planning a living trust now, should you ignore the tax planning hoping the tax will be repealed? You shouldn't count your tax eggs until they hatch. Wait until Congress really acts before assuming that the tax will be repealed. To assume that the tax will be repealed, given the financial data in the preceding paragraph, could be a costly planning mistake. If the tax is repealed, the nontax planning discussed in this book (which is most of this book) will still apply. You will still want protection in the event of disability. You will still need powers, living wills, and wills. Insurance trusts to protect the proceeds of large insurance policies will still make sense. Repealing the estate tax, if done, won't make your hard-earned assets safer from creditors, so asset protection will still be essential.

Asset Protection Planning

Everyone should give some consideration to protecting assets. What good will it be to avoid probate and save estate taxes if you're sued and have no assets left to be taxed? Many of the trusts, corporations, and other entities established as part of your plan can help protect assets as well. Reviewing your casualty insurance coverage is essential.

EXAMPLE: A common asset protection technique for family businesses is to divide different types of assets, each of which has a different risk profile, in distinct entities. For example, real estate where the family business is operated may be owned by a limited liability company. Equipment used in the business may be owned in an S corporation. The real estate and equipment entities may lease their respective assets to a third entity, a C corporation or more commonly a limited liability company, which serves as the operating entity. This approach can help insulate one asset from lawsuits against other assets.

Personal Goals

Don't forget yourself and the other people your plan is to benefit. Personal goals, religious feelings (or the lack thereof), medical decisions, and so forth, all should be addressed. These can affect every aspect of your estate plan and can be reflected in many aspects of a revocable living trust:

- Specify a religious or other preference for nursing home or other facilities in the event of disability.

- Make charitable bequests.
- Incorporate religious provisions in distribution clauses.
- Direct the payment of burial and funeral expenses in accordance with specific religious or personal preferences.
- Give investment provisions either a social or religious orientation.

Investment Planning

Are your assets allocated to minimize risk and maximize return? Do your investments meet your personal financial goals? How will funds in trusts you establish for yourself (e.g., if you are disabled and the successor trustee of your living trust invests your assets)? How will trust funds for children be invested? What about funds in the applicable exclusion trust under your will?

Summary of Revocable Living Trusts and Estate Planning

Each of the topics previously noted above should be considered in formulating and implementing your comprehensive estate plan, which may include your revocable living trust. The more comprehensive your approach, the more likely you and your loved ones will achieve your goals. This book will focus on revocable living trusts as part of planning your estate. However, always keep in mind the broader definition and objectives of the planning process. A revocable living trust, alone, despite what the hype would have you believe, can never suffice without other steps.

SAFE-KEEPER POUR-OVER WILL

The most common approach to integrating an estate plan that includes both a will and revocable living trust is to draft a pour-over will. On death, any probate assets (presumably only those assets that could not be identified or that had a legal or other impediment to a lifetime transfer to the revocable living trust) would be poured over from the probate estate (i.e., as governed by the will) into the revocable living trust.

In many cases, particularly with the simplistic do-it-yourself form books sold to nonlawyers, the will is a simple two-page document that does little more than appoint an executor and state that any assets be poured into the revocable living trust. This approach is wrong. The correct approach is to draft a comprehensive will, including all typical boilerplate provisions and details on how your assets are to be distributed. With computers, this process involves negligible time and cost. If you use the common two-page pour-over will approach, what happens if you accidentally or intentionally destroy your living trust without revising the will? The simplistic pour-over will would result in the equivalent of your dying intestate—without a will.

This can destroy any planning that had been completed. Since the will has no details as to how your assets should be distributed and the trust doesn't exist after you revoke or destroy it, the assets governed by the will should be subject to the laws of intestacy. These are state laws that indicate where your assets will be distributed on death.

It is also advisable to have a comprehensive will in that any actions to be taken by the executor may be facilitated by having a will with broad fiduciary power provisions. These could include special powers to deal with business assets and make tax planning decisions. Because the recommended approach to preparing your will offers many safeguards, this type of will is called a Safe-Keeper Will. It will keep your loved ones safer.

If you do not use the pour-over Safe-Keeper Will and transfer all of your assets to your revocable living trust while alive to avoid probate. Are you willing to risk an intestacy proceeding if any probate assets are identified (which is generally the situation), or another issue arises? Who can make tax decisions and other decisions in the absence of an executor? Will the IRS accept the decisions of the successor trustee under the revocable living trust? Practically, there would be little alternative since in such situations all assets would be within the control of the trustee. To address these and other potential administrative problems, you should always have a comprehensive will that states in some detail many powers and rights given to the executor.

Do not pour over the assets for the benefit of the surviving spouse into that surviving spouse's revocable living trust unless that trust is specifically structured to qualify for the marital deduction. Instead, the distribution to the surviving spouse should be to a QTIP (a trust for your spouse which qualifies for the unlimited estate tax marital deduction), QDOT (a special trust required if your spouse is not a citizen of the United States), or outright (i.e. to her directly, with no trust). The surviving spouse can then distribute the assets received to his or her revocable living trust. If the surviving spouse is disabled, then the agent under the surviving spouse's durable power of attorney can contribute the distributions received from the deceased spouse's revocable living trust to the surviving spouse's revocable living trust. When this type of planning is pursued, your spouse must also have a comprehensive Safe-Keeper Will to avoid problems in the event he or she dies before assets are transferred to his or her living trust.

There are many other examples of problems with the simple pour-over will used by most living trust promoters. The bottom line is, be sure you have a comprehensive will. The following sample language illustrates the pour-over provision from a Safe-Keeper Will.

SAMPLE SAFE-KEEPER WILL LANGUAGE:

1. My net residuary estate I give, devise, and bequeath to the Fiduciary in office at the time of my death under a certain Trust Agreement entitled *LIVINGTRUST-NAME made the *DATE OF LIVING TRUST, between myself and

*LIVINGTRUST-COTRUSTEE as Co-Trustee, to be held, administered, and disposed of by my Fiduciary in accordance with the provisions of said Agreement.

2. In the event that for any reason the above named trust is held or found to be invalid, or if for any other reason the assets of my estate cannot be properly transferred to such trust, then, in such event, all the rest of my residuary estate shall be disposed of in accordance with the following provisions:

* Incorporate all dispositive residuary provisions here in conformity with those of living trust.

DURABLE POWER OF ATTORNEY

A power of attorney is the most important, and also the simplest and least expensive, estate planning document. It is a contract in which you grant another person, often your spouse, the power to act on your behalf if you are ill, injured, or unavailable for any reason. The person you grant this authority to is called your attorney in fact, or agent. Your agent has the important responsibility of seeing to your financial matters if an emergency prevents you from taking the necessary actions. Powers of attorney are an essential estate planning tool. Because of the simplicity, ease of preparation, and nominal cost, you and you family members or loved ones should all have powers of attorney.

A revocable living trust is not a substitute for a power of attorney. Even if you already have a living trust, you should still prepare and sign powers of attorney. Your living trust will only control the assets that you took the necessary legal steps to transfer to it. A power of attorney, however, if broadly written, can give your agent access to all of your non-trust assets. Since a durable power of attorney immediately terminates on your death, it can never be considered a substitute for a will or trust arrangement.

If you are disabled, a power of attorney can authorize your agent to make gifts and take other actions to minimize your estate tax. This can also be done, and perhaps with greater control, under your Comprehensive Living Trust (see Chapter 20).

EXAMPLE: Father began a regular gift program where each year he and his wife join in making gifts of stock to each of their four children, their children's spouses, and their 10 grandchildren. The gifts are each $20,000 in value, the maximum amount that can be given away each year without any gift tax being due (see Chapter 20), for a total of $360,000. Father falls ill in December and is unable to sign the necessary documents to make a transfer for the year so the couple makes no gifts in that year. The couple could incur an unnecessary additional estate tax cost of as much as $216,000 because this gift was not made. If the generation-skipping transfer tax were also considered, the additional tax cost could increase substantially. Had Father prepared an appropriate power of attorney, his agent might have been able to handle the paperwork to make the gifts and eliminate this unnecessary estate tax burden. A living trust can be used to make gifts.

Types of Powers of Attorney

There are many choices to consider when preparing a power of attorney document. A "durable" power of attorney remains effective even though you are disabled. This is generally the only type of power you will want. A provision expressly stating that the power of attorney will remain valid even if you become disabled must generally be included in your power of attorney. This, as illustrated in the preceding example, is one of the most important reasons for a power of attorney. A "springing" power of attorney is one that only springs into being when you become disabled. This prevents your agent from having any authority until you are actually disabled and need assistance. The drawback to using a springing power of attorney is that your agent will have to prove you've become disabled. This can sometimes present problems, or, at minimum, additional work and delays for the agent. People often use a springing power because they don't feel comfortable granting such power to the person they are naming as agent. You should not grant any power of attorney unless you trust the person named. If trust is not then an issue, why risk restricting the power of attorney until you become disabled? This could raise questions as to whether the power of attorney has become effective (i.e., whether you are disabled). If you are setting up a revocable living trust that will hold most of your assets, the decision process for your power of attorney may change. If most assets are in your trust, maybe you would feel more comfortable naming an agent whose power is effective immediately (i.e., when you sign the document) rather than springing into effect later.

NOTE: The rules differ from state to state. Be certain to consult with an attorney in your state to learn the specific rules that apply to you. For example, some states (Florida) limit to certain close relatives the people you may name as an attorney in fact. In some states (California), it may be advisable to file (record) the power of attorney in the appropriate governmental office.

Most powers of attorney are "general" powers. This means they include a broad range of provisions to address almost any imaginable situation. In some cases, however, you may want a "special" power of attorney. This is a power of attorney limited to a few specified uses. For example, you may want to grant a limited power of attorney to a close colleague to authorize him or her to perform certain functions relating to your business when you are ill or otherwise unavailable. A business power of attorney may even provide for compensation. This should be considered an important planning component for every closely held business.

Standard or "form" powers of attorney use a recognized statutory form. Some state laws prescribe use of a particular form of power of attorney. These laws may state that people must accept a form prepared in accordance with the law. In these cases, even though you should sign a customized power of attorney form prepared by your attorney since it can offer additional provisions and flexibility that the preprinted standard forms can't, you should also sign a power of attorney on the preprinted form since this will be more readily accepted in some instances. The time and cost to prepare and sign a form power of attorney is nominal. Be careful, however, as some attorneys charge hundreds of dollars for even a preprinted power of attorney that might take their secretary 10 minutes to type. If your attorney says you don't need both, it might be because the attorney has simply typed up the standard form on a word processor and is overcharging you for not much more than a standard form.

Although there is no reason your banks and brokerage firms should not accept the power of attorney your lawyer prepares, they may not readily honor it. Often, a bank may be willing to honor a durable power of attorney you provide, but will first require its legal department to review it. The resulting delays may be problematic. To address this concern, you can sign standard forms from each bank and brokerage firm you deal with.

You should note that the standard bank and brokerage forms, as well as most standard state forms, will not contain any special provisions to coordinate with your Comprehensive Living Trust. Therefore, always have a comprehensive durable power of attorney tailored to your specific needs, that addresses your trust.

Terms to Include in Your Power of Attorney

To coordinate your power of attorney with your Comprehensive Living Trust plan, you should incorporate several clauses and steps. Be sure to address these expressly with your attorney since many attorneys will not routinely address these issues.

- You should name one or more alternate agents as a precaution in the event that the primary agent (e.g., your partner or spouse) is unable or unwilling to take the necessary actions. Give careful consideration to the persons named under each document. Should they be the same people? Different people? Different combinations of people? In many cases, it's best to name one person at a time to serve as the sole agent of your power of attorney to make it easier for the agent to take action. If there are two agents, both have to sign. Often two co-agents are named to serve to provide safeguards.

- If you own real estate in any state other than the state in which you live, it may be necessary to have a power of attorney written in compliance with the laws of that state. The alternative is to transfer that property to your Living Trust or to an entity (e.g., a limited liability company) as described in Chapter 17.

- Your agent should sign the power of attorney agreement indicating his or her agreement to act in the manner described in the document.

- The power could place restrictions on the scope of the agent's actions. For example, you may only permit the payment of certain emergency expenses; you may permit or not permit the sale of assets, and the making of gifts.

- The power should authorize in some detail your agent to deal with the IRS on a broad range of tax matters.
- The power should include the right to transfer assets to your revocable living trust.
- Possibly include the right to amend your living trust, but carefully consider whether this is appropriate. Also, consider the relationship of the persons designated as agent under your power of attorney and as successor trustees under your living trust. There may also be tax consequences to giving this power if your agent is also a beneficiary under your trust. It is best to review this clause, and all of its ramifications, with your estate planner.
- Consider authorizing the right to form a revocable living trust on your behalf. While this is a good clause to include, and preferably with sufficient detail to make it practical (e.g., that the agent forming a living trust must use the same provisions as your will for distributing your assets), it's far better to prepare a living trust while you are able to make all the decisions yourself.
- Gift powers authorizing gifts to your intended heirs are essential. Without this provision, the IRS may not recognize any gifts made as valid, and neither may the laws of your state. This can create a host of problems. It is important to carefully limit a gift provision so it is clear which people can receive gifts and the maximum amounts that can be given. Be certain that the gift provisions of your power of attorney are coordinated with those in your living trust. You probably don't want both the trustee and the agent to accidentally make gifts in the same year exceeding the maximum $10,000 (to be indexed for inflation) in tax-free gifts that can be made each year. You could include, for example, a reminder that the trustee should consult with the agent before making gifts.
- Consider the impact of using a funded (i.e., significant assets are transferred to your living trust) versus unfunded living trust. The funded trust is usually better and avoids worries over the powers granted to your agent under a durable power. If most assets have been transferred to your funded living trust, there will be few assets left over which the agent under your power of attorney has control.

LIVING WILL AND HEALTH CARE PROXY

Why Do You Need a Living Will/Health Care Proxy?

Deciding how you should be cared for in the event of grave illness is an extraordinarily difficult and emotional decision. Making your wishes for health care treatment known in the event you are unable to communicate your decisions when you are gravely ill has become an integral part of estate and personal planning for everyone. Without advance preparation, living wills, and health care proxies (the forms used to communicate your health care wishes), your preferences may not be followed. Your family or loved ones could face gut-wrenching decisions with no solace in knowing what you would have wanted. Also, since a Comprehensive Living Trust is such a broad, all-encompassing planning document, decisions made in your living will, health care proxy, and living trust should all be coordinated to minimize problems. Living trusts often contain no details related to health care. This can be a tragic mistake, as the following discussion will demonstrate. While neither document is a substitute for the other, coordination of the provisions in both will best assure that your wishes are carried out with the least difficulty.

Thinking about and discussing terminal illness and death can never be a pleasant or easy matter. However, your failure to provide your loved ones with guidance now, while you are able to, may cause them to have to second-guess what you would have wanted done. That would be a difficult and emotionally traumatic task for them. It is essential to communicate guidelines for your care in the event of a medical emergency or terminal illness. With legal authority, even if your family and other loved ones know your feelings, they will face more difficulties and perhaps find it impossible, to carry out your wishes. The result may be that doctors, courts, or others may, despite trying to ascertain and fulfill your wishes, take steps that are the opposite of what you would want. Your personal preferences, religious concerns, family, and other personal relationships should all be considered.

What's the Difference between a Living Will and a Health Care Proxy?

A living will is a statement of your health care wishes. A health care proxy is a durable power of attorney for medical matters. With the health care proxy, you appoint someone as your agent to make health care decisions. Some states do not afford the same recognition to a living will as they do to a health care proxy. For a living will to be valid, the decisions made may have to present "clear and convincing" proof of your wishes. General statements as to "no heroic measures" and the like, which are typically used in living wills, may not suffice. You should therefore sign both a living will and a separate health care proxy and have each of them witnessed and notarized separately.

The health care proxy (power of attorney for medical directives) is essential since it provides a mechanism for your chosen representatives to make decisions if, when, and where the need exists. It is impossible to foresee every future illness or treatment your doctors may prescribe. By appointing a person to act in your behalf, these decisions can be based on your condition at that time, the available medical procedures and advice, and your wishes.

Whom Should You Name as Your Health Care Agent?

Who is to be your health care agent? This decision can be difficult. Many loved ones, however sensitive to your feelings, may simply not be able to make the very difficult decisions that might become necessary.

Can you name two or more people to make a joint decision? It is recommended that you never require joint action by two or more people to make a decision. Some state laws may prohibit this as well. Do not necessarily assume that the person you select will be able to carry out your wishes. Many people simply do not have the emotional composition to "pull the plug" or to make other heart-breaking decisions. Many prospective agents may have religious, moral, or other personal reasons for not being willing to carry out certain wishes. You should discuss these important matters with every agent or successor agent in advance. Request their permission.

Be very careful in naming a child to make decisions. Many children, even those who have long ago passed the age of majority, find it extremely difficult to make a pull-the-plug decision for a parent. If you are to name children, a more important issue is can they bear this responsibility? Rarely is it advisable to name a child under age 25. If you have more than one child, whom do you name? Remember, some states prohibit joint agents. Further, requiring more than one signature might just assure that the required decisions can never be made in time.

Consider your state's health care statutes (laws) at your local library for any requirements that your state may impose on health care agents.

Religious considerations may play a role in choosing your agent.

Should your agent under your health care proxy and living will be the same person as the successor trustee under your living trust? While they could be, there is no reason for them to be. In fact, it may be better that they are not. Also, in your living trust, you may name two people to serve jointly as successor trustees, whereas you should not name joint agents under your living will or health care proxy. Since the successor trustee is being named primarily to deal with financial matters, there is no reason to name the same people. However, your successor trustees under your living trust should have sensitivity to health care and related issues since they will control the purse strings to finance health care decisions.

Additional Decisions You Must Make

You should give thought to many issues when directing your attorney to prepare your living will and health care proxy:

- Should mechanical means of prolonging life be used?
- You should specifically state whether you would permit your agent to ever withdraw artificial nutrition and hydration. If you do not wish to have artificial feeding, even if discontinuing it could hasten death, this should be specifically stated. Many states will not permit the

cessation of nutrition or hydration unless the form specifically authorizes it. Some states require that if your health care proxy is to permit the agent to withdraw nutrition or hydration, the form must be separately signed by that provision.

- State your feelings and wishes about health care, treatment, quality of life, refusal or acceptance of medical treatment, and so forth.

- Organ donations are a vital step to help save the lives of others. Seriously and carefully give thought to permitting organ donations.

- If you want any specific eulogy, service, or steps taken, specify it in your living will. If you want a traditional religious ceremony, say so. Your revocable living trust can also include such provisions, but be sure they are consistent. Preferably, list them only in your living will and direct your successor trustees to cooperate with the decisions made by your agent under your living will.

- Religious considerations can also be vitally important. For those with strong religious convictions, it is imperative to specifically address religious concerns to avoid having your beliefs compromised when you may be unable to express your desires. Never assume that your lawyer or any standard form addresses these concerns.

- What about pain medication and other treatments or procedures to reduce pain? Should they be administered even if they hasten death? Is there any adverse religious implications if pain relief hastens death?

Silence Is Not Golden: Discuss Your Living Will Decisions

As important as the documents you sign is the process through which you determine what they should contain. The process should include discussions about your feelings with your family, doctor, and religious adviser if applicable. All may be involved in the decisions concerning your health care if you should ever be unable to express your own wishes. They cannot be expected to carry out your desires unless you first inform them of your feelings. The more openly you can discuss your feelings with family, the more likely that you will ease the burden of the decisions they could face. While your religious adviser can assist your doctors and family in reaching a decision in accordance with applicable religious tenets and your personal beliefs, an awareness of your feelings can help guide your family and physicians. Communicating your beliefs and feelings is one of the most important steps, and this can't be done with by signing a quick-fix form with your lawyer.

LETTER OF INSTRUCTION

It is essential to communicate your personal desires and objectives to family, friends, and loved ones. Many of these decisions are too personal, variable, or simply inappropriate for inclusion in your legal documents. Many of these decisions cannot be enforced legally so you will be relying on the respect of loved ones to carry them out. Some of these decisions are too vague to reduce to clear legal terms. Finally, as these personal decisions change over time, a nonbinding informal letter can be revised by you anytime, and at no cost. This might (but check with your advisers) enable you to avoid the expense of revising expensive legal documents.

An essential step in implementing your Complete Living Trusts Program is preparing a letter of last instruction to your successor trustees, heirs, and others. Your instructions as to how personal jewelry and other items should be distributed could be included. Since this can change frequently it is often too costly and difficult to continually amend your will to address jewelry and similar personal property. Funeral and burial instructions can be described in this letter (but don't be inconsistent with what you've included in your living will). This is important since a will is often not available in time to relay this information. Finally, you should include some guidance to a prospective guardian as to the care and raising of your children. This guidance will be so helpful that you should push yourself to get through the pain of writing such a letter.

You can keep a copy of this letter in your safe-deposit box, give a copy to your executor, and keep a copy with your original will. Because of the highly personal nature of this letter, a form would really not be of much help. Take the time and try to address the issues important to you.

CHILD EMERGENCY MEDICAL FORM

A child medical authorization form addresses an important and almost always ignored need. There is a gap in most estate plans concerning minor children. Guardian appointments under a will only take effect on the death of the parents. The parents' living wills only address the parents' health care matters. If the parents are on vacation, not reachable, or disabled, who can make a decision concerning a child's medical treatment? Also, when the child is in the hands of a caregiver and the parents cannot be reached, critical personal or medical information may not be known. This form attempts to close this gap. See www.laweasy.com for a sample.

SUMMARY

This chapter has provided a brief review of some of the many tax and legal considerations that you must address in your overall estate and financial plan. These other documents, and the tax issues discussed, must all be coordinated with your revocable living trust.

Part Three

TAX PLANNING AND YOUR COMPLETE LIVING TRUSTS PROGRAM

8 THE JUST-IN-CASE (DISCLAIMER) LIVING TRUST

WHAT IS THE JUST-IN-CASE LIVING TRUST?

Most living trust programs and estate planning documents generally assume that if your aggregate estate (i.e., what you own and what your spouse owns, if you are married) is less than the $650,000 (1999) applicable exclusion amount (what you can give away tax-free), that tax planning (typically in the form of a bypass trust) is not really necessary. This is a potentially costly, and often inappropriate, conclusion. If your estate is estimated at less than $650,000 (or whatever the applicable exclusion amount will be in the year you are doing your planning), perhaps you can ignore tax planning. However, if your estate then exceeds the applicable exclusion amount in the year you die, a tax will be due. The safer solution in many cases is a technique called a "disclaimer bypass trust." This distribution scheme would provide for the distribution of all assets to the surviving spouse outright. However, if your surviving spouse were to disclaim (files the required documents with the probate court within nine months of your death saying she did not want to accept all the assets bequeathed to her under your will), then the assets disclaimed would be distributed into a bypass trust. The bypass trust language would be provided in your will in a manner allowing activation only after your spouse's disclaimer. This technique can preserve the benefit of the applicable exclusion and provide the opportunity to save estate taxes just in case it proves to be advantageous at the time of your death. Hence the title "Just-in-Case Living Trust." The estate tax consequences of this are discussed later in more detail; however, other benefits should also be noted.

The importance of the disclaimer bypass trust extends beyond merely estate tax planning. If your surviving spouse remarries, having assets held in a bypass trust will protect the assets you bequeath her from her new spouse. Having your assets held in a trust will assure that the remaining assets will ultimately be distributed to your heirs, not to the heirs designated by your wife's new spouse. If your surviving spouse is disabled, the assets can be managed in the structure of the bypass trust for her benefit. If there is a lawsuit or claim against your surviving spouse, the trust will provide an important measure of protection for the assets held in the trust. This contrasts with assets held directly in your spouse's name, which will not be protected.

To understand the "disclaimer bypass trust," which is at the heart of the "Just-in-Case" Living Trust, you need to understand some basic estate tax rules, even if your estate is too small to worry about the tax rules. This is because the structure of the trust will be based on tax planning concepts.

WHAT IS THE APPLICABLE EXCLUSION AMOUNT?

To understand the Just-in-Case Living Trust, you must understand what the applicable exclusion amount is. To do so, you have to first understand, in simple terms, the gift and estate taxes. Unlike the income tax, which is familiar to everyone, the gift and estate taxes are transfer taxes. The gift and estate taxes are assessed on the value of property transferred. A primary difference between the gift tax and the estate tax is that the gift tax is assessed on transfers during your life (inter vivos transfers), whereas the estate tax is assessed on transfers following your death (testamentary transfers). These include assets bequeathed under your will. The gift tax and estate tax are integrated. The same progressive tax rate scale applies to combined transfers.

The gift tax and the estate tax share many similar concepts, in particular a single applicable exclusion amount (formerly loosely called the "unified credit"). This exclusion permitted anyone to give away up to $650,000 in 1999 (increased by the 1997 Tax Act in phases up to $1 million by 2006) in assets during their lifetime (as gifts) or at death (e.g., under your living trust). You can gift $650,000 in 1999 in taxable gift transactions (i.e., above the $10,000 annual gift exclusion explained in Chapter 20) while you are alive. But if you do, your estate will not have any applicable exclusion amount left when you die to shelter your remaining assets from the estate tax (unless the credit increases between the year of the gift and the year of your death). If you use the opposite approach and use none of your applicable exclusion amount during your lifetime to offset taxable gifts, your estate would have the full applicable exclusion amount available to offset the tax on $650,000 of assets transferred at your death. This doesn't mean you don't make gifts, just not taxable ones. This applicable exclusion amount is not affected by gifts you make using the $10,000 annual exclusion amounts. Thus, this $650,000 amount is a single aggregate exclusion. You can give away, in the aggregate during your life and under your will following your death (or through a revocable living trust), a total of $650,000.

HOW THE DISCLAIMER BYPASS TRUST WORKS

Your "Just-in-Case Living Trust" should include a disclaimer bypass trust. The classic estate tax plan for a married couple uses a bypass trust under the will of each spouse. On the death of the first of you and your spouse, if assets are titled properly, your bypass trust would have assets transferred to it (funded). It is called a "bypass" trust since the assets in it bypass your surviving spouse's estate. Up to approximately $650,000 (1999) of assets may be placed in this trust. When you use this approach, you and the tax advisers to the estate must prepare a balance sheet for both the decedent and the surviving spouse to determine whether the combined estate is likely to exceed the exclusion amount. If it will, you should consider encouraging the surviving spouse to disclaim assets into a bypass trust assuming your living trust permits this.

For some decedents, the maximum $650,000 (1999) of assets that can avoid estate taxation as a result of the applicable exclusion amount are not available to fund a bypass trust. When this occurs, consider having the surviving spouse disclaim some portion or all the IRA or pension assets to the extent that the secondary beneficiary designation and/or the decedent's will result in the assets passing to the bypass trust. This is complex and requires professional advice.

Several options exist for setting up a bypass trust. Your trustee can be given the right, or even the obligation to pay income to your surviving spouse, and/or children and/or other heirs (although if you include grandchildren, additional tax complications will apply). Principal invasion rights can be included so long as they are limited sufficiently to avoid the assets in the bypass trust from being taxed in your surviving spouse's estate. An estate attorney can help you make these technical tax decisions. The income and principal of your disclaimer bypass trust can be distributed to or for the benefit of any beneficiaries you wish. Typically, the income and principal are distributed for the benefit of the surviving spouse and any children or other heirs in the discretion of the trustee (called a "sprinkle power"). Some taxpayers prefer to limit distributions solely to the surviving spouse. Many different approaches are possible, and an approach should be tailored to meet your personal goals. On the death of the surviving spouse, the remaining assets in the trust can be distributed to the children or other heirs, either with no strings attached, or if the children are young, perhaps in another trust until they reach a specified age.

Sample Language:

a. I give, devise, and bequeath my net residuary estate to my spouse, if my spouse should survive me for Sixty (60) days.

b. If my spouse shall disclaim and renounce any portion or all of the preceding bequest, then such disclaimed and renounced portion, but not in excess of the amount specified in the following provision, I give, devise and bequeath to the Bypass Trust provided in the provision of my Will, below. [Later provisions of your will would then include details of the bypass trust.]

The remainder of your estate over the applicable exclusion amount can then be distributed outright (i.e., with no further trust) or in a special marital (QTIP) trust to your spouse. These additional complications are discussed in the following section.

SALVAGING THE PLANNING IF YOUR LIVING TRUST DIDN'T INCLUDE A DISCLAIMER OR REGULAR BYPASS TRUST

If your living trust doesn't have such an arrangement, you might still use a disclaimer, but the surviving spouse won't have any access to the assets. She would disclaim any rights to the assets, and the assets would pass under your trust to the next named beneficiaries as if your spouse had predeceased you.

EXAMPLE: Assume that the decedent's trust simply bequeathed all assets outright to the surviving spouse; the surviving spouse could disclaim up to $650,000 (increasing to $1 million by 2006) of assets. The assets the surviving spouse disclaimed would pass as provided for in the trust, as if the surviving spouse had died prior to the decedent. Thus, the beneficiary contemplating exercising a disclaimer must carefully review the will before proceeding. In a typical simple trust for a family, the children usually inherit on the death of the last spouse/parent. Thus, if the surviving spouse were to disclaim, the assets so disclaimed would pass directly to the children and bypass her estate entirely. This, if the estate were large enough, would save potentially hundreds of thousands of dollars of federal estate taxes on the wife's later death.

If all your assets pass outside probate as a result of beneficiary designations or joint ownership, insufficient assets may be available to fund the disclaimer bypass trust included in your Comprehensive Living Trust and the estate tax benefits may be lost. Depending on state law and other factors, disclaimers may be the method of solving these problems.

To be effective, disclaimers must meet the requirements of state law (typically, the state where you were domiciled at death). For a disclaimer to be effective, it must also comply with the requirements of the federal estate tax laws under Internal Revenue Code Section 2518. These include:

- It must be irrevocable (the beneficiary disclaiming can't change his mind later).
- It must be in writing.
- It must be unqualified. The beneficiary can't place any conditions on the disclaimer.
- The person disclaiming can have controlled or benefited from the property before the disclaimer.
- The beneficiary, except for your spouse, cannot have any benefit from the property disclaimed after the disclaimer.
- Once disclaimed, the property must pass to the next beneficiary without any directions from the beneficiary disclaiming or any benefit to him or her.
- The disclaimer must be completed within nine months of the decedent's death, or within nine months of the disclaiming beneficiary's attaining age 21.

NOTE: For more information and sample forms see Martin Shenkman, *The Probate Guide* (New York: John Wiley & Sons, 1999), Chapter 18.

SUMMARY

This chapter explains how the Just-in-Case Living Trust works and how it can benefit you. In contrast to most of the simplistic living trust plans that offer tax planning or no tax planning, the Just-in-Case Living Trust offers an important compromise. It grants your heirs the benefit of hindsight to determine whether the estate tax planning bypass trust should be used. Because of the many nontax benefits this approach offers, few living trusts should be drafted with less tax planning language incorporated. If a living trust you presently have, or are considering signing, does not have at least this type of protection, ask your estate planning attorney why. If the answer is not satisfactory, consider changing attorneys.

9 THE FAMILY TAX PLANNING LIVING TRUST

INTEGRATING BASIC ESTATE TAX PLANNING INTO YOUR FAMILY TAX PLANNING LIVING TRUST

For aggregate family estates that may exceed the applicable exclusion amount ($650,000 in 1999, scheduled to increase to $1 million by 2006, but don't be surprised if Congress changes the amount before then), the simplistic approach used in many living trusts is inadequate. The Just-in-Case Living Trust described in Chapter 8 will probably not suffice, and even for smaller estates, additional planning may be necessary if the family is a second or later marriage. The solution is the Family Tax Planning Living Trust described in this chapter. The Family Tax Planning Living Trust combines the bypass trust, marital trust, and possible trusts for children. This combination of trusts to be formed following your death, under the legal structure of your living trust, can minimize or eliminate taxes, protect your surviving spouse, assure an inheritance for children of a prior marriage, and so forth. To understand the workings of this type of living trust, you must know the basic rules of the applicable exclusion, bypass trust, and marital trusts, insurance planning, annual gifts, and other tax planning techniques. The applicable exclusion and bypass trust were introduced in Chapter 8. You might want to review that discussion first, since this chapter builds on that information.

THE BASICS OF ESTATE TAX PLANNING

To save estate taxes, your comprehensive plan should take into consideration a host of tax planning concepts, including some of the following:

- You are permitted to give away up to $10,000 per year (the amount is indexed to inflation) without using up any of your $650,000 applicable exclusion and without incurring any gift tax. This tax benefit is called the *annual exclusion*. You can also pay tuition and medical expenses without limit if you pay the medical care providers and school directly. Use your annual gift tax exclusion to give away assets most likely to appreciate. Since the annual exclusion is used or lost each year, it is a common foundation for many estate plans. Often, annual gift amounts are combined with other techniques. When a married couple each makes gifts, $20,000 per donee can be given away. Even with a small group of intended heirs, this simple technique can enable many estates to avoid tax entirely.

- Remove life insurance proceeds from your estate by having beneficiaries, or trusts for their benefit, own and be beneficiary of, irrevocably, the life insurance. This is the cornerstone of many estate plans. Since insurance can be such a large amount, this type of planning should always be considered. Although it is quite common, the many technical complications make it necessary to consult an estate planning specialist.

- Divide the ownership of assets with your spouse to take maximum advantage of the applicable exclusion amount each of you is permitted to transfer without any gift or estate tax cost. This concept was discussed in Chapter 8 in the context of assuring assets are available to transfer at death to a disclaimer bypass trust. For the Family Tax Planning Living Trust, the same planning concepts must be addressed in the context of funding a regular bypass trust (i.e., one that works automatically without the need for your surviving spouse to disclaim).

- Your will and revocable living trust include proper planning for maximizing the benefits of the applicable exclusion amount through the use of a *bypass* (also called *credit shelter, applicable exclusion,* or *A*) trust. In contrast to the disclaimer bypass trust discussed in Chapter 8, the Family Tax Planning Living Trust will automatically be funded. This means that there will not be any need for your surviving spouse to disclaim assets for this planning to occur.

- Have your will or living trust take advantage of deferring estate taxes through the unlimited estate tax marital deduction. This concept was briefly introduced in Chapter 8 and will be elaborated on in later discussions in this book. Simply, assets given outright (i.e., without the restrictions of a trusts) or in one of several types of special trust, will avoid any tax on your death. These assets, whether in a special trust or given outright to your surviving spouse, will be taxed on her death in her estate. The benefit, however, is that no tax will be due until her later death.

- Plan to reduce income taxes of trusts through careful selection of investments, and monitoring of distributions. This is why a sprinkle bypass trust which has your spouse and other heirs as beneficiaries is preferable.

FAMILY TAX PLANNING FOR MARRIED COUPLES

Combining Applicable Exclusion Amount Planning with the Unlimited Marital Deduction

As introduced in Chapter 8, a bypass trust is included in your living trust, and family assets are owned, so that on the death of the first of you or your spouse, the maximum amount of assets ($650,000 in 1999) are transferred to a bypass trust to benefit the surviving spouse, without being taxed in her estate.

The bypass trust type of planning can be tailored to work for unmarried partners; the marital planning cannot be since no estate tax marital deduction will be available.

What happens if your estate (the estate of the first spouse to die) exceeds the maximum applicable exclusion amount? The answer for married couples is simple: the excess is bequeathed to the spouse in a manner that will qualify for the estate tax marital deduction. This avoids any tax on the first death. Thus, the applicable exclusion amount and the unlimited estate tax marital deduction have resulted in a classic zero tax approach for most married couples on the first death. This combined planning technique consists of each executing a will (or revocable living trust) that includes a bypass (credit shelter) trust. The remainder of the estate is, under this typical planning arrangement, distributed outright (i.e., with no trust) to the surviving spouse, or in a special trust which qualifies for the estate tax marital deduction (called a QTIP trust, short for Qualified Terminable Interest Property trust). The QTIP is especially common in second or later marriages to assure that the intended children or other heirs benefit on the death of the current spouse. If your spouse is not a citizen, you will instead need to use a special trust for noncitizen spouses (called a QDOT trust, short for Qualified Domestic Trust). Several other types of trusts can qualify for the marital deduction, but they are less commonly used and therefore are not discussed in this book.

CAUTION: Special considerations apply if the surviving spouse is not a United States citizen, or if community property is involved. These rules are complex and you should seek the advice of an estate planner familiar with these rules. For additional details on this QDOT trust and other types of marital trusts, see Martin Shenkman, *The Complete Book of Trusts* (2nd ed.) (New York: John Wiley & Sons, 1997).

MARITAL TRUST PLANNING

There are several ways you or your estate can qualify for the gift or estate tax marital deduction. In planning to use this deduction, review with your estate planner the pros and cons of deferring estate tax. In some instances, it may be advantageous to use less marital deduction and actually incur some tax on the death of the first spouse. This could be done, for example, to take advantage of the lower graduated estate tax brackets.

GENERAL TAX RULES GOVERNING BEQUESTS TO YOUR SPOUSE

An unlimited marital deduction is available for qualifying distributions to a surviving spouse. It is not available to someone who is not married to you under law. Thus, a lifetime partner will not qualify for these benefits. This deduction is available where the following requirements are met for a transfer to, or for the benefit of, your spouse:

- The property that is intended to qualify for the marital deduction must pass from you to your surviving spouse. The property must be transferred under your will (or under your state's laws of intestacy if you died without a will), as a result of joint ownership between you and your spouse, pursuant to a general power of appointment, by a beneficiary designation, or under your living trust.

- The rights and property transferred to your spouse cannot be what is called a terminable interest. This is an interest that will terminate or fail as the result of the passing of time, the occurrence of an event or contingency, or the failure of an event or contingency to occur. A bequest for a term of years (my spouse shall have the use of our yacht for 15 years) is a terminable interest and therefore does not qualify for the marital deduction. Several exceptions from this terminable interest rule are critical to the use of trusts for transfers to your spouse. These are discussed later in this chapter. The most commonly used exception to this rule denying a marital deduction for property interests which may terminate, however, is the exception provided for QTIP property.

OUTRIGHT (I.E., NO TRUST) GIFT OR BEQUEST

Where your estate makes a transfer to your spouse—outright and free of any restrictions or trusts—that qualifies for the marital deduction, the amount transferred to your spouse is deducted from the value of your gross estate. The primary issue in evaluating the use of an outright (i.e., not in trust) marital bequest is whether you are comfortable losing control to the surviving spouse of the proceeds of your estate. What if your spouse remarries following your death? Where will your assets ultimately be distributed? Personal concerns are often paramount. The estate plan should be tailored to meet these objectives with the least tax interference possible. In most cases, this requires the use of one or more trusts.

Another factor to consider in evaluating an outright marital bequest versus a transfer of assets to a QTIP trust is that the marital deduction must be claimed if the assets are distributed outright. If the assets are distributed in trust, your executor has the option to claim, or to forgo, the marital deduction. This additional flexibility can be important. This flexibility also benefits Generation Skipping Transfer (GST) tax planning. This sophisticated tax planning is introduced in the discussion of the Multigenerational Living Trust in Part Four.

QTIP MARITAL TRUST

The qualified terminable interest property, or QTIP, trust is the most popular form of marital deduction after the simple distribution of assets outright to the surviving spouse. The key advantage is that the assets transferred to a QTIP trust qualify for the unlimited estate or gift tax marital deduction, but you can control where the assets are ultimately distributed (e.g., your children from another marriage). Thus, your estate can qualify for the estate tax marital deduction without your having to give complete control over the assets to your spouse.

To qualify for QTIP tax benefits, the trust must meet the following requirements:

- The surviving spouse must be entitled to all income from the trust for life.
- No person can have the power to appoint the trust assets to any person other than your surviving spouse prior to her death.
- Income from the trust must be paid to your spouse at least annually.
- Your executor must elect to qualify the trust for the marital deduction.

On the death of the surviving spouse, the entire value of the QTIP property is included in your surviving spouse's gross estate. These assets will be taxed at her top marginal tax brackets. Your surviving spouse cannot give away these assets to avoid this tax result. If she tries, a gift tax could be triggered for the entire principal balance given as well as for the value of the income interest.

MARITAL DEDUCTION FOR SPOUSE WHO IS NOT A CITIZEN

If your spouse is not a United States citizen, the unlimited estate tax marital deduction will not be available if you do not take special steps. Thus, the use of a QTIP trust, as described earlier, will not defer estate tax. While a credit provision can mitigate this result to some extent, the best answer, short of becoming a United States citizen, is to use a special trust for noncitizen spouses. The credit works as follows. If you bequeath property to your spouse, who is not a citizen, that is subjected to the estate tax, but would not have been taxed had your surviving spouse been a citizen, a credit will be available. On the death of your spouse, her estate will receive a credit for the tax paid by your estate on the earlier transfer to her which did not qualify for the marital deduction.

The key planning opportunity where your spouse is not a citizen involves the proper use of trusts. Where the assets are passed into a qualified domestic trust (QDOT), the marital deduction will be available without limit. To qualify, a QDOT must meet the following requirements:

- *Trustees.* At least one of your trustees must be either a United States citizen or corporation. This requirement must be contained in the trust documents. Provisions should be made for alternate trustees to assure compliance with this requirement. For example, a final alternate should be a United States bank or trust company.
- *Income.* The surviving spouse must generally be entitled to all of the income from the trust, payable at least annually.
- *Regulations.* The trust must meet additional requirements prescribed by IRS regulations which are intended to assure that the trust assets will not escape United States taxation.
- *Election.* Your executor must make an irrevocable election on the United States estate tax return with respect to the trust. This rule provides flexibility in that your executor is not required to make the election. The executor's right to make, or not make, this election, should appear in your will or the QDOT trust.

Estate tax will be levied on distributions of principal (corpus) from the QDOT other than annual income distributions. This tax will be calculated as if the amount distributed had been included in your estate (i.e., the first to die, the citizen spouse). This calculation adds all prior distributions from the QDOT to your taxable estate to push the tax on the QDOT distributions into the highest federal estate tax brackets. This calculation and tax requirement also will somewhat complicate the administration of the QDOT. An exception is provided for certain hardship distributions. In addition, a tax will be assessed on the property remaining in the QDOT on the death of the second spouse. This tax is calculated in the same manner.

Where a trust does not meet the requirements of a QDOT, the IRS may provide the flexibility of reforming the trust so that it does qualify.

PLANNING FOR MARRIED COUPLES WHEN ONE SPOUSE OWNS MOST ASSETS

A special technique can help address planning when one spouse owns most assets and for personal, asset protection, or other reasons dividing assets equally is not an acceptable solution. This technique, called an "inter vivos QTIP trust" (not a revocable living trust) is likely to become a more commonly used estate planning technique as taxpayers with larger estates, and the ever more common second (and later) marriage, seek to assure maximum use of both spouses' applicable exclusion amounts while protecting assets for the children of a prior marriage.

Here's how this technique could be applied. First a bit of background. You can make unlimited gifts of assets to your spouse (if he or she is a United States citizen) without any gift tax cost because gifts to your spouse qualify for the unlimited marital deduction. If yours is a second marriage, however, you may not want to give a large portion of your assets to your spouse since ultimately she may bequeath them to her children from a prior marriage. The common solution for this problem is to use a marital trust, called a Qualified Terminable Interest Property (QTIP) trust. When you bequeath assets to this type of trust, your spouse must receive all income of the trust at least annually for his or her lifetime. On his or her death, the beneficiaries you name will inherit the assets. The benefit of this approach is that the assets bequeathed to the trust for your spouse will avoid any estate tax on your death because they will qualify for the unlimited estate tax marital deduction. On your spouse's later death, the assets will be distributed to your children from your prior marriage. This QTIP technique is valuable because you can qualify for estate tax deferral and still control the assets.

A twist on this technique provides a planning opportunity that is likely to see much greater use following the 1997 Tax Act, the inter vivos QTIP. In the same second marriage scenario, assume that you have the lion's share of assets. Therefore, you may easily be able to fund your bypass (credit shelter) trust using the new increased applicable exclusion amount. However, any assets you own in excess of that amount will be taxed heavily if not bequeathed to your spouse. Your spouse, on the other hand, owns assets worth substantially less then the maximum she could use to fund a bypass trust, thus wasting a significant portion of her applicable exclusion amount. The challenge, then, is how can you use some of your spouse's otherwise wasted applicable exclusion amount to save estate taxes, by taking maximum advantage of the applicable exclusion amount, while assuring that the assets pass to your children from your first marriage? One possible solution is to establish an inter vivos QTIP trust.

EXAMPLE: Sam and Susan are married. Both had prior marriages with children from those marriages that they each want to eventually benefit. Sam has $2.4 million net worth, Susan only $200,000. Sam gives $400,000 (which he can add to in later years) to a QTIP trust that he establishes now (i.e., while he is alive, not under his will) for the benefit of Susan. On Susan's death, these QTIP assets are taxable in her estate where the tax will be offset by the applicable exclusion amount (eventually $1 million). The QTIP assets will then pass to Sam's children from a prior marriage. Had Sam not engaged in this planning the $400,000 could have been reduced by nearly half as a result of estate taxes. What was the cost of this huge estate tax savings? Susan would have a life interest in the income of the assets transferred to the trust. While this may dissuade some taxpayers from pursuing this planning, the huge tax savings, for many, will outweigh the delay.

TAX CONSIDERATIONS FOR NONMARRIED TAXPAYERS

Nonmarried couples face several difficulties in planning for their estates that traditionally married couples do not. These additional problems stem from the bias that the tax and property laws have in favor of married couples. There is no right to transfer unlimited assets without gift or estate tax cost to a nonmarried partner as there is for a spouse.

The gift and estate tax laws are extremely biased against nonmarried partners. The tax laws provide especially favorable treatment to married couples. As a result, every couple can readily avoid any estate tax on the death of the first spouse. Any husband or wife can transfer on death to the surviving spouse unlimited assets without any tax cost. The concept behind the favoritism shown married couples is that they are viewed for tax purposes as a partnership, a single economic unit. All assets of the marital economic unit will be subject to the estate tax after the death of the two spouses. This same principle is behind the filing of a joint income tax return by a married couple. While this concept reflects logic and equity, these same benefits are denied to any couple whose relationship is not under state law a marriage. Although these nonmarried couples may be as much of a single economic entity as a married couple, the tax laws do not recognize this. There is no unlimited "partner" deduction equivalent to the unlimited marital deduction even though nonmarried partners are often as much of a single economic unit as married couples.

A spouse can generally make unlimited transfers of property to the other spouse during life as gifts, or after death through intestacy or under a will. All of these transfers are free of federal and state gift and estate taxes. However, this right is not afforded to nonmarried partners. This presents substantial and costly problems to nonmarried partners. Nonmarried or married couples alike can bequeath up to $650,000 (1999) to anyone they choose without any estate tax cost. If your estate is not in excess of this amount, you will not face any federal estate tax problem (although there can still be significant state level transfer tax costs). If your estate exceeds this amount, the federal tax cost will be substantial. You cannot transfer unlimited assets above this amount to your partner (as you could if the relationship were treated like a marriage). You must take other tax planning steps to protect assets in excess of $650,000 (1999) to avoid horrendous tax consequences and to assure that your partner will in fact receive the assets.

Possible suggestions to address the potentially costly problem of a significant estate tax on the death of the first-to-die partner include:

- The partner with the most significant assets can purchase life insurance to cover this estate tax. The insurance should be owned in an irrevocable life insurance trust to remove the proceeds from the reach of creditors and to keep the proceeds out of the taxable estate of the first nonmarried partner.

- Begin an aggressive gift program to reduce the wealthier partner's taxable estate.
- Use the tax-oriented trusts and other techniques discussed in Part Four of this book: grantor retained annuity trusts (a similar technique called GRIT may be available), charitable lead trusts, and so forth.

As a result of these limitations, nonmarried couples should begin a gift program early. In addition, the techniques discussed in this book to discount gifts (lack of marketability discounts, limited partnerships, grantor retained annuity trusts, etc.) should be evaluated with a tax expert.

SUMMARY

This chapter has explained the general use of the Family Tax Planning Living Trust, and in particular, it has described the estate tax planning incorporated into this type of trust. This generally includes a bypass trust to preserve the applicable exclusion amount available on the death of the first spouse (or partner). It will also generally include gift-giving provisions to enable your trustee to take advantage of the annual $10,000 (indexed) gift tax exclusion (and perhaps the right to make distributions for tuition and medical expenses direct to qualifying providers). Finally, it may include a marital trust (QTIP, or QDOT or other type) if the survivor was legally married to you at death.

10 OPERATING YOUR FAMILY TAX PLANNING LIVING TRUST

YOU MUST MONITOR YOUR FAMILY TAX PLANNING LIVING TRUST WHILE YOU ARE ALIVE

Estate planning documents are not a step you can take and then forget about. You will always have vital responsibilities to fulfill while you are alive. Failing to do so will, at best, leave the effectiveness of your planning to chance. At worst, it can result in easily avoidable tax costs that can decimate your estate. It can result in the wrong people receiving your hard-earned assets and in heirs receiving unprotected assets that are exposed to many risks. It can provoke family feuds. While the famed Hatfields and McCoys battled for reasons unrelated to estate planning, poor planning or follow-up can duplicate that acrimonious relationship among your heirs.

If you do not title assets properly, the bypass trust may not be funded fully (see Chapter 8). For example, if you leave assets in joint name with your spouse or other heirs, the bypass trust, which is the cornerstone of the Family Tax Planning Living Trust, may not be utilized to the fullest extent of your applicable exclusion. Further, assets not properly transferred to your living trust may be distributed to your spouse or other heirs outright and not in the protective trusts you want. To obtain the many tax and nontax benefits, carefully review with your estate planner the ownership (title) to each of your assets. Also, review the beneficiary designations on any assets for which you can name a beneficiary. These include insurance policies, annuities, many types of employee benefits, individual retirement accounts (IRAs), and other types of retirement accounts. Just as importantly, you personally must monitor how the value and ownership of assets change over time. You cannot expect your estate planner, accountant, insurance agent, or attorney to do this for you unless you arrange for a periodic meeting. Once you understand the basic tax concepts in Chapter 8, you should be equipped to at least identify potential issues.

EXAMPLE 1: Your estate and the estate of your spouse aggregated $500,000 when your living trust estate plan was completed. Your estate planner may not have included any type of bypass trust in your documents. The titles to assets may have been ignored. This may not have been an issue at the time, or for the foreseeable future. Subsequent to the signing of your documents, your net worth increased to $1 million. This could have resulted from the purchase of an inexpensive term life insurance policy from an organization you joined, growth in the value of your business or stock portfolio, or any number of factors. If you don't inform your estate planners of the changes, they cannot review your assets, documents, and plan to suggest the changes you should make to protect your family.

EXAMPLE 2: When your documents and planning were completed, your family net worth was $1.4 million. An estate tax would be due on the death of the last of you and your spouse if no planning were done. Your estate planner helped you divide assets approximately one-half to each of you and your spouse so that whoever died first, there would be sufficient assets to fund the bypass trust. When assets were divided, the house was put in your name, valued at $700,000 and the stock portfolio in your spouse's name. The stocks doubled in value. However, a zoning change in your neighborhood made property values plummet by half. The title to assets is way out of kilter. If you die first, much of your applicable exclusion will be wasted. You must monitor assets and consult with your advisers as to steps to take. You could, if you felt comfortable understanding the concepts involved, simply have transferred some of your spouse's securities to your name.

EXAMPLE 3: When your estate plan was completed, your planner discussed the concepts of Chapters 8 and 9 with you. You were to change the ownership of securities and beneficiary designations on several accounts. You failed to follow up. Your plan won't work.

The key point to the preceding examples is the same. You must be responsible to follow up on the steps your planners suggest, monitor changes in assets and other personal factors, and notify your advisers if there have been changes. Financial factors are not the only issues to be alert for. Changes in the financial, marital, or other circumstances of your intended heirs can suggest the need to review and revise documents. Changes in your health or personal circumstances can necessitate changes in insurance coverage. If you don't assume an active role, in time your plan is likely to fail to meet your objectives.

Tax planning is far from the only issue you must monitor. If you've formed a living trust to avoid the issues probate can raise, you must monitor changes in assets, and perhaps more importantly, new assets you receive. If you don't arrange to transfer newly received assets (e.g., an inheritance) to your living trust, you will not obtain the benefits you had hoped for. If your risks for lawsuits change, you need to consult with your advisers concerning the planning concepts discussed in Part Five.

The ideal approach is twofold. First, become educated so you understand the process. This book will help. Making sure you understand the advice of your professionals is essential. Second, you should monitor changes and tasks you are responsible for and periodically review them with your estate planning team—accountant, insurance agent, lawyer, and perhaps others. This doesn't have to be an expensive process. While a meeting once a year (or more frequently if significant changes occur) with all of your advisers around a single table is the ideal, you can accomplish the same goals on a shoestring budget. Provide each planner with three concise and clear documents: a current list of family members and other important people in your plan (indicating marital status, age, and any notable health or financial issues), a current balance sheet (indicating categories of assets, who owns them, and who the beneficiaries are), and a summary of your current goals and concerns. These three documents should highlight changes that have occurred since your documents and planning were last reviewed. Request that each adviser call you for a brief phone conversation to determine whether additional planning or steps are necessary. You can simplify the process and control costs even more if you include a list of current documents and planning steps you have in place to save the advisers the expense of retrieving and reviewing your files.

YOUR FAMILY TAX PLANNING LIVING TRUST FOLLOWING DEATH

Your Living Trust May Terminate

Your living trust is intended to function primarily during your lifetime and then, at your death, to serve as a conduit for transferring assets to the heirs you've selected and to trusts for their benefit. Once this postdeath transition is completed, your living trust will no longer hold any assets. This doesn't mean that your heirs or successor trustees throw away your trust document. The trusts (bypass, QTIP, children, other) that your attorney included in your living trust will be activated. The guidelines for the operation of each of these trusts is included in your living trust document. Thus, the document will remain extremely important until all testamentary (formed following your death) trusts included in your living trust have themselves concluded and terminated assets. This could be a short period until the death of your surviving spouse, or if dynasty trusts are formed as part of a Multigenerational Living Trust (see Part Four), it could be forever (unless the trust runs out of assets before "forever" is over!).

Following death, your successor trustees will obtain control over assets in your trust (assets outside your trust, unless they have designated beneficiaries, will require action by the executor appointed under your Safe-Keeper Will), pay expenses, and distribute assets to fund your bypass (applicable exclusion) trust and marital (QTIP/QDOT) trust.

If you've transferred all of your assets to your trust, your estate may avoid the need for a probate process. However, don't assume that none of the concepts of probate will apply. Probate, as explained in Chapter 1, is simply the process of having your will admitted to the court and obtaining a document (letters testamentary) issued to your executor, authorizing him to manage your estate. Probate also may entail filing estate tax returns, transferring title to assets, distributing assets from your living trust to heirs and obtaining receipts and releases from them, accounting for assets in your trust, and investing assets following your death.

NOTE: See Martin Shenkman, *The Complete Probate Guide* (New York: John Wiley & Sons, 1999) for detailed explanations, forms, checklists, and other helpful tools.

Filing a Federal Estate Tax Return

If you've transferred all assets to your Family Tax Planning Living Trust, your estate may entirely avoid probate and no executor may be appointed. The successor trustees under your living trust will then be responsible for filing the necessary federal estate tax return if your estate is worth more than the applicable exclusion amount that applied in the year of your death ($650,000 in 1999, increasing to $1 million by 2006). This tax return is essential to properly fund and qualify the bypass and marital trusts. This return should never be filed without the assistance of an attorney with substantial probate experience. The amounts are always too large, and complex issues can often arise, even in simple estates.

Your successor trustees must take the appropriate steps on the estate tax return to qualify a QTIP or other marital trust for the estate tax benefit of the unlimited marital deduction. This election may be essential to assure that there is no tax on the death of the first spouse. This election has many twists and complications that should be reviewed by your successor trustees with a probate attorney. The Multigenerational Living Trust discussed in Part Four raises additional tax planning steps for the marital trust. Depending on the circumstances, your successor trustee might consider extending the deadline for filling the federal estate tax return for six months when a QTIP trust is funded. If your surviving spouse dies during this period, then the QTIP election can be made for only the portion of the estate of the first spouse to die equal to the amount that would have been taxed at the maximum marginal tax rate. The portion of the QTIP trust that would be taxed at the lower progressive estate tax rates, from 37 percent to 55 percent, would not be covered by the QTIP election. Thus, a tax would intentionally be incurred at the lower estate tax rates on the death of the first spouse.

If you have a Family Tax Planning Living Trust but your estate was small enough that it didn't have to file a federal estate tax return, your successor trustee should still seek the formal advice of an estate planning attorney. This will assure that any issues are identified and addressed and that sufficient records are maintained to determine the income tax consequences if assets that your bypass trust or other heirs received are later sold. If no return is required, the costs should be dramatically less, perhaps no more than merely a consultation or two. But they should be obtained.

Selecting Assets to Fund Each Trust

The applicable exclusion amount, as explained in Chapter 8, permits your estate to avoid tax on the first $650,000 in 1999 (increasing to $1 million for decedents dying in 2006). This is accomplished through the funding of the bypass trust under your Family Tax Planning Living Trust. The income and principal of this trust can be distributed to or for the benefit of any beneficiaries. Typically, the income and principal are distributed for the benefit of the surviving spouse or partner, and any children or other heirs in the discretion of the trustee (called a "sprinkle power"). Many people limit distributions to solely the surviving spouse. There are many possibilities. The key is that the distribution provisions of your bypass trust should meet your personal and nontax goals as closely as possible while still preserving the estate tax benefit of avoiding having the bypass trust assets taxed in your surviving spouse's or partner's estate.

On the death of your surviving spouse or partner, the remaining assets in your bypass trust are then distributed to your children or other heirs. The key benefit of this planning is that the surviving spouse or partner can have access and benefit (albeit restricted as compared to outright ownership if the assets were bequeathed directly instead of in the bypass trust) without those assets being later taxed in the surviving spouse's estate. The remainder of your assets (i.e., your estate) are usually distributed outright or, in the case of a spouse (not a partner for which no marital deduction is available), in a marital or QTIP trust. The marital portion will be taxed in your surviving spouse's estate on her later death. The bypass trust assets will not be taxed in her estate, no matter how large in value they grow. Therefore, choose assets most likely to appreciate when selecting assets to fund the bypass trust and the QTIP or other marital trust. This would have the growth occur outside the surviving spouse's or partner's estate.

Operating Your Bypass Trust

Once assets are transferred to your bypass trust, the trustee or co-trustees (if you named two or more people to be in charge of the trust at the same time) will invest the trust assets, file income tax returns, and distribute income and/or principal from the trust to the beneficiaries you indicated in your Family Tax Planning Living Trust. Ideally, the trustees should consult with an attorney to be certain that they understand the requirements of administering the trust and all the terms of the trust as set forth in your living trust. They should also consult any letter of instruction that you've left. Although the letter isn't legally binding, most trustees will try to carry out your wishes as best as they can.

In performing their duties, the trustees should communicate regularly and in writing with the beneficiaries of the trust. This is especially important if it's a sprinkle trust with many beneficiaries. They should seek information about the beneficiaries' financial situation and need for distributions now, and in the future. The trustees will have to determine if you had a preference that your surviving spouse be favored over children or others when distributions are made. They should consult with investment advisers or financial planners to be certain that the trust assets are invested in a reasonable fashion considering the needs of the beneficiaries, the terms of the trust, and your stated objectives. For some bypass trusts the objective is growth so your children or other heirs will ultimately inherit the most. In other cases it may be income to support your surviving spouse and minor children currently. If the trustees don't have the expertise, they should hire, at the expense of the trust, the necessary experts. This may include an accountant to assist with income tax planning and filing the necessary income tax returns. It could include an appraiser to value nonmarketable assets if necessary. It might include a business consultant if your living trust transferred business interests to a trust. It may also include a lawyer for any legal issues.

Operating the Marital Trust

Once assets are transferred to your QTIP or other marital trust, the trustee or co-trustees (if you named two or more people to be in charge of the trust at the same time) will invest the trust assets, file income tax returns, and distribute income and/or principal from the trust to only your spouse, and to no other beneficiaries while she is alive. Ideally, the trustees should consult with an attorney to be certain that they understand the requirements of administering a marital trust in accordance all of the terms of your living trust. This is especially important for the marital trust because if all of the requirements described earlier, including distributions of all income to your spouse, are not followed, the estate tax marital deduction could be lost and could trigger a potentially huge estate tax.

In performing their duties, the trustees should communicate regularly and in writing with your spouse who must be the only beneficiary of the trust. If the trustees are permitted to make principal distributions (income must be distributed) they should seek information as to your spouse's financial situation and need for distributions now, and in the future. These distributions could have an adverse tax affect in a Multigenerational Living Trust. Also, principal distributions may defeat your goal of controlling where the assets ultimately go since your spouse will control all monies distributed to her. They should consult with investment advisers or financial planners to be certain that the trust assets are invested in a reasonable fashion considering the requirement of the tax laws to distribute all income to your spouse at least annually (the trust may require more frequent distributions), needs of your spouse for discretionary principal distributions, as well as the remainder beneficiaries (the heirs who receive the assets left in the QTIP trust after your spouse dies), the terms of the trust, and your stated objectives. If the trustees don't have the expertise, they should hire, at the expense of the trust, the necessary experts, as described earlier.

SUMMARY

This chapter has provided a brief overview of the operations of your Family Tax Planning Living Trust and has highlighted the few important differences between this trust and the Foundation Living Trust discussed in preceding chapters. The key differences are the mandatory bypass trust to preserve the estate tax benefits of the applicable exclusion amount and the possible use of a QTIP or other type of marital trust. Most importantly, this chapter has again demonstrated the need for your ongoing monitoring and involvement in the planning process. You cannot simply sign documents and assume all your goals will be met. You must regularly review your plan and follow up with your advisers. Finally, this chapter has discussed many options for writing these trusts. The choices available should make it clear that you want documents tailored to your personal goals, not mere boilerplate off a word processor.

11 INSURANCE AND CHILDREN'S TRUSTS SUPPLEMENT YOUR FAMILY TAX PLANNING LIVING TRUST

WHY ADDITIONAL TRUSTS MAY BE NEEDED TO SUPPLEMENT YOUR FAMILY TAX PLANNING LIVING TRUST

If your estate could be large enough to warrant the estate tax planning incorporated into the Family Tax Planning Living Trust, additional tax planning may be advisable. The additional tax planning may take many forms, but the two most common are the use of an insurance trust to avoid large insurance proceeds becoming taxable on your death (or the death of your spouse) and trusts to protect annual gifts, which can be as large as $10,000 (indexed) per person ($20,000 if your spouse also makes gifts), from minors or other beneficiaries needing supervision. This chapter provides an overview of these two common planning techniques. Also, just as with the bypass and marital trusts discussed in previous chapters, the insurance trust and children's trusts offer many nontax benefits such as protecting trust assets from creditors, divorce, and other risks, as well as providing an organized method of managing assets in the event the beneficiary cannot.

INSURANCE TRUSTS

Insurance is an integral part of many, if not most, estate plans. Contrary to what most people expect, however, insurance often causes substantial estate tax problems. Thus, proper planning for insurance is a critical part of any Family Tax Planning Living Trust program.

AUTHOR'S STRATEGY: My life insurance is held in a trust as discussed in this chapter. If you're young, term insurance is often available very inexpensively from organizations or professional societies you belong to ("cheap" may be more descriptive), or you may even purchase your own policy. If you have children, that extra coverage is worth having. If you and your spouse die, however, the government, not your children, may become your biggest beneficiary—all because of the cheap term insurance. The use of an insurance trust avoids this tax problem and protects the insurance for your family. I don't want to pay insurance premiums to enhance government tax revenues. I want those premiums to benefit my family. Also, I've seen what happens when someone dies. "Well wishers" can besiege the family trying to help and may include everyone from sincere friends to snake-oil salespeople with wild investments. You can gain some protection against all by having assets held in a trust.

Insurance Is Not Tax Free without an Insurance Trust

Life insurance trusts are one of the most important trusts but are too often not used by those needing them most. Why are they so often overlooked? Because most taxpayers erroneously assume that life insurance is tax free. It is not estate tax free unless you plan properly. Life insurance is taxable in your estate if you owned the policy, named your estate beneficiary, or retained what is called an "incidence of ownership," such as the right to change the beneficiaries. Even if life insurance escapes taxation on your death because it is paid to your spouse, it only escapes because of the unlimited marital deduction discussed in Chapters 8 and 9. On the later death of your spouse, 55 percent of the insurance proceeds remaining could be paid in estate tax. Because life insurance trusts can help you avoid this estate tax bite, they are an extremely powerful planning tool. Even people of modest means can often benefit from an insurance trust.

EXAMPLE: The Youngs have negligible net worth. They own a home which is fully mortgaged. They have two children. Because of their limited resources and great needs (i.e., the two children), Mr. and Mrs. Young each purchase a $1 million term life insurance policy. Because of their young ages, the premiums are very inexpensive. If both Mr. and Mrs. Young are killed in an automobile accident, their children may have to pay $350,000 or more in estate taxes!

Although almost any trust can own insurance policies and receive insurance proceeds, what is generally thought of as a life insurance trust is a trust that is formed to own only life insurance policies on your life.

The use of a life insurance trust can be illustrated with a simple example:

NOTE: Your estate is worth $2 million. Assume that your estate taxes and expenses are estimated at $800,000. You purchase an $800,000 life insurance policy to cover the cost. The policy, however, is included in your estate since you own it at death. Thus your estate has been increased to $2.8 million, and your taxes and expenses have increased to $1.2 million. Thus, one-half of the insurance proceeds could be lost to additional tax costs. As an alternative, you could set up an irrevocable life insurance trust to purchase the policy. Since the policy is owned by the trust from inception, the proceeds will not be included in your estate. Your estate remains valued at $2 million and your taxes and costs remain at $800,000. But in addition, your trustee now has a pool of $800,000 that can be used to purchase nonliquid assets from your estate thus providing your estate with cash to meet its tax and expense obligations. The value of the assets then held in the trust can be used to provide for the needs of your loved ones. This can be an advantage over having the beneficiaries own the polices: more control, protection from the creditors of the beneficiaries, protection from becoming a marital asset in the event a beneficiary divorces, and so forth.

Benefits of an Insurance Trust

Advantages of an irrevocable insurance trust can include:

- Insurance proceeds can be excluded from both your estate and your spouse's estate, thus completely escaping transfer taxes at your generation. To assure that the insurance proceeds are removed from your estate as the grantor of the trust, you as insured must not possess any significant powers. Your surviving spouse can receive some or all of the annual income from the insurance trust and distributions of the principal in the trust subject to certain limitations (to avoid causing the trust to be included in her estate).

- If you engage in multigenerational tax planning as described in Part Four of this book, the insurance trust can be an ideal way to transfer and leverage assets for the benefit of your grandchildren and later generations.

- Trust assets are protected from claims by creditors if the trust includes a spendthrift provision limiting beneficiary's rights and the beneficiary, if also serving as a trustee, has his rights limited (e.g., as a trustee he cannot make distributions to himself as a beneficiary). Thus, physicians and other professionals and business persons seeking to protect their assets should consider this technique as part of their overall asset protection strategies.

- Investments from insurance proceeds retained in the insurance trust are protected from claims by a divorcing spouse (e.g., an insurance trust with your child as beneficiary could be protected from equitable distribution claims of your child's ex-spouse). In some states, however, the law may permit the income earned on the trust to be counted toward child support and alimony requirements.

- There is flexibility in selecting the choice of applicable law when a trust is used to own insurance. This could be useful to take advantage of differences in state laws.

- For those concerned about publicity, the insurance proceeds included in the trust are not included in your probate estate. So if there is no legal challenge to the trust, the insurance proceeds and how they are to be distributed should not be made available for public knowledge.

- Assets can be managed to protect the insurance proceeds for the ultimate care and use of the beneficiary. You assist a minor or disabled beneficiary by carefully selecting the trustees who will invest the ultimate insurance proceeds.

Typical Use of a Second-to-Die Insurance Trust

Perhaps one of the most common uses of an irrevocable insurance trust is to hold second to die or survivor's insurance. In a typical estate plan, here is how this technique works. Assume that your estate is worth $2.3 million. The proper use of applicable exclusion or bypass trusts in the wills for you and your spouse (and retitling of assets to be certain those trusts are funded) can remove $1.3 million ($650,000 in 1999 times two for you and your spouse) from your combined taxable estates. Ignoring expenses, that leaves a $1 million taxable estate. Assuming a 50 percent estate tax bracket (the rates are actually graduated) a $500,000 second-to-die (survivor's) insurance policy is purchased by the irrevocable insurance trust you and your spouse establish (i.e., you and your spouse are grantors). On the death of the last of you and your spouse, the $500,000 insurance proceeds are paid to the trust. The trustee can then invest the proceeds and use them to care for your heirs, to purchase assets from your estate, or loan your estate the money to pay the tax, thus assuring your estate of sufficient cash to pay any estate tax due. A key benefit is that this $500,000 asset will be preserved outside your taxable estate. Your heirs get $2.3 million.

Provisions to Include in the Insurance Trust

Revocable versus Irrevocable Trusts

Most life insurance trusts are carefully structured to be irrevocable (you cannot change the trust once signed) to assure that the proceeds will not be included in your estate (or your spouse's estate if first or second-to-die insurance is involved). This is the opposite of your living trust, which can be changed by you at anytime before you become disabled or die. In some instances, however, insurance will be placed in a revocable trust. Be certain that you have carefully reviewed the consequences of using an irrevocable trust with your tax adviser before using this approach. Where a revocable living trust is used, there is no gift tax cost on the transfer of money or policies to the trust because the gift to a revocable trust is considered incomplete for gift tax purposes. The transfer won't be complete, and no tax cost can be triggered until you give up control over the trust assets. Why use a revocable trust? It can help you achieve any of the benefits that the living trust can provide: management, avoidance of probate, confidentiality, and so forth. However, it cannot provide estate tax savings. If the insurance involved is insurance only on your life, and the proceeds will be payable to your spouse, there will be no estate tax cost on your death as a result of the unlimited marital deduction offsetting the insurance included in your estate. Further, if your spouse is young or you have young children, the insurance proceeds may be spent before her death so that there will be no estate tax cost at that time either. Where your estate is less than the $650,000 (1999) applicable exclusion this will not create any additional cost. The important benefit that the revocable insurance trust can offer in situations where tax costs are not a concern is that you can change it when circumstances change. If you divorce, you can change beneficiaries. You cannot change an irrevocable life insurance trust.

Grantor versus Nongrantor Trust

Under the tax law grantor trust rules, an insurance trust will be deemed to be a grantor trust to the extent that the income of the trust is used to pay insurance premiums on the grantor's life, or where income is paid to or for the benefit of the grantor or the grantor's spouse, or is accumulated for later distribution to grantor or grantor's spouse. Because of this, most insurance trusts are not funded during the insured's lifetime with any significant assets other than the insurance policy.

Selecting a Trustee

The trustees of your insurance trust can come from the same list of people listed as trustees in your living trust, but there is no requirement that they be. It is preferable that your spouse is not the sole trustee of an insurance trust if she is also a beneficiary. Instead, consider naming her as a co-trustee along with an independent person. Where a second-to-die policy is purchased, neither you or your spouse should be a trustee.

Crummey Power

The first key tax planning benefit of using insurance trusts is the removal of the insurance proceeds from the estate tax, as described previously. The second key tax benefit is that you can avoid using up any of your $650,000 (1999) applicable exclusion when you make gifts to the trust each year so that the trust has money to pay insurance premiums. The most common approach to achieving this second important tax goal is to have the trust document include a technique called a "Crummey power," the name coming from a famous court case sanctioning the technique. In addition to including the appropriate language in the trust, each time you gift money to the trust, the trustee should deposit the money in the trust bank account and issue a formal written notice to the beneficiaries reminding them of their right to withdraw a portion of the gift under the Crummey power. After a period of time specified in the trust, typically 30 to 60 days, the trustee can then pay the insurance premium. The lawyer who sets up your insurance trust can provide you with guidance for this.

NOTE: For a more detailed discussion, see Martin Shenkman, *The Complete Book of Trusts* (2nd ed.) (New York: John Wiley & Sons, 1998).

Distribution Provisions

The provisions that address how the insurance proceeds should be distributed are important since in most cases the trust will be irrevocable and the amounts involved large. For insurance on your life to benefit your spouse, the issues to consider are similar to those discussed in Chapters 8 and 9 for the bypass trust. If children or other minor beneficiaries are named, consider a broad range of issues. Since the proceeds may not be paid for many years into the future, and anticipating the circumstances your family or loved ones may face is so difficult, it's often best to give more, rather than less, flexibility to your trustee. You can do this by providing substantial discretion to the trustee to allocate income and principal of the trust to the beneficiaries most in need. Should a child have special needs, a well-drafted insurance trust can give the trustee the invaluable means to apply the money where it is most needed. If grandchildren (or other skip persons) could be beneficiaries, be certain too that your estate planner has carefully considered the generation-skipping transfer (GST) tax discussed in Chapter 12.

Trustee Powers

The trustee can be provided authority to invest in any assets, including real estate, closely held business interests, and other assets your estate will own. The trustee should be authorized to purchase insurance and take any steps necessary to maintaining the desired insurance in force. This could include the use of income or principal to pay for premiums (but see earlier comments concerning grantor trust status), the right to purchase additional policies, and so forth. However, the trustee should not be required to pay any debt or expense of your estate. It is generally preferable not to require the trustee to purchase or maintain any insurance policy.

Powers to Deal with Insured's Estate

This could enable your trustee to purchase assets from your estate to provide cash needed to pay estate taxes. If your estate includes valuable property, the trust could use insurance proceeds to purchase these nonliquid assets, thus providing your estate with the cash necessary to meet expenses and estate taxes. When the trustee is granted this right, it may be advisable to have the trust document give the trustee broad powers for the management, lease, improvement, and so forth of the property.

Marital Tax Savings Clauses

If you die within three years of transferring the insurance to your trust, the insurance proceeds will be included in your taxable estate. There is a backup approach that can salvage an estate tax benefit. If you are married, transfers to your spouse can qualify for the unlimited marital tax deduction. Thus, your life insurance trust can provide that if the insurance is to be included in your estate as a result of your dying within three years of making the transfer, the proceeds will be transferred into a trust that qualifies for the marital deduction. This may be a qualified terminal interest property trust, more commonly called a QTIP. To qualify, several requirements have to be met, including that the spouse is entitled to all the income from the trust, at least annually, for her life (see Chapter 8).

Operating Your Life Insurance Trust

Apply for Insurance Coverage

Have the trustees complete and sign (in their capacity as trustees) all applications and forms from your insurance agent. You should take any required medical examinations to qualify for the insurance desired.

Obtain a Tax Identification Number

The trustee should obtain a federal tax identification number by filing Form SS-4 with the IRS.

Transfer Existing Insurance Policies to the Trust

If you are planning to transfer existing insurance policies to your life insurance trust, contact your insurance agent and request a written estimate of the value of the insurance policies being transferred, the balance of any loans outstanding, and the amount of the policy that can be borrowed against. Your insurance agent should be able to provide you with a calculation of the value of the insurance given, in accordance with a prescribed IRS formula. The value of the policies is important because, if it is too large (which can occur on large dollar whole life or similar policies), there could be a gift tax cost on making the transfer. To successfully accomplish this objective, the policy, and all incidence of ownership in the policy, must be given away. Further, this gift must be accomplished at least three years prior to your death. If not, the insurance proceeds will be included in your estate and will be subject to estate tax. To remove the death benefit of an insurance policy you own from your estate, you must effectively transfer all economic benefits of ownership of the policy (e.g., to the insurance trust). An "incidence of ownership" means the right to borrow the cash value, change the name of the beneficiary, assign the policy to another person, borrow against the policy, and so forth. To eliminate all incidence of ownership, and remove the proceeds of an insurance policy from your estate, you must assign the policy a new owner and surrender every power over the policy and all the benefits the policy can provide. You must irrevocably give up all these rights. Where you transfer insurance to a trust, you should not have a reversionary interest equal to more than 5 percent of the value of the policy. That is, there cannot be more than a 5 percent possibility that the insurance policy or its proceeds may return to you.

You Should Make a Gift to the Insurance Trust

The gift should be sufficient to pay the first insurance premium and to maintain a bank account for the trust.

The Trustees of Your Insurance Trust Should Open a Bank Account

Your trustee should take a signed copy of your trust agreement and your tax identification number to a bank and open a bank account. Deposit a nominal amount to get the account started, or a larger amount if your trustee will have to pay an insurance premium.

The Trustees of Your Insurance Trust Must Issue Crummey Power Notices

Your insurance trust will probably include an annual, noncumulative, demand or Crummey power. This technique was explained earlier.

Trustee Should Pay Premiums

Your trustee should pay for the periodic insurance premiums.

NOTE: For a more detailed discussion of insurance trusts, see Martin Shenkman, *The Complete Book of Trusts* (2nd ed.) (New York: John Wiley & Sons, 1998).

CHILDREN AND MINORS' TRUSTS

The second most common type of trust used in connection with your "Family Tax Planning Living Trust" is a trust for a child, or other minor or dependent. The primary purpose of this type of trust is to hold annual gifts or other significant receipts of the beneficiary where the beneficiary is too young or otherwise incapable of managing assets. Although this discussion will generally refer to the trust as being for a child, the trust could be for any beneficiary. One of the only significant issues that requires different treatment is naming a beneficiary who is a grandchild or later descendant. This would require the additional consideration of the generation-skipping transfer (GST) tax discussed in Part Four.

Trusts Are Key in Planning for Children

When people think of trusts, one of the first types of trusts thought of is trusts for children. This is natural since an essential characteristic of trusts is that they provide for the separation of ownership and management of an asset (in the trustee) and the beneficial enjoyment of that asset (the children as beneficiaries). With children, who have important financial needs for their education and care, and the immaturity that requires another to manage their assets, trusts are often ideal. The need to provide for management of assets and to protect the children from themselves, a potential divorce, or creditors, makes trusts the ideal approach to providing for your children and other heirs.

The desire to help your children, reinforced by the high gift, estate, and GST tax rates often provides a strong incentive to make gifts to take maximum advantage of the annual $10,000 (indexed for inflation) gift tax exclusion. If the gifts are likely to be significant, the next question is whether the gifts will become large enough that you should use a trust. This is primarily a question of costs. It can cost typically between $750 to $2,000 for a child's trusts. A trust for a grandchild may be a bit more depending on the complexity of the GST planning. A dynasty trust, which is to continue in perpetuity, is likely to be substantially more. Much will depend on how customized and comprehensive the trust document will be. In all cases, however, if you are completing multiple trusts, say trusts for all five of your children, the cost for the additional trusts is often nominal because the terms of the documents are almost identical. Even if you spend $1,800 for the first trust and $50 for each additional child's trust, the cost per child is only $400, not much for the protection involved.

Gift and Estate Taxes Encourage Children's Trusts

The gift and estate tax rates reach more than 50 percent. With the generation-skipping transfer (GST) tax, the rate can exceed 75 percent. To avoid these costly taxes, you should consider taking advantage of the exclusions and special rules available. You can give away up to $10,000 (indexed for inflation) per year to as many different people as you wish. This right is noncumulative. If you do not give a $10,000 gift in one year to a particular donee, you cannot give more than $10,000 in the next year. Thus, a cornerstone of estate planning for many people is to make the maximum annual $10,000 gifts to as many family members as possible. If you pursue a gift program on a regular basis, year after year and the funds are well invested, it does not take long to transfer sizable amounts of money to each beneficiary. When children are involved, a trust is a natural step to protect this large and growing nest egg.

EXAMPLE: One of the most common trust arrangements is illustrated as follows: Grandfather establishes an "Education Trust" for Grandchild. Grandfather makes $10,000 annual gifts to the trust, which are invested and saved for Grandchild's college and graduate school education. Often the trust funds will not be needed for education if sufficient other assets are transferred or if Grandparents take advantage of the other common gift tax exclusion—paying any amounts to educational institutions directly for tuition. The trust will then typically distribute the principal amounts to Grandchild in approximately equal increments at ages 25 and 30 and the balance at 35 (or not infrequently, at older ages). If the trust is started when Grandchild is 5, the principal in the trust alone can be $300,000 by age 20 if both Grandparents make annual gifts. This amount is far too large to leave in a child's control at a young age of say merely 18 or even 21.

When setting up a trust for a child or other heir, you must take care to address the gift tax consequences of a gift to a trust since they are more complicated than the gift tax consequences of a gift made directly outside any trust. It is difficult to avoid a current gift tax (or use of your unified credit) by qualifying for the $10,000 per year annual gift tax exclusion. To avoid gift tax, the gift must be a "gift of a present interest." This can be done through the use of what is called a Crummey Power (described earlier in this chapter), or using a special trust known by the Internal Revenue Code Sections creating the "2503(c) or 2503(b) Trust," described later in this chapter.

In addition to the complexities caused by the gift tax annual exclusion rules, there are two potential income tax problems. If the trust is not properly structured, there is a risk trust funds could be used to meet your legal obligation to support the child. Where trust income or assets are used for educational, medical, or other obligations that the law requires you as a parent to provide for, the income earned by the trust may be taxed to you instead of the trust. The second problem is the trust income tax rates. Once the trust realizes a modest level of income, its income is taxed at the maximum tax rates. Thus, investments have to be carefully planned. Often this will include growth-oriented stocks, mutual funds managed to minimize current taxable income, and tax-exempt bonds. So long as you are cautious to address these issues with your tax adviser, the use of trusts to hold assets of minors is an ideal planning device.

TIP: In some situations, you can use a family limited partnership or limited liability company to control assets given to children. The advantage of these entities over a trust is that they are not irrevocable in that the agreements governing them can be modified in the future. More cautious taxpayers actually combine the two techniques. They will transfer assets to a family limited partnership or limited liability company and then form trusts for the benefit of their children to own the limited partnership interests or the limited liability company membership interests. This approach, while more complex, affords even greater protection, tax planning possibilities (by permitting lack of marketability discounts and other techniques), and protection. See Part Five.

"Kiddie Tax" Must Be Considered in Planning Gifts to Children

When planning gifts to children or trusts for the benefit of a child, the Kiddie Tax must be considered. If you use a trust for your child, the Kiddie Tax will apply to distributions from the trust. The trustee of a child's trust will have to weigh the benefits of retaining income in the trust and subjecting it to high trust tax rates, versus distributing the income to the child so that the Kiddie Tax may apply.

The Kiddie Tax rules provide that unearned income of a child who has not reached age 14, which is above a certain amount, is taxed at the top tax rate of the parents, which could be 39.6 percent or even higher.

Where any parent's estate planning involves gifts to their child under age 14, the careful selection of an appropriate investment strategy can minimize the burden of the Kiddie Tax. Any assets are appropriate until the level at which tax applies is reached. After that point, invest in assets that will appreciate rather than generate current income. This can include growth stocks, raw land, Series EE United States bonds. After the child reaches age 14, when the Kiddie Tax will no longer apply, these assets can be traded for income-producing assets. Investments in tax-exempt bonds also avoid the Kiddie Tax.

Although the Kiddie Tax can be a costly trap for children under age 14, the costly estate tax rates of up to 55 percent can make gifts to a child under 14 still advantageous if your net worth is large enough. When these gifts are made, the most common approach is to plan the gifts to comply with the requirements of the annual $10,000 exclusion from the gift tax, to avoid any gift tax implications.

Types of Trusts for Minors

Tax Considerations in Selecting a Minor's Trust

When trusts for minors are formed during your lifetime, the key tax concern is qualifying gifts to the trust for the annual $10,000 (as indexed) gift tax exclusion. The annual gift tax exclusion permits every taxpayer to give away up to $10,000 per year to any person without incurring a gift tax and without using up any of their once-in-a-lifetime $650,000 applicable exclusion. To qualify for this benefit, a gift must generally be a "gift of a present interest." A gift in trust will only qualify where your child, or the other beneficiary, is entitled to receive all the income currently or to withdraw up to the $10,000 (or lesser amount) that was given to the trust, or the special rules of Internal Revenue Code Section 2503(c) are met. The manner in which this goal is accomplished helps determine how the trust should be structured.

Income Only Trust (Section 2503(b) Trust)

One type of trust for minor children that permits gifts to qualify for the annual gift tax exclusion is formed under the provisions of Internal Revenue Code Section 2503(b). It is often called by that section number or, alternatively, is referred to as an income only trust.

This trust must require that all of the trust's income be distributed annually to your child or other beneficiary. This will permit you to make a gift of up to $10,000 per year and qualify for the annual gift tax exclusion. The child will then be taxed on all of the income earned by the trust. The assets in the trust will have to be income producing for the IRS to respect the arrangement (e.g., raw land that is not leased will not qualify). This type of trust offers additional flexibility over the 2503(c) special minor's trust, to be described. In the income only trust, the remainder beneficiary (the person who gets the trust property after the trust ends) does not have to be the same person who receives the trust income while the trust is in existence. If different beneficiaries are named, great care must be taken in how the trust agreement is worded. If the child-beneficiary receiving certain income during the existence of the trust has an emergency, should the trustee be permitted to dip into trust principal for this child? If this is done, it will reduce the amount available to the person receiving the assets when the trust terminates. Clear rules advising what the trustee should do are important.

Right to Withdraw under Crummey Power

Perhaps the most common manner to structure a trust for a minor to qualify for the annual exclusion is the use of a Crummey power arrangement. With the exception of a special trust for minor children to be discussed, you will not qualify for the annual $10,000 gift tax exclusion on gifts to a trust that can accumulate income. However, a gift to a trust will qualify as a gift of a present interest (i.e., you will qualify for the annual exclusion) up to the amount that the child can withdraw each year from the trust. This is called an "annual demand power," or a "Crummey power," and was explained in Chapter 11. This right gives the child beneficiary the absolute right to presently enjoy the gift made by the parent. Even if the child doesn't exercise this right, so that the money remains in the trust, the existence of this right enables the parent to avoid any gift tax. There are numerous complications to this type of planning that should be reviewed carefully with the attorney assisting you with estate planning.

Special Trust for Children under Age 21 (Section 2503(c) Trust)

There is yet another manner in which you can plan a trust so that gifts to the trust will qualify for the annual gift tax exclusion. If neither of the preceding trusts appeal to you in light of the child you are planning for, you should consider this third approach. The law provides for another special rule that permits you to transfer $10,000 per year to a trust; the trust can accumulate the income and you can still qualify for the annual gift tax exclusion. To qualify, however, the trust must meet several requirements. The trust must be set up to benefit a minor child. The trustee must have the ability to use the income for the benefit of the minor child without restriction. The trust assets must be invested in income-producing assets (stocks, bonds, and CDs, not raw land). If the child dies prior to age 21, the trust assets must be distributed to the child's estate, or in a manner that the child appoints. When the child reaches age 21, the trust must be distributed to the child. This latter requirement is the reason that this trust is not commonly used. Most custodial accounts can hold assets to age 21. The primary reason many parents opt for trusts is to protect and manage the income until a later age. If all of the principal must be distributed at age 21, the primary benefit of using a trust is defeated.

All is not lost however. There is no requirement that the child actually take the assets at age 21, merely that the child have the right to do so. Thus, the child can be given the right to require that the assets of the trust be distributed when he or she reaches age 21, but voluntarily choose not to take the money. This option, however, does not compare favorably to the Crummey power arrangement. If a child who is beneficiary of a Crummey power trust exercises the right to take the money (something the parent will probably intend not be done), the most the child can take is often $10,000. Contrast this with a Code Section 2503(c) trust. At age 21, the child legally can demand the entire trust! Is this a risk worth taking?

Trusts for Grandchildren

If you plan significant gifts to grandchildren, you should consider establishing trusts for their benefit. When forming grandchildren trusts, the issues and options discussed earlier for children's trusts are identical. The same decisions must be made to qualify for the annual gift tax exclusion. When planning grandchildren's trusts, however, an additional layer of complexity must be addressed, the generation-skipping transfer (GST) tax (see Part Four).

Trusts for Children with Special Needs

Where a child has special needs as a result of a handicap or illness, trusts represent the most important tools to protect the child. This is because a trust arrangement can provide for the care of your child for many years into the future, even when you are no longer able to assist. These trusts, however, can raise several unique issues.

A complex patchwork of government programs can provide benefits for a special child. Thus, the difficult goals for many families are to preserve wealth for the family unit as a whole without undue depletion to meet the needs of the special child, maximize the availability of public and other program resources available to the special child, and assure that the special child's needs are met.

These are not simple goals. They can often be contradictory. The laws and entitlement programs not only are complex, but change frequently. These trusts are also subject to all the concerns and problems of avoiding creditors described in detail in several chapters in this book.

Trusts can also be set up to hold assets, in part for the benefit of the special child, and to provide for distributions to or for the benefit of the special child. The trusts are typically created under your living trust after your death. They are not as commonly set up while you are alive because the rules to qualify gifts to them for the annual gift tax exclusion contradict the objectives of a special needs trust. If the special beneficiary is given the right to income, or to principal under a Crummey power, perhaps medical and other health care or government providers could reach the assets. The critical provisions of any trust will be those that determine when distributions can be made. In a special needs trust, these provisions are written to limit the trustee's rights to make distributions and limit the special beneficiary's legal access to trust assets for the purpose of making it as difficult as possible for government agencies to reach the assets to pay for the special beneficiary's care. Many special needs trusts include a provision indicating that the trust's income and assets cannot be distributed to or for the benefit of the special child where the distributions or expenditures would jeopardize qualification for government benefits or distributions from charitable organizations. Your trust can clearly state that the trustee is not to make distributions that can be met from other government or charitable sources. Rather, only the gaps in those programs and additional items for personal comfort should be provided for.

Where the state or other government agency can reach the trust assets, a more extreme provision sometimes is included that will terminate the trust and require the distribution of all of the assets in the trust to children other than the special child. The objective here is to dissuade government agencies from suing the trust for reimbursements for medical care. The effectiveness of such a provision, however, is not guaranteed.

When planning any trust for a special child, you must consider each of the available government or charitable programs, along with its requirements and qualifications. Medicare and Social Security are two important federal programs. Social Security can provide benefits where the special child is totally disabled. Medicare provides for limited basic medical coverage. Supplemental Security Income (SSI) Medicaid, welfare, and other programs may be available as well. To qualify for these need-based programs, the income and assets of the child/recipient must be quite limited. Assuring qualification for these, and any other, need-based programs is a cornerstone of such planning. The trust arrangement that you set up must not result in the child being considered to have more income or assets than the requirements to qualify for these programs permit, or the benefits will be lost. Various states have additional programs, such as cost of care type programs, that may also be available. These should all be reviewed with an experienced estate or financial planner.

SUMMARY

This chapter discussed the two most common estate tax and asset protection techniques used when the bypass trust and marital deduction (whether in trust or outright and free of trust) alone may not suffice. These two techniques, the insurance trust and the child or minor's trust require documents separate and independent from your Family Tax Planning Living Trust. These documents are complex, raising many legal and tax issues and should only be prepared by a qualified estate tax attorney.

Part Four

THE MULTIGENERATIONAL (GST) LIVING TRUST

12 THE GENERATION-SKIPPING TRANSFER (GST) TAX

WHY CONSIDER MULTIGENERATIONAL TAX PLANNING?

What Is Multigenerational Tax Planning?

A Multigenerational Living Trust is a living trust estate plan designed to protect assets and tax benefits for your heirs (including grandchildren and possibly future generations) as well as for yourself and your children.

There are four degrees to which your Multigenerational Living Trust can take multigenerational planning.

Degree 1—As an Afterthought

When you set up your Multigenerational Living Trust, your primary objectives may be avoiding probate, protecting yourself in the event of disability, and protecting your spouse in the event of your death. The multigenerational aspects of the planning may be appealing, but not a major priority. If this is the case, you'll probably engage in the estate tax planning of the Family Tax Planning Living Trust and perhaps may include contingent trusts for the benefit of your grandchildren in your will. A contingent trust is a trust that is only used if a contingency, such as your child dying or disclaiming, happens. If a child dies before you, then that child's share of your estate could be bequeathed in trust to that deceased child's issue (i.e. your grandchildren). Barring that undesirable contingency, you can build a valuable planning opportunity into your will. If a child disclaims (because he doesn't need the money or is in the midst of a lawsuit or divorce), the inheritance he disclaims will go to his children in trust.

Degree 2—Intentional but Simple Planning

You may want to provide some assured measure of protection for grandchildren. You could bequeath specific amounts to them under your Multigenerational Living Trust. The most common approach, however, is to set up trusts while you are alive to hold annual gifts for their benefit. These trusts would be similar to the child trusts described in Chapter 11. However, to assure that they qualify for the GST tax annual gift tax exclusion, they would have one grandchild beneficiary per trust and the trust would assure that if the grandchild died before all assets were distributed, the trust assets would be taxed in the grandchild's estate.

Degree 3—More Substantial Planning for Grandchildren

In most multigenerational estate plans, the planning focuses solely on the transmission of wealth two generations down (i.e., to grandchildren) but not further. This can be exceptionally valuable planning because it can protect the assets while your children have access to it, but can assure that your children can pass the remaining assets on to their children without incurring the wrath of the estate tax. This type of planning can be accomplished by establishing, typically after the death of you and your spouse, a trust for each of your children to last for their respective lives. While your child is alive, he or she could have access to the trust income and assets subject only to limitations to assure that the assets are not taxed in their estates. Each child could designate in his or her will how his or her children (i.e., your grandchildren) would receive the assets. This could include their designating the percentages each of their children inherit, whether the amounts would be in trust, and so forth. This is quite broad access to the trust assets and a fairly substantial measure of control. However, properly structured, the assets would have a reasonable measure of protection from your children's creditors and would not be taxed in their estates. You've effectively given your children the ability to use what they need and pass on the rest estate tax free.

Degree 4—Perpetual Trust Planning

Comprehensive multigenerational planning focuses on taking maximum advantage of GST tax planning and the use of trusts. This type of planning will typically involve transferring assets to a trust up to the maximum amount you can give away without incurring GST tax. This amount will then be held in trust for the benefit of your descendants as long as possible. If your descendants have need for money, the trustees can make distributions. To the extent your heirs don't need money, the assets will stay in trust, protected, as long as possible. This approach maximizes the estate and asset protection planning benefits. The only other limitation on this type of trust is the rule against perpetuities, if your state law has such a rule. This rule provides that at some specified time, say 100 years, every trust in that state must end. For many people, this is a sufficiently long time. However, if you want to maximize the multigenerational planning benefits, you should organize the trust in a state that has eliminated this restriction (see later discussion). Unless you live in a jurisdiction that has eliminated the rule against perpetuities, or have a large estate, it is unlikely that you would need to establish your trust in such a jurisdiction.

Generally, the only trusts warranting formation in those jurisdictions are for extremely large estates that want to take advantage immediately of the $1+ million GST exemption rather than waiting for death. The advantage is that any growth in assets during your lifetime would also be protected from estate and GST taxes.

Multigenerational Planning Benefits Include Far More Than Merely Tax Savings

Benefits of multigenerational planning are substantial. Using many Multigenerational Living Trusts, however, raises some complex issues—tax, legal, and other. The possible advantages of this type of planning include the following:

- *Dynasty.* If the trust is based in a state (jurisdiction) whose laws permit trusts to continue forever (in perpetuity), then the trust can continue for future generations of yours until the assets are exhausted. This long-term time horizon makes the trust more complex to prepare since there are many additional issues to address.

- *Asset Protection.* If the assets of the trust are distributed to the beneficiary at a certain age, a lawsuit or divorce after that age may have a better likelihood of reaching those assets. If assets stay in trust longer, they stay protected longer. This can require a more comprehensive approach to preparing the terms of the trust. For example, instead of simply distributing money from the trust to enable a child to purchase a house, the better approach in a longer term GST or dynasty trust may be to have the trustee loan the child or grandchild money to buy the house, or even to buy the house in the trust and permit the beneficiary to use the house. This keeps the assets protected. This more comprehensive approach is rarely used for a trust that will make substantial distributions by age 30 or so.

- *Control.* The longer assets are held in trust the greater control you can exercise over how the assets are used, who will use them, and when the beneficiaries will be able to access them. You might wish to assure that your grandchildren will have the financial wherewithal to attend college even if your children prove to be fiscally irresponsible. Multigenerational planning accomplishes this.

- *Long-Term Investing.* With multigenerational planning, your investment time horizon is far longer. This can facilitate a more aggressive investment posture than perhaps may be appropriate for a trust with a shorter term time horizon.

- *State Tax Savings.* Many multigenerational trusts are established in states that have favorable, or even no, income tax charged on trust income. Over a long number of years, this modest annual savings can generate substantial additional value to trust beneficiaries.

Where to Consider Forming Your Multigenerational Trust

If your Multigenerational Living Trust includes planning only for grandchildren, but not further heirs (i.e., you are not attempting to set up a dynasty trust), the most likely state would be the state where you reside and under whose laws your living trust is formed. However, if you want a longer term multigenerational trust, it may be necessary to form the trust in a different state. This could be done while you are alive, as a trust independent of your living trust, or following your death (or the death of your spouse) under the provisions included in your Multigenerational Living Trust.

Which state you should use is an issue to discuss with an estate planning attorney. Several states have eliminated the rule against perpetuities that had restricted the number of years a trust can continue. The following states, among others, have eliminated the rule against perpetuities: Alaska, Delaware, Idaho, Illinois, New Jersey, South Dakota, and Wisconsin.

Expect the trend to continue with more states joining the list. You should consider where you live, whom you will name as trustee, the state income tax consequences to a trust being located in a particular jurisdiction, and the requirements for the laws of that state to apply if it is a state other than where you live. In most cases, at minimum, you will have to appoint a bank or trust company in that other state as a co-trustee for that state's laws to apply to govern your multigenerational trust.

Of these jurisdictions, Wisconsin and Idaho have significant state income taxes. Even though the rates are small relative to the federal income tax rates applicable to trusts, over the long time horizon of the trusts being considered, these taxes will have a substantial and adverse impact.

In each of the preceding states (jurisdictions), it is possible to form a trust to facilitate the transfer of wealth down multiple generations without the further imposition of transfer taxes. This can be accomplished while still permitting each generation substantial use of the trust assets. A key technique to accomplish this is for the trustee to permit a beneficiary the use of trust property, rather than distributing the trust property to the beneficiary. For example, the trustee could purchase artwork or a vacation home and permit the beneficiaries to use these assets. Since the beneficiary has not been given title to the asset, the asset can remain in the ownership of the trust and continue to pass on to later generations without incurring additional transfer tax costs. This approach can enable these assets to continue to pass on free of any gift, estate, or GST tax costs. Once an asset is distributed out of the trust these benefits will be lost.

To accomplish the treatment of assets as described, the investment provisions of the trust must exempt these types of purchases from any applicable state or other statute or regulation (e.g., the Prudent Investor Act) that would otherwise require the diversification of the trust assets and so forth. The trustee powers should also include sufficient detailed powers authorizing these transactions.

WHAT IS THE GENERATION-SKIPPING TRANSFER TAX AND WHY DID CONGRESS ENACT IT?

To understand the importance of multigenerational tax planning, you must understand the basics of the tax system that affect it. The gift and estate taxes, described in Chapters 8 and 9, are not the only taxes you may face when making gifts with the use of trusts. The generation-skipping transfer (GST) tax is an expensive and complicated transfer tax that can affect wealthy taxpayers making transfers by gift or at death to grandchildren or other people the tax laws consider to be more than two generations beyond the donor. The GST tax is charged on every gift or other transfer of property that meets the requirements of being a generation-skipping transfer. The GST tax is calculated as a flat 55 percent tax rate on the taxable amount of a generation-skipping transfer. While the GST will not affect most taxpayers, those it does affect can be shocked by its impact.

The purpose of the GST tax is to equalize intergenerational taxation of property transfers where planning is attempted to avoid the estate tax. The GST was designed to prevent the very wealthy from passing assets through many layers of generations, transfer tax free, often through the use of trusts.

EXAMPLE: You are a grandfather. To simplify calculations, assume all taxes are at a maximum 50 percent flat rate. Your estate is $4 million. On your death, you leave your daughter and sole heir your entire estate. She pays $2 million, assuming the 50 percent tax rate. On her death, she leaves her entire $2 million estate to her son and sole heir. Her son, your grandchild pays a $1 million tax again assuming a 50 percent flat rate. Thus, from your $4 million estate, only $1 million reached your grandchild. To avoid this harsh result, you decide to split your estate 50/50. $2 million to your daughter and $2 million to your grandchild. This approach would save the estate tax your daughter would have to pay on some portion of the assets she ultimately bequeaths to your grandchild. To prevent this end run around the estate tax system, Congress enacted the GST tax.

HOW THE GST TAX WORKS

Calculating the GST Tax

Once it has been determined that a gift, bequest, or other transfer is subject to the GST tax, the GST tax must be calculated. The first step is to determine the value of the property involved. The property is generally valued at the time the transfer occurred. However, if the transfer was a direct skip (to be explained) and the property was included in your gross estate, the special valuation rules your estate uses will apply to the GST as well. These rules could permit your executor to value the property at the date six months following your death rather than at the date of your death, which is the general rule. Where the transfer also triggers a gift tax, the amount of GST tax paid by the donor is treated as a further gift subject to the gift tax.

The GST tax is assessed at a flat rate equal to the maximum estate tax rate, presently 55 percent. This tax rate is actually multiplied by the "inclusion ratio" which is briefly explained later in this chapter.

Overview of Transfers That Trigger the GST Tax

The GST tax can apply to a broad range of property transfers. For the GST tax to apply, a taxable event must occur. The simplest example is your gift of property to your grandchild. This is because this gift is a transfer of property to a person who is considered to be a member of a generation at least two generations below you. In simple terms, you're generation 1, your child is generation 2, and your grandchild is generation 3. This type of transfer is called "a direct skip." The grandchild in this simple example is referred to as a "skip" person, since a generation is skipped getting to him. This concept of a skip person is important to understanding other aspects of the GST tax as well.

Two other types of transfers also trigger GST: A taxable distribution and a taxable termination. A taxable distribution occurs when a trust has been set up for several people, some of whom are skip people (e.g., grandchildren) and some of whom are not skip people (e.g., your children). Since it is unclear who will receive the trust assets, no GST tax is charged while the assets stay in the trust. Once the trustee makes a distribution to a skip person (i.e., a grandchild), then the GST tax can apply. This is called a "taxable distribution" since it is a distribution that triggers GST tax. To take this example a step further, when all the nonskip people die (e.g., your children) or can no longer receive distributions under the terms of the trust, then only skip people remain as beneficiaries. This is analogous to the termination of the trust and the distribution of all assets solely to skip people. When this occurs, the GST tax will apply. This type of transaction is called a "taxable termination" because the interests of all nonskip people have terminated and the tax is triggered.

EXAMPLE: An applicable exclusion trust is formed under your Multigenerational Living Trust for the benefit of your surviving spouse and descendants. Descendants include grandchildren who are skip persons. However, your spouse and children are not skip persons so that the trust is not a skip person. The GST would only apply if there is a distribution to your grandchildren or later descendants (a taxable distribution) or on the death of your wife and children the trust ends and is distributed to grandchildren or later descendants (a taxable termination).

Disclaimers are a common postdeath estate tax planning technique described in Chapter 8 as part of the Just-in-Case Living Trust. A disclaimer can, however, trigger surprise and costly GST tax consequences if the ultimate beneficiaries are skip people.

Earlier, it was indicated that a skip person is a person who is two or more generations below you. This simple explanation needs to be expanded for you to understand the workings of the GST. A skip person could include your grandchild, or a trust for the benefit of your grandchild. A trust is considered a skip person where no distributions can be made to nonskip persons. A nonskip person is a person who is less than two generations below the generation of the person making the gift (e.g., your child or sibling).

While a grandchild or later descendant is obviously a skip person, the law is much broader and more complex. A skip person can include any individual (not only a direct descendant) who is more than a specified number of years younger than the person setting up the trust or making the gift. For nonlineal descendants, a generation is considered to be 25 years. A person born within 12.5 years (i.e., ½ of the 25 years) of your birthday will be treated as being of your generation. A person who is more than 12.5 but less than 37.5 (i.e., 12.5 + 25 years, which is considered a generation) is considered to be in the same generation as your children would be (assuming you had children). Persons more than 37.5 years younger are considered to be in the same generation as your grandchildren would be (assuming you had grandchildren).

HOW TO PLAN TO MINIMIZE THE GST TAX IMPACT ON YOUR TRUST

There are several basic GST planning techniques to avoid the harsh tax results illustrated in this chapter. You should review these techniques with your estate planner when setting up your Multigenerational Living Trust.

Annual per Donee Gift Tax Exclusion

You can still give up to $10,000 (indexed) per year to any person, including every grandchild, without triggering the GST tax. If your spouse joins you in the gift, you can give $20,000 per year. Thus, over a period of years, you can transfer substantial assets to your grandchildren with no GST tax cost. Again, however, the GST can be tricky. The requirements to qualify a gift to a trust for a grandchild or other skip person for the annual $10,000 GST exclusion are more stringent than the requirements discussed in Chapter 11 to qualify for the annual $10,000 gift tax exclusion for a gift to a trust for a child. For a gift to a grandchild (i.e., GST) trust to qualify for the GST annual gift tax exclusion, in addition to the gift tax requirements (such as a Crummey power), it must meet other requirements. Thus, a transfer might qualify for the annual $10,000 gift tax exclusion, but not for the GST tax. The $10,000 annual exclusion is only available for GST tax purposes on a gift to a trust if, during the life of the grandchild (other skip person) who is beneficiary of the trust, payments cannot be made to any other person. Thus, the commonly used sprinkle power (trustee has discretion to pay income and principal to anyone from a listed group of beneficiaries) won't qualify. This is why a single or pot trust for several grandchildren will not qualify. An additional requirement is that if the beneficiary dies during the term of the trust, the trust assets must be taxable in the beneficiary's estate. This means that if the grandchild dies before the term of the trust ends, the assets would not be included in the grandchild's estate.

Transfers for Educational and Medical Benefits

You, or the trustee under your Multigenerational Living Trust, can gift unlimited amounts of money to pay for a grandchild's education or medical benefits. With a large family, and the high cost of quality medical care and education, tremendous amounts can be transferred for the benefit of later generations with no GST tax implications. This technique should be carefully reviewed before incurring the expense, and problems, of setting up grandchildren's trusts.

This exclusion for medical and tuition payments can be used to protect distributions from trusts from the GST tax. For example, assume an applicable exclusion trust is included in your Multigenerational Living Trust that permits distributions to your spouse and descendants generally in the trustee's discretion (a sprinkle power). Since a distribution to a grandchild could trigger GST tax (or use of your GST exemption, to be explained) this may not be desirable. Consider instead having the trustee to limit distributions for the benefit of grandchildren (i.e., skip people) solely for qualifying medical and tuition payments. This approach could provide for maximum flexibility without triggering GST tax.

If you have no other significant multigenerational planning (i.e., you won't use your GST exemption for a better purpose), your successor trustee could allocate some of your GST exemption to your applicable exclusion trust. If this is done properly, no distributions from that trust will ever trigger GST tax. The next section discusses this exemption amount.

One-Million-Dollar + Exemption

The primary protection from the GST is a one-time exclusion (similar to the one-time gift and estate tax applicable exclusion). You can gift up to $1,010,000 (the 1999 amount, which is indexed for inflation) to your grandchildren with no GST tax cost. Your spouse can make a similar transfer to the grandchildren. Thus, a wealthy family can gift over $2 million to grandchildren without the application of the GST. As explained earlier, the gift doesn't have to be solely for grandchildren. The applicable exclusion trust can be for grandchildren as well as your spouse and children. If your successor trustee allocates a GST exemption amount to this trust on your estate tax return, then distributions from that trust will never cause a GST tax. This approach, however, wastes your GST exclusion anytime your spouse or children receive a distribution since distributions to them did not need the protection of your GST exemption to avoid GST tax.

While this exemption can eliminate the GST tax for most taxpayers it does not mean that taxpayers should not concern themselves with the GST since ignoring the GST can still be costly. Also, to use these large $1 million + exemptions advantageously takes careful planning. You cannot ignore the GST planning in a Multigenerational Living Trust plan because it may be critical at a future date. A simple example will illustrate.

EXAMPLE: On your death, your trustee transfers $650,000 to an applicable exclusion trust for the benefit of your spouse and all descendants. Your trustee does an outstanding job investing and 10 years later the trust is worth $3 million. Your children have been successful in their own right and have no need for the assets. Had your trustee allocated $650,000 of your $1,010,000 GST exemption to the trust when it was formed, no distributions from that applicable exclusion trust, no matter how large, would ever trigger GST tax. Thus, the GST exemption can protect amounts much larger than the exemption itself. Most importantly, proper use of the exemption can protect trusts no matter how large they grow in future years. Given the long-term time horizon for multigenerational planning, this can be extremely important.

Once a portion or all of your GST exemption is allocated to a particular property transfer, the protection of that allocation will stay with the property in trust. Thus, if your GST exemption is allocated to property given to a trust, that trust will remain protected from your GST tax in future years.

EXAMPLE: You set up a $1 million trust fund for your grandchildren and great-grandchildren. You allocate your entire $1 million GST tax exemption to the trust. The assets of the trust appreciate to $10 million before being distributed in a taxable distribution or termination. None of the transfers of the $10 million in trust property to your grandchildren and great-grandchildren is subject to the GST tax. If instead you had allocated only $500,000 of GST exemption to the $1 million in assets, the inclusion ratio would be 50 percent and $5 million [50 percent inclusion ratio × $10 million taxable] would be subject to GST tax.

Multigenerational GST Planning Example

With proper planning over time, a substantial amount of net worth can be transferred to grandchildren without triggering the GST tax.

EXAMPLE: You have four children and nine grandchildren. You and your spouse set up separate trusts for each of your grandchildren, each properly structured so that $10,000 gifts will qualify for both the gift and GST tax annual exclusions. You and your spouse give, combined, $20,000 per year to each grandchild's trust. This amounts to $180,000 per year. Over a 10-year period (not even counting the earnings, which would have made the trust balances grow substantially), you will have given away $1.8 million to your grandchildren. This is in addition to any amounts you could have given to each of your children and their spouses (which could have amounted to an additional $1.6 million over the same 10 years). Finally, in each of your wills, you and your spouse can provide for a $1 million GST exempt trust. The two trusts will total, after the last of you and your spouse dies, $2 million. Thus, over a 10-year period, you have transferred $3.8 million to trusts for your grandchildren. Planning, however, is essential.

If additional estate tax planning techniques are used in making the gifts in the preceding example to the trusts for your grandchildren, the amounts transferred can be increased substantially beyond what the example indicates. For example, if stock in a closely held business, or interests in a family limited partnership (FLP), rather than cash, is given to the grandchildren's trusts, the gifts may qualify for a lack of marketability or minority discount that can enable the transfer of more economic value than the equivalent cash amount (see Part Five).

NOTE: For a detailed discussion of the GST tax, see Martin Shenkman, *The Complete Book of Trusts* (2nd ed.) (New York: John Wiley & Sons, 1999).

SUMMARY

This chapter has presented an overview of multigenerational planning in the context of formulating your revocable living trust and estate plan to meet your needs and objectives, as well as the needs and objectives of your heirs. This type of planning can provide tremendous asset protection and tax benefits, but requires sophisticated tax and legal assistance to succeed.

13 DRAFTING THE MULTIGENERATIONAL LIVING TRUST

WHY YOU NEED SPECIAL DRAFTING FOR A MULTIGENERATIONAL LIVING TRUST

Special complications and issues must be addressed in drafting a trust intended to continue for generations. This chapter highlights some of them. While you must have a lawyer who is an estate planning specialist prepare your Multigenerational Living Trust, a familiarity with the key concepts will help you minimize costs by making decisions in advance and enable you to be discriminating in accepting advice.

The key to the Multigenerational Living Trust is that the distribution provisions must include distributions for grandchildren or further descendants designed to maximize your GST tax benefits within the confines of your personal goals. The trust document will also have to include sufficient rights and powers for your trustee to be able to implement the multigenerational planning. This could include the power to divide trusts, allocate the GST exemption, and so forth. These are all technical tax points which your estate planning attorney will handle. The discussions in the preceding chapter provided an overview of basic GST tax concepts. This chapter addresses many of the nontax issues involved.

RECITAL/WHEREAS CLAUSES

The introductory paragraphs of your Multigenerational Living Trust should state the general purposes and objectives of the trust, and in particular, should indicate the objectives of your multigenerational planning. For example, if your real objective in setting up a trust is to provide for your grandchildren's education, and you're not particularly concerned if funds are left for later or other purposes, say so. This will give a much different focus to the trustee than if you state your goal is to provide a legacy for all future generations of your family. These somewhat sketchy statements should be expanded in a personal, nonbinding letter of instruction to your successor trustees.

SPENDTHRIFT PROVISION

This provision is key to the asset protection planning intended in most Multigenerational Living Trusts. Usually, in this type of planning there is an objective of protecting assets over a relatively long period for family members or loved ones. By restricting any beneficiary's right to appoint assets of the trust or encumber them, you will help safeguard those assets.

CHANGE IN SITUS

What if you want to have a trust set up in perpetuity, but don't want to make the commitment now to form a trust in a state that has eliminated the rule against perpetuities (i.e., the rule that requires a trust end at some time); is there an option? Yes, but there is no guarantee that it will be effective. You could grant your trustee the right to change the location (situs) of a trust from the state it is organized in, to any other state. This might, although legal commentators don't all agree that it would be effective, give the flexibility for the trustee to change the trust to a state that has eliminated the rule against perpetuities. A change in situs to a jurisdiction with a lower (or no) state income taxation (or other taxes applicable to a trust) will be a desired goal in some circumstances. It is not clear, however, that the relocation of a trust from one state to another will assure that the former state will not assert jurisdiction over the trust even following the relocation.

FIDUCIARIES OTHER THAN TRUSTEES

In Multigenerational Living Trusts, the very long time period for which trusts may continue requires more planning to assure that the trust will operate effectively. Most trusts are established with the intent that in some number of decades they unwind. Multigenerational planning can result in trusts continuing for many generations, even in perpetuity. To assure reasonable operations over such a long time period, additional steps might be warranted. These include naming additional persons who have perhaps quasi-fiduciary status. They are not trustees, yet they have positions of importance. The proper blending of these additional positions and that of the trustees will increase the flexibility and security of your trust arrangements.

- *Trust Protector.* Your trust could designate a person to have a position called a trust protector that is uniquely different from that of the trustee. The trust protector can be a valuable concept although it has not been commonly used in trusts formed in the United States. This is changing. A trust protector is an individual with limited rights expressly provided in the trust document. These could include the right to change trustees, situs (where the trust is located), or governing law.

- *Investment Adviser or Committee.* An individual, institution, or group of individuals can be given the authority to invest trust assets. This has historically been a function of the trustee, but if your state has enacted a more modern version of the prudent investor act, a different person independent of the trustee can be named. For example, you may need to name an institutional trustee in a particular state to take advantage of the favorable laws in that state, to have the objectivity of an institution, and so forth. However, you may have a particular money manager or firm you have worked with and would like to continue to involve in your investment decisions. This can be done by limiting the scope of responsibility of the trustee and designating someone else to assume responsibility for investment decisions.

- *Distribution Committee.* If you are setting up a trust for a child, it might be pretty obvious to you how and when money should be distributed. Pay for college, contribute something for starting a business and buying a house, and distribute what's left at age 35. Now when your children are still teenagers, try that same thought process for a trust intended to benefit grandchildren and great-grandchildren. Much tougher to make a decision, probably impossible. You could leave distributions up to the trustee, but will Aunt Jane even be around then? One solution is to have a distribution committee appointed that could consist of perhaps the oldest of the beneficiaries at each generation. This would assure that senior family members would be making decisions.

PERPETUITIES

Many if not most trusts will be established for a limited number of years. If a perpetual term is used, however, money can be distributed when needed, but if not needed, it can stay within the protective shelter of the trust. If you form your trust in a state with a limitation on how long a trust can exist (rule against perpetuities), a perpetuities savings clause should be included to assure compliance with the states statutes in the event any trust property becomes subject to those rules.

BENEFICIARIES' USE OF ASSETS

The trustee should also have the authority to purchase assets and then permit the beneficiaries to use the assets, in lieu of distributing the assets directly, in order to preserve the perpetuities, GST tax, and asset protection benefits. For example, if a child of yours needs $250,000 in help to buy a house, the trustee could, if you've had the trust prepared to permit this, simply distribute the money to your child. However, if the child is sued or divorced, the $250,000 can be reached. If the child is successful and faces an estate tax, the $250,000 could end up subject to a 55 percent estate tax and worse, GST tax. On the other hand, if the trustee can instead buy the house and let your child live in it, the money remains protected.

BENEFICIARIES

It is important to name classes of persons who can be defined and identified in the future as a result of the duration of the trust. Clarity is important especially in a multigenerational trust.

DISTRIBUTION PROVISIONS

A typical trust will require the income to be distributed, for example, to the child beneficiary annually. Principal is typically distributed at specified ages, say one-third at ages 25, 30, and 35. However, mandatory income or principal distribution provisions can destroy the asset protection benefits the trust is hoped to afford. Also, if the trust is intended to be GST exempt, mandatory distributions would represent leakage of GST benefits back into a taxable estate. This is why it was suggested earlier that the trustee be given the right to purchase assets that can be made available to the beneficiaries.

The trust distribution provisions may also provide that the trust estate, the assets, be maintained as a single pot for the duration of the trust. Alternatively, the "pot" could be divided at each generational level into additional shares on a per stirpes basis. This, however, could be problematic as future generations are added since the number of separate shares could mushroom. The distribution provisions should address what should happen if a particular generational line should cease.

TRUST TERMINATION

"In perpetuity" is a long time. Some flexibility should be given to the trustee to terminate the trust and distribute trust assets if the trust is uneconomical, impractical, or otherwise inappropriate to operate. This could be especially important if the trust distribution provisions require that the trust estate be divided at each generational level into separate trusts. At some point if the growth in trust principal does not exceed the distributions and divisions sufficiently, the trustee could end up administering scores of small and uneconomical trusts.

TRUSTEE SELECTION

Trustee selection for a multigenerational trust involves several factors that differ from those considered for a typical trust. If the trust is to exist over several generations, or especially if it is to exist perpetually, an institution that can exist perpetually should be named trustee or perhaps co-trustee. To establish a sufficient legal connection, called nexus, with the domestic asset protection trust jurisdiction, you should use an institution in that jurisdiction. These types of asset protection trusts permit you to be a beneficiary although the assets may not be reached by your creditors and may be excluded from your estate for tax purposes. If you're seeking to have a specific state's law apply to your trust, you may have to select an institution or person in that jurisdiction to be trustee. You can also build flexibility into the trustee selection in several ways. The use of a trust protector to name successor trustees and even to replace trustees, was already noted. You can also give the beneficiaries some limited right to replace trustees. For example, you can grant the beneficiaries by perhaps majority or unanimous vote the right to change one institutional trustee for another. You may want to limit the circumstances in which this is done, or perhaps limit the number of times trustees can be changed per year or other time period.

GOVERNING LAW

When selecting the jurisdiction to govern, consider the following (as well as any other applicable) characteristics of the available state statutes:

- Little or no state income tax or other tax on trust assets, activities, or investments. Even a modest tax percentage, when compounded over decades and longer, will have an extremely negative impact on the value of trust assets.

- The degree to which state law would involve itself in trust activities (except if actually requested by the beneficiaries).

- State spendthrift statute and the attitudes of that state's courts toward spendthrift provisions in trusts.

- Generally legal environment of the state toward asset protection planning, trust planning, and related legal matters and trends.

- Status of the state's statutes governing limited liability companies (and family limited partnerships). How many members are required to form an LLC (e.g., can a one-member LLC be valid)? This is important if there is a goal not to involve others, a desire to support lack of marketability and minority interest discounts, and so forth.

- The state's statute's asset protection benefits (and in particular) how they have been viewed by the courts governing the case.

Once a jurisdiction is selected, circumstances could change such that it is advisable to change to another jurisdiction and governing law. These provisions are sometimes called jurisdiction skipping provisions. This can be reserved as a power to the trust protector, or handled otherwise.

PROVISIONS ESTABLISHING AND MAINTAINING NEXUS

Several provisions in the trust can be tailored to help establish sufficient connection to a particular state so that state law can apply to govern your trust (nexus). An institution based in a particular state could be appointed as trustee to establish nexus. The trust can require a specified portion of assets to be invested in that jurisdiction to establish or demonstrate nexus. Specified services or actions important to the trust, such as accounting records and tax filings, can be addressed in that jurisdiction. The governing law can be stated to be the particular state. Your estate planner can advise you as to the minimum steps you must take.

ACCOUNTING AND TAX PREPARATION

You may want to address several administrative matters in your trust. State law may require that certain accounting and reporting functions be performed in that state if the trust is to be based there. If so, the trust document could require this. Should the trust protector be entitled to reports? Should the trust protector have any rights or powers to affect this process? This should be specified in the trust.

SUMMARY

This chapter has provided an overview of some of the many provisions to be included in your Multigenerational Living Trust when you are addressing multigenerational and GST planning goals.

14 OPERATING YOUR MULTIGENERATIONAL LIVING TRUST

YOU MUST MONITOR YOUR MULTIGENERATIONAL LIVING TRUST WHILE YOU ARE ALIVE

Estate planning documents are not a step you can take and forget about, as discussed earlier concerning the Family Tax Planning Living Trust. This can be even more critical when your living trust contains multigenerational planning since mistakes will have so many more years over which to veer off the track of your intended objectives. Thus, careful monitoring while you are alive, so that you can take steps to refine your plan is vital.

If you do not title assets properly, the bypass trust may not be funded fully in your Family Tax Planning Living Trust. In your Multigenerational Living Trust, more than title is important. Even if assets are owned properly between you, your spouse or partner, and other heirs, planning could be jeopardized. The structure of your assets must also be properly handled. For example, if you have real estate in one state, but your trust is organized in a different state to benefit from the more favorable laws of that state, the state law where your trust is based will not apply to real estate in another state. You may have to transfer the real estate to an entity, such as a limited liability company (LLC) and have the interests in the LLC owned by your trust, not the real estate directly.

Further, assets not properly transferred to your living trust may be distributed to your spouse or other heirs outright and not in the type of protective trusts you want. This problem was addressed in the discussion in Chapter 10 concerning the Family Tax Planning Living Trust. With the Multigenerational Living Trust, the tax consequences can be even worse since not only may you end up with a lousy estate tax result, you can be jeopardizing the GST tax result as well. Thus, you personally must monitor changes in the value and ownership of your assets over time. You cannot expect your estate planner, accountant, insurance agent, or attorney to do this for you unless you arrange for a periodic meeting.

TRANSFERRING ASSETS TO YOUR MULTIGENERATIONAL LIVING TRUST

Select Assets Consistent with Long-Term Growth

When selecting assets to transfer to your Multigenerational Living Trust, choose assets that are most likely to appreciate, since the time horizon is so long. However, don't transfer only high-risk, high-growth assets if it may be necessary to make distributions in the foreseeable future. This could force the sale of assets at an inopportune time. You should also carefully review the assets you intend to transfer to your trust with the institution that will serve as a co-trustee. Since institutional co-trustees are so common with multigenerational planning, you should give consideration to the restrictions of working with an institutional co-trustee. Many institutional trustees either will not want to accept certain types of assets that they view as too risky or will insist on a rather comprehensive investigation (due diligence) process before accepting those assets into the trust. This can create both costs and time delays. You should also consider the ability of the institutional co-trustee to reasonably help you manage such assets.

Real Estate and Tangible Property Could Lose Planned Benefits

As previously noted, you may not want to transfer real estate or tangible personal property to a multigenerational trust if the trust is organized under the laws of a different state. Owning real estate or tangible personal property (e.g., art) that is located in a different state could be problematic. The trust may not legally be able to accept title, or if it does, the state law of the state where the property is physically located may apply. One possible approach is to have the assets transferred to a family limited partnership (FLP) or limited liability company (LLC) or other entity and then transfer the ownership interests in that entity to your Multigenerational Living Trust. Be sure to review the issues involved with your estate planner and any institutional co-trustee.

MAINTAINING PERPETUITIES BENEFITS

Changes in the financial, marital, or other circumstances of your intended heirs can suggest the need to review and revise documents to the extent feasible. Changes in the health or personal circumstances of your intended heirs can necessitate changes in planning documents, investment philosophy, insurance coverage, and other matters. If you don't assume an active role, your plan is likely, given enough time, to fail to meet your objectives. This is the same warning discussed in the context of the Family Tax Planning Living Trust. With multigenerational planning, however, the situation is even more complex. You must address changes in circumstances for yourself and all heirs, and attempt to foresee how the changes will play out over a long time horizon. Even more difficult, you must enlist the involvement of your heirs since their input is often vital in such multigenerational planning. Finally, in addition to trustees, you may have investment advisers, trust protectors, and others to deal with.

YOUR MULTIGENERATIONAL LIVING TRUST FOLLOWING DEATH

Following death, your successor trustees will obtain control over assets in your trust (assets outside your trust, unless they have designated beneficiaries, will require action by the executor appointed under our Safe-Keeper Will), pay expenses, and distribute assets to fund the trusts provided in your Multigenerational Living Trust.

As discussed in Chapter 10, your successor trustee will most likely be responsible to file a federal estate tax return for your estate if your estate is sufficiently large. The same principles will apply if you have a Multigenerational Living Trust, only the complications will be greater. The GST exemption will almost assuredly have to be allocated to certain trusts on your estate tax return, and this should be done in a manner that best leverages and preserves GST benefits for the appropriate trusts. Depending on the amount of assets transferred to a trust, the trustees may have to divide trusts into two components so that one component will be completely protected by the amount of the GST exemption allocated to it. This decision process involves assuring that the inclusion ratio for the GST-exempt trusts is zero. This is a complex topic that your trustees should review with the estate planners they hire.

As discussed, the decisions as to which assets to transfer to which trusts are complex and are designed to direct growth to the trusts likely to avoid tax for the most years and preferably for the most generations.

Trust protectors, investment advisers, and distribution committees all have to be informed of the trust's formation, assets, tax consequences, and so forth.

SUMMARY

This chapter has provided an overview of some of the unique issues that arise in the context of operating a multigenerational trust. These are complex and require addressing many difficulties in addition to the ones discussed in Chapter 10.

Part Five

THE COMPREHENSIVE
LIVING TRUST PROGRAM

15 WHAT IS THE COMPREHENSIVE LIVING TRUST PROGRAM?

IMPORTANCE OF COMPREHENSIVE LIVING TRUST

The comprehensive component of your living trust is the final stage or level of living trust planning. If you have business or real estate assets, are a professional, or are otherwise concerned about liability exposure, the comprehensive techniques discussed in Part Five are essential for your protection. If your estate is significantly larger than the applicable exclusion amount, more sophisticated tax planning may be necessary. Since each level or phase of living trust in the "Complete Living Trusts Program" builds on the prior phases, it is assumed that if life insurance and a life insurance trust, or annual gifts and possibly trusts for children, were warranted, these steps will have already been taken. It is also assumed that a bypass and marital (QTIP) trusts are included in your Family Tax Planning Living Trust. Each of these techniques can protect your assets and save estate taxes. Thus, at this phase of planning, you should be evaluating more complex tax planning techniques. These will almost always require the formation of entities and/or trusts independent from your living trust.

Whether or not your estate is substantial in size, if you face significant risks from malpractice, divorce, or other sources, or you have unusual personal or business problems, additional planning will be necessary. This will often take the form of creating additional entities, such as limited liability companies (LLCs) and family limited partnerships (FLPs), to hold certain assets. These entities can be used to limit liability, secure control, provide income and estate tax savings, and achieve other benefits.

The living trust books and seminars that have proliferated of late tend to give at most some sidenote to these techniques or ignore them completely. The Comprehensive Living Trust Program properly addresses all of your personal, tax, legal, and financial goals, and shows you how to integrate these planning measures with your overall living trust program.

CONCEPTS COMMON TO YOUR COMPREHENSIVE LIVING TRUST PLAN

Several principles are common to most of the more advanced planning necessary to implement your Comprehensive Living Trust Plan.

Principles of Asset Protection

To protect assets, planning focuses on separating risk into separate legal entities to prevent a domino effect. If you own a rental property, obviously you should have adequate liability insurance and an umbrella policy, and should minimize risk by removing hazards, being certain snow is shoveled promptly, and so forth. But you should do more. Ideally, each property should be owned in a separate entity. Typically today an LLC or FLP would be used, depending on the state law involved. Historically, many people used S corporations, but for real estate these were never, and are not, the ideal tool. If there is a lawsuit on a particular property that is not covered by insurance, the claimant should only reach the value of that property, not all of your other assets. For this planning to succeed, you must adhere to the formalities of the entity involved.

Once this level of planning is in place, you can take further steps to insulate your assets. This can include structuring the ownership of all your assets in a manner that makes it more difficult for creditors to reach them. This can involve a combination of techniques such as having all investment and other assets held in entities that make it difficult for a creditor to reach. You can transfer assets to special trusts that provide further disincentives to claimants.

A living trust alone will not provide any meaningful asset protection benefits. You can still use your living trust as a foundation of your overall plan, but it alone will not suffice. You will need to form and maintain additional entities. These entities can, if you wish, be the assets owned in your living trust. This comprehensive approach of forming additional entities to properly meet your goals, and integrating these entities into your living trust plan, is referred to as a "Comprehensive Living Trust." If your estate is sufficiently large to warrant more substantial tax planning strategies, the tax reduction techniques are generally consistent with the asset protection objectives you may also be considering. If your estate is not sufficiently large to justify more complex estate tax reduction techniques, don't overlook the importance of asset protection. Even nontaxable estates should take steps toward self-preservation.

Estate Tax Reduction

You should always evaluate and, if appropriate, implement the tax planning techniques noted earlier—bypass trust to secure your applicable exclusion and that of your spouse's (if applicable), annual gifts, and the removal of insurance from your estate—before undertaking more sophisticated planning. Once the benefits of those techniques are exhausted, then more sophisticated techniques must be employed. Some of these techniques rely on leveraging the applicable exclusion and annual gifts already discussed, to squeeze more benefits from them. Other techniques incorporate time value of money, charitable giving, and other techniques to maximize the value of assets you can transfer. But essential to all these tax reduction techniques is that you must be willing to part with assets. Each of these techniques is consistent with the asset protection goals you may also be pursuing.

SUMMARY

This chapter has provided an overview of the Comprehensive Living Trust Program and explained the basic concepts that are used to integrate asset protection and more substantial tax reduction into your living trust planning.

16 DRAFTING THE COMPREHENSIVE LIVING TRUST

GENERAL DRAFTING ISSUES AFFECTING THE COMPREHENSIVE LIVING TRUST

If you need to expand your Foundation Living Trust or Family Tax Planning Living Trust or Multigenerational Living Trust to address more substantial asset protection and/or tax savings, special modifications of your living trust document are essential. Dealing with these additional issues will assure the coordination of your overall plan and enable your trustee to deal with any complications and entities that may result. This chapter describes many of these special modifications. In all cases, you must have your estate planner handle these issues. You should note that none of the popular living trust forms or books include any of these planning concepts.

BUSINESS POWERS

If you own business interests and your stock, LLC membership interests, or limited partnership interests will be owned by your living trust, your trustee must have the authority to deal with these assets. Most living trusts have sufficient powers to address many of the most common business issues. Almost every trust has language stating that the trustee has the right to perform every act that state law permits a trustee to perform. However, it's best not to rely on these provisions alone. It is safer to craft specialized provisions that address as many likely business type issues that can arise in as specific detail as feasible. This is important to minimize the likelihood of your successor trustees having to obtain legal advice as to whether they have the authority to take certain actions. If the trust document is not precisely clear, third parties, such as banks or brokerage firms, may require a formal legal opinion that the trustee has the right to act in the transaction involved. This is both costly and time consuming. Worse, the result may be a finding that a particular matter is not permissible.

Listing detailed business powers is only the start. Every entity in which you own an interest should have a reasonably comprehensive agreement governing its operations. For a corporation, this agreement is called a *Shareholder Agreement*. For an LLC it is called an *Operating Agreement*. For a partnership, it is called a *Partnership Agreement*. Don't be penny-wise and pound-foolish and try to save fees by not having an agreement. The best living trust in the world will do little to avoid legal entanglements and other problems if your estate is composed primarily of interests in real estate and business ventures for which there are no agreements governing your relationship with your partners.

Finally, you should give careful consideration to the trustee and other fiduciaries you name in your living trust. Do the people you've named have sufficient ability to deal with your business interests? If not, consider naming pairs of successor trustees so that there will always be at least one trustee with the ability to handle business issues.

S CORPORATIONS

Most closely held business interests have historically been formed as S corporations to gain tax advantages and to limit the owners' liability. The "S" indicates that the corporation has elected to be taxed under subchapter S of the Internal Revenue Code. Briefly, this means that the shareholders will be personally taxed on income and gain, not the corporation. This avoids the double tax that can plague closely held corporations which have not qualified for such favorable tax benefits.

While S corporations have considerable benefits, few business endeavors are organized as S corporations now. Instead, family limited partnerships (FLPs) and limited liability companies (LLCs) have become the most common approaches. However, because of the tax cost of converting an existing S corporation into an FLP or LLC, most closely held businesses will remain organized as S corporations. Your living trust document must deal with the many complex special requirements these corporations have to comply with to preserve the income tax benefits. If the document doesn't, the favorable tax status for the entire corporation, not just the shares you own, can be lost.

Thus, your living trust agreement should include special language overriding other provisions of your trust when necessary to comply with S corporation requirements. One of the key aspects of this planning is that only special types of trusts generally can qualify to own stock in S corporations. Your living trust will qualify for owning S corporation stock while you are alive. However, the bypass trust included in most Family Tax Planning Living Trusts will not. Many child and grandchild trusts, including those typically included in a Multigenerational Living Trust, will not meet the S corporation requirements. Thus, additional provisions should be included to modify these trusts if they happen to own S corporation stock.

Many common trusts cannot own stock in an S corporation. If stock in an S corporation is transferred to a nonqualifying trust following the death of the grantor of the revocable living trust, the S corporation could lose its favorable tax status as an S corporation. This means it could be taxed as a C corporation with income subject to corporate taxes and then individual taxes—a double tax bite that an S corporation generally avoids. The typical bypass trust used in many estate plans (Chapter 8) can create serious problems if the decedent owned (outright or in a revocable living trust) shares in an S corporation. A trust to which S corporation stock is transferred pursuant to the terms of a will can only be an S corporation shareholder for two years (60 days under old law), or the S corporation status will be lost. This will not occur if the beneficiary trust meets certain requirements (which many do not).

Qualified Subchapter S Trusts

The most commonly used trust that can qualify to hold S corporation stock is the Qualified Subchapter S Trust (QSST). A newer type of qualifying trust, which is less frequently used, is called the *electing small business trust*.

For a trust to qualify as a QSST to own S corporation stock, it must meet strict requirements. If any of these requirements are not met, then the trust will generally cease being a QSST on the date any requirement is no longer met.

Many of the trusts that are created to qualify for the marital deduction for federal gift and estate tax purposes can also meet the requirements of a QSST. For example, the Qualified Terminable Interest Property (QTIP) trust discussed in Chapter 9 can be a QSST.

Many of the typical trusts established for the benefit of minors will not qualify for QSST treatment without modification. Thus if the grantor of a revocable living trust includes trusts for minors in his or her revocable living trust to hold assets following death, these trusts will have to be properly planned for. This is because many of these trusts give the trustee the authority to accumulate income rather than pay it currently to the minor. The provisions of many minors' trusts can be drafted to meet the QSST requirements. However, this must be done when the revocable living trust is first drafted.

QSST Requirements

Election

The income beneficiary (such as your child) must elect to be taxed as the owner of the S corporation stock for income tax purposes. This is because the income beneficiary will be taxed on his or her share of the income from the S corporation. The election must be made within 2½ months of the trust becoming a shareholder, or within 2½ months of the beginning of the first tax year of the S corporation. Where this election is not properly made, the IRS may determine that the S corporation's election is not valid. The IRS has, in some situations, reinstated the S corporation's election where it deemed the failure to comply to be inadvertent.

Tax Reporting

The concept of an S corporation is that all income and tax consequences generally flow through to the individual shareholder. A trust is permitted to be a shareholder where this result is not fundamentally changed. Thus the single beneficiary of the QSST trust will be treated as if he owns the portion of the trust that consists of stock in the S corporation. The effect of the election is to treat the beneficiary as the deemed owner of the S corporation stock. This means that the S corporation's income allocable to the shares of stock owned by the QSST flow directly to the beneficiary as if he were the shareholder. The trustee can simply attach a copy of the tax form 1120-S, Schedule K-1, it receives from the S corporation to the tax form that the trustee issues to the beneficiary reporting his income—Form 1041, Schedule K-1.

Required Income Distributions

During the life of the current income beneficiary, the trust's income must be required by the terms of the trust agreement to be distributed to one beneficiary. This beneficiary must be a person who is qualified to be a shareholder of an S corporation (a nonresident alien cannot qualify). This means the trustee cannot have the power to sprinkle trust income to different beneficiaries. Where a trust holds assets other than stock in an S corporation, this requirement need only be applied to the income generated by the S corporation stock owned by the trust.

To determine the income that must be distributed, the fiduciary accounting income as calculated under the provisions of the trust agreement is used. If the trust agreement contradicts state law, then the terms of the trust agreement may be overlooked in making the calculation. Where an S corporation doesn't distribute all its income, the trust will not be required to distribute income that it did not receive. This distribution requirement will not necessarily destroy the trust's status as a QSST where the trust requires that all income be distributed, but the trustee simply fails to do so. Where the trust agreement does not require that all income be distributed, it is sufficient that local law requires it.

Beneficiaries

There can only be one beneficiary. Any distributions of trust assets (corpus) during the life of the current income beneficiary can only be made to that one beneficiary. This requirement, however, does not imply that any amount of the trust's assets must actually be distributed. Where distributions of trust assets do occur, they can be made in the discretion of the trustee, so long as they are only distributed to the income beneficiary. For example, if you set up a trust for the benefit of your spouse, you could give the trustee the right, in the trustee's sole discretion, to distribute trust assets where necessary to maintain the health of your spouse. A trust will meet this requirement even if the trust agreement requires that all trust assets be distributed when a certain event occurs (e.g., the child benefi-ciary reaches age 35).

End of Required Distributions

The current income beneficiary's income interest in the trust must end at the earlier of his or her death, or the termination of the trust. The trust can, however, end at an earlier date (e.g., when your child who is the ben-eficiary reaches age 30).

Distribution on Termination of QSST

If the trust ends during the current income beneficiary's life, the trust as-sets must all be distributed to the current income beneficiary.

ESBT—Electing Small Business Trusts

Electing small business trusts (ESBTs) are another option meeting S corporation requirements and provide an alternative to the QSST dis-cussed above. An ESBT can be shareholders of S corporations after 1996. For a trust to qualify, all of the ESBT's beneficiaries must be individuals or estates (i.e., partnerships, corporations, etc. cannot be beneficiaries). Certain charities can be contingent remaindermen (i.e., the beneficiaries who receive trust income or assets if all prior beneficiaries die or cease to qualify as beneficiaries). ESBTs can provide greater flexibility than QSSTs in that they can have many current income beneficiaries. This means several different people can receive income each year from the trust. QSSTs require a separate trust for each beneficiary. However, an ESBT must pay tax at the maximum rate on all income.

ENVIRONMENTAL ISSUES

Environmental issues are a major concern for anyone investing in real es-tate. Your trustee should be given broad authority to refuse to accept any real estate contributed, given, or bequeathed to your trust or any of the trusts formed under your living trust (e.g., a bypass trust, child's trust, etc.). The trustee should also be given authority to authorize and pay for from trust assets any type of environmental or related testing that the trustee deems advisable. The worst result would be for the trustee to accept property with an environmental problem that then subjects all of your as-sets to lawsuits or claims.

SPENDTHRIFT PROVISION

A spendthrift provision is a clause in a trust that prohibits the benefi-ciary from assigning trust assets, and taking certain other steps. If you are concerned about liability issues, your living trust won't provide much protection for you. After all, you will almost always have the unfettered right to revoke or modify the trust, so a restriction applicable to you can't mean much (it is also inconsistent with your right to revoke). However, if you have a spouse or partner who will leave you assets, those assets should be left to you in trust (e.g., bypass trust, marital trust, etc.) with a spendthrift provision. If you are concerned about protecting assets you leave to children or other heirs, you probably want those trusts (all formed under your living trust) to include spendthrift provisions.

COMPREHENSIVE POWERS TO DEAL WITH UNIQUE ASSETS

If you have unusual assets, such as art or antiques, review with your estate planner steps to specifically address these assets in your living trust document. You may want to give specific authority to the trustees. You probably should always provide detailed suggestions on how to deal with these types of assets in your nonbinding letter of instruction.

SELECTION OF SKILLED TRUSTEES

When you engage in planning that involves a Comprehensive Living Trust program, carefully review the qualifications, skills, time availability, and other attributes of your trustees to be certain that they can cope. Consider these issues in helping your estate planner plan the provisions of your trust concerning a trust protector, distribution committee, and the like.

SUMMARY

This chapter has provided an overview of a few of the important modifications you should make to your living trust document to engage in the asset protection planning and more complex tax planning that a Comprehensive Living Trust Program entails. You must coordinate your living trust document with this incremental planning, or your plan simply won't work.

17 INTEGRATING ADDITIONAL SOPHISTICATED TAX PLANNING AND ASSET PROTECTION TECHNIQUES INTO YOUR COMPREHENSIVE LIVING TRUST PROGRAM

WHY SOPHISTICATED TAX PLANNING TECHNIQUES AND ASSET PROTECTION TECHNIQUES ARE DISCUSSED IN THE SAME CHAPTER

Many people whose needs, goals, or objectives cause them to consider the Complete Living Trusts Program may find that additional entities and tax planning techniques are necessary. This chapter highlights some and addresses their application to planning for a living trust.

DOMESTIC ASSET PROTECTION TRUSTS

Why Is There a Need?

Many Americans are extremely concerned over the potentially devastating effects of a lawsuit. These worries are not confined to doctors worried about malpractice suits. All professionals, investors, business owners, and almost anyone with any significant net worth has this fear. To use this technique, you set up a special trust in Alaska or Delaware (with perhaps some additional states to follow). These states have passed special laws permitting you to set up an irrevocable trust to protect your assets while you still remain a potential beneficiary of the trust. If you can receive benefit from trust assets under the laws of most states, your creditors would have the right to reach the trust assets to the same extent that you could. Thus, if in theory you could receive all trust assets, your creditors could as well.

How to Implement an Asset Protection Trust

To implement this type of planning, an irrevocable trust is formed, often with dynasty planning to continue in perpetuity and with consideration of allocating a portion of your GST exemption (as discussed in Chapter 12) to the trust. A gift can be made from your revocable living trust to this dynasty trust. A gift tax return will almost always have to be filed on forming such a trust.

Characteristics of Asset Protection Trusts Generally

Asset protection trusts have several common characteristics to enable them to provide asset protection benefits.

Spendthrift Trust

A spendthrift trust is a trust the assets of which a beneficiary cannot appoint prior to those assets being distributed to the beneficiary. Spendthrift protection is sometimes afforded by operation of law. In many jurisdictions, a spendthrift clause must be added to the trust agreement in order to have spendthrift protection. Spendthrift trusts are generally resistant to the claims of your creditors. However, you could not have engaged in a fraudulent conveyance when forming or funding the trust. For example, if you know you have a claim outstanding, you can't quickly transfer assets to such a trust before the lawsuit is concluded and hope to protect them. This planning must be done in advance, before the claim arises. The trust should also be immune from attacks by the creditors of the beneficiaries. Exceptions, however, are provided for the IRS, the provision of necessities, and so forth.

Fraudulent Conveyance

Conveyances made prior to your bankruptcy can be set aside. These include conveyances where your objective was to delay, defraud, or otherwise hinder creditors. If you received less than adequate consideration (e.g., a gift transfer) the transfer could be set aside. Finally, if you were insolvent or were made insolvent at the time of the transfer (i.e., assets less than liabilities), the bankruptcy code or state law may require that such transfers be made available to creditors.

In most jurisdictions, assets transferred to a trust in a transfer intended to defraud your creditors are deemed to be a fraudulent conveyance and are not protected.

Independent Trustee

The trustee of an asset protection trust should not also be a beneficiary of the trust. Often an institution will be used.

Nexus and Contacts with Host Jurisdiction

There must be some minimal level of contacts with the host jurisdiction, especially if you reside in another jurisdiction, to give credibility to the argument that the trust has sufficient contacts with the jurisdiction offering the favorable asset protection statute. The scope of contacts can vary from jurisdiction to jurisdiction, but the general rule must be that the greater the contact with the host jurisdiction the more likely the trust to withstand a challenge that jurisdictions laws do not apply. Contacts can include a trustee in that particular jurisdiction, assets in that jurisdiction, or performance of certain key trust functions in that jurisdiction.

Are You a Likely Candidate for an Asset Protection Trust?

Who are the prime persons for this type of planning? Generally, an elderly widow or widower with a $3 million to $10 million estate, who is uncomfortable making large gifts, but can benefit substantially from significant planning. This type of taxpayer could, for example, gift the applicable exclusion amount of $650,000 (1999) to the Delaware trust and remain a discretionary beneficiary. If the investments are successful, these funds will compound outside your estate. If your worst fears are realized, and medical and other living costs deplete your remaining estate, you'll have the trust to fall back on.

CHARITABLE LEAD TRUSTS

Overview of Charitable Lead Trusts

A charitable lead trust (CLT) is a sophisticated estate tax planning technique to use when the tax planning techniques of the Family Tax Planning Living Trust (including the insurance trust and minor trust) aren't enough to reduce your estate taxes to the level you want. The CLT is also a tremendous tool to use to pass on the values of philanthropy to your heirs. The reduction in tax cost is achieved because your heirs must wait a number of years (you pick the number, the longer the bigger the tax break) to receive the assets. While they are waiting, an annual payment is made to the designated charity.

EXAMPLE: You give $250,000 to a charitable lead trust. A designated charity will receive annual payments (often an annuity payment) for each year of the trust. Following the end of the trust, which will occur after the number of years you determined when setting it up (usually 20+ years), your heirs will receive the trust assets. The value of the trust assets is likely to be much greater than the $250,000 contributed because of the growth in the assets at a rate greater than the annual payments made to the charity. The benefits of this technique are that the value of the gift you are making to your children, for purposes of calculating the gift tax due on the transfer, is reduced by the value of the income interest paid for the specified term of years to the charity. For a 25-year 7 percent trust, the value of the gift would almost be negligible for tax purposes.

You can form a CLT while you are alive (inter vivos). This was illustrated in the previous example. A key purpose for an inter vivos CLT is to reduce the gift tax on the gift to children or other remainder beneficiaries. Where a CLT is to be formed during your lifetime, you should be certain that neither you, nor your family or dependents, will need that income during the term of the trust. A CLT can also be a testamentary trust formed under your will. A CLT under your will can provide an excellent tool to reduce estate taxes, with no effect on your access to the money while you are alive.

CLT Taxation

Most people assume that the CLT is a tax-exempt charitable trust, since it benefits one or more charities. However, a CLT is a taxable entity, and can, depending on the outcome of property and other transactions, be liable for an income tax. A CLT only avoids taxation where the amounts paid to charity, and hence deductible by the CLT, are sufficient to offset any income tax otherwise due by the CLT. When planning the investments for your CLT, one of the goals is to time income realization (e.g., capital gains) so that they don't significantly exceed the amount given in that year to the charity. This minimizes or avoids any current income tax. This is also why it is generally not advisable to gift only highly appreciated stock to a CLT. If your CLT is organized as a grantor trust as a result of your having kept certain rights and controls over the trust, the income will be taxed to you. This more sophisticated variation is, however, beyond the scope of this book.

Gifts to CLTs do not qualify for the gift tax annual exclusion. Thus, except to the extent that the gift tax charitable contribution deduction can offset the value of the property transferred, you must pay the current gift tax or use your $650,000 (1999) applicable exclusion. Similarly, if you form the CLT under your will, an estate tax might be due. The key point in both cases is that the CLT technique will dramatically reduce the taxable amount.

CLTs and Your Multigenerational Living Trust Plan

A basic principle of using trusts to plan for the generation-skipping transfer (GST) is to plan a trust so that it has an inclusion ratio of zero. This means that none of the trust assets will be subject to the GST. This rule gets tricky to apply when planning for CLTs. Should the calculation be made when the trust is formed or when the noncharitable beneficiaries receive their interests? This is critical because the gift tax value of the trust when formed is always quite small because it is reduced by the value of the charity's interest. When the noncharitable beneficiaries receive the trust assets at the end of the CLT, there is no reduction since no charity will have any interest in the assets any longer and the assets will have, if all goes as intended, grown substantially.

The tax laws contain a special rule applicable to the charitable lead annuity trusts (CLATs) GST tax inclusion ratio so that the determination cannot be made until such time as the charitable interest ends. With a CLAT, the fixed annual payment is determined when the trust is formed, say 7 percent of the $250,000 principal. If a 25-year CLAT is used, the determination will be made at the end of year 25. Thus, if grandchildren or further descendants are to be the beneficiaries of a CLT then the unitrust version, a charitable lead unitrust (CLUT), must be used since the allocation of the GST amount can occur on funding of the trust. Since with a CLUT, the percentage paid to the charity is based on the value of assets each year (e.g., 7 percent of the value of the assets as determined each year, not just when formed), the charity ends up sharing in any appreciation, so your heirs get less. Therefore, you pay a price to use a CLT in multigenerational planning.

CHARITABLE REMAINDER TRUSTS

Tax Benefits of a CRT

A charitable remainder trust (CRT) is a commonly used advance estate tax reduction technique. If you use a CRT, you would donate property (e.g., real property, stock, business interests) to a charity and receive a charitable contribution tax deduction in the year of the donation. The charity will receive the property at some future time after the CRT ends. During that time, the CRT makes periodic payments to you. You select the number of years (or your life or even your life and say the life of your spouse) for which the CRT will exist and make payments to you. The longer the number of years, the more money you get back, but the lower your current income tax charitable contribution deduction. In addition to the income tax deduction, none of the value of the CRT assets will be taxed in your estate. This is because the assets will be distributed to charity. But, there is a significant price to pay for these benefits: your heirs don't inherit any of the assets. So why consider a CRT? Because the income and estate tax savings are often so substantial that you can purchase life insurance to make up what the heirs have lost and everyone wins. For people who don't have children or other heirs for whom they feel tremendously responsible, the CRT is an even more powerful tool. For many people, the idea of turning a nonincome-producing asset into a monthly or quarterly check is very appealing.

Types of Charitable Remainder Trusts

Where the gift of a remainder interest is made in trust, it must be in the form of an annuity trust or unitrust payment. A charitable remainder annuity trust (CRAT) will provide a fixed annuity to yourself, or the people you designate in the trust agreement, as the income beneficiaries. The minimum rate of return to them cannot be less than 5 percent and it must be a fixed or determinable amount. The beneficiaries' income is calculated based on the fair market value of the property transferred to the trust. Once the trust is established, no further contributions can be made to it. Where the trust income is insufficient to meet the required annual return, principal must be invaded. A charitable remainder unitrust ("CRUT") provides a form of variable annuity benefit to its income beneficiaries. The minimum rate of return to the income beneficiaries must be 5 percent. This rate of return is calculated on the fair market value of the property determined on an annual basis. This requires an annual appraisal, which for any property that is difficult to value (e.g., closely held business interests and real estate), could be prohibitively expensive. For this reason, an annuity trust approach is likely to prove more appropriate when such assets are to be contributed. The trust may provide that if the annual income earned by the trust property is insufficient to meet the required distribution to the income beneficiaries, principal may be invaded. If principal is not required to be invaded, than the trust must provide that the deficit will be made up in later years. Once a unitrust is established, additional contributions may be made in later years under certain conditions.

Tax Consequences of a CRT

If you set up a CRT, you will receive a deduction for income and estate or gift tax purposes. The deduction is based on the present value of the charitable remainder interest. *Present value* means that the value of your deduction is reduced through a mathematical calculation to recognize the time value of money—the time until the charity will receive the assets. This contribution deduction is calculated using IRS tables and some rather complex formulas. These methods consider the value of the property transferred, the ages of the income beneficiaries (e.g., you and your spouse), and the payout rate. The actual value of the tax deduction will depend on numerous factors including your marginal tax bracket, the income interest you will receive, and other factors.

In addition to the current income tax deduction, you may also receive a valuable estate tax benefit. If you are one of the income beneficiaries of the charitable trust, the value of the trust will be included in your gross estate when you die. Since the interest will pass to the charity however, there will be an offsetting estate tax charitable contribution deduction. Thus, the value of the property donated will be effectively removed from your estate.

If you die before your spouse, the value of the CRT will be included in your gross estate because you will have owned an income interest for your life from the CRT. However, since the interest will pass to your spouse, there will be an offsetting estate tax marital deduction. On the death of your surviving spouse, the value of the charitable remainder trust will be included in her gross estate. However, since the interest will pass to a qualified charity, there will be an offsetting estate tax charitable contribution deduction.

GRANTOR RETAINED ANNUITY TRUSTS AND UNITRUSTS

Grantor retained annuity trusts (GRATs) and grantor retained unitrusts (GRUTs) are trusts designed and intended to leverage gifts made during your lifetime to magnify the estate tax reduction. Closely held business interests, real estate, or other assets likely to appreciate in value faster than the interest rates the IRS requires you use to calculate the tax benefit are typically transferred to a GRAT or GRUT.

EXAMPLE: You give property to a GRAT for the benefit of your heirs. You receive an annuity payable to you annually for 10 years at 12 percent. The longer the number of years and the higher the rate of annuity paid back to you, the lower the gift tax value of the assets given to your heirs through the trust. At the end of the specified number of years, the GRAT ends and your heirs receive the property with no further gift or estate tax. If the asset given to the GRAT was interests in a closely held business that appreciated at 22 percent per year, you would have removed a substantial value and appreciation from your estate.

Qualification as a GRAT or GRUT is only required for transfers to certain family members. For example, they do not apply if you're an uncle and you give property to a trust and retain an interest, with the property thereafter passing to your niece. The requirements apply to transfers to children or other lineal descendants, such as grandchildren only. They do not apply to a nonmarital partner; thus this can present a tremendous planning opportunity for nonmarried partners to make up for the inherent unfairness in most of the gift and estate tax system.

If the income of the GRAT were not sufficient to meet the required payout to the donor, GRAT assets would be distributed in kind. So if you gave stock in a family business to the GRAT, some shares of stock could be distributed back to you.

Two Types: GRATs and GRUTs

GRATs and GRUTs are the two types of these trusts that you can use. The key difference, as with the CLUT and CLAT described previously, is in how the periodic payments are calculated. Your GRAT is required to pay an annuity amount equal to a specified percentage, 7 percent as an example, of the value of the GRAT's assets determined as of the date of the trust agreement. This payment must be made in each taxable year of the trust's term, which can be any period (e.g., 3 years). This payment amount is required to be made at least annually, regardless of the amount of income actually earned by the trust, to you as the donor for the term. A grantor retained unitrust, or GRUT, in contrast, has the payment percentage, say 7 percent, applied to the value of the assets in the trust each year. Thus, a larger percentage of the appreciation of the trust assets will be paid back to you. As with the CLT discussed earlier, there are important consequences to your multigenerational planning depending which type of trust you use, GRAT or GRUT.

The following pointers will help you discuss with your tax adviser which of the two trusts, GRAT or GRUT, will be preferable in your particular situation. You must select one approach exclusively for any trust. The different approaches cannot be combined in a single trust:

- If the assets in the trust are readily valued, such as marketable securities, a GRUT is relatively simple to use. However, because a GRUT (unlike a GRAT) requires annual valuation of trust assets, if the assets are difficult to value (e.g., a closely held business interest), then a GRUT could be quite burdensome to use.

- If the interest rate for the periodic payment is set at a rate greater than the applicable federal rate that the tax laws require you use in determining the value of the gift, a GRAT will result in a lower gift value. This is because the calculations under a GRAT assume that each year a piece of the GRAT principal will have to be distributed back to you to meet the payment. In contrast, a GRUT will result in a greater current gift tax cost because when a GRUT is used, the annual percentage is applied to each year's principal balance of the trust. If the trust principal is reduced by payments back to you as grantor in excess of the assumed earnings, each year's payments to you will decline. Hence, less principal will be repaid in a GRUT.

- If the periodic payment is set at a rate less than the applicable federal rate required by the tax laws to be used in determining the value of the gift, then the GRUT will result in a lower current gift tax cost by applying the same analysis as in the previous paragraph.

Tax Consequences of a GRAT and GRUT

A GRAT/GRUT must have its own tax identification number, but it doesn't file an income tax return since the GRAT/GRUT income is reported on your personal income tax return. A gift tax return will also be required. The gift you make to your heirs through a GRAT/GRUT cannot be protected by the $10,000 (indexed) gift tax annual exclusion. However, you may avoid any current gift tax by the use of your applicable exclusion amount ($650,000 in 1999). For example, if the gift tax value of the assets you transferred to your GRAT/GRUT were $300,000, you would simply reduce on your gift tax return the $650,000 applicable exclusion amount to $350,000.

If you survive the term for the GRAT/GRUT, the GRAT/GRUT property should pass to your heirs without further gift or estate tax consequences. However, if you do not survive the fixed term of the GRAT, a portion (or according to the IRS all) of the GRAT/GRUT property will be included in your estate for estate tax purposes.

GRATS/GRUTS AND YOUR MULTIGENERATIONAL LIVING TRUST PLAN

To avoid the generation-skipping transfer tax, you have to allocate your $1 million (as indexed) GST exemption to protect all trust assets. When you use a GRAT, you cannot allocate exemption until the end of the GRAT. This is extremely unfavorable to you because by then the value of the assets probably will have increased substantially. You have to wait because of a technical tax trap known as the "estate tax inclusion period," or more lovingly, "ETIP." Your accountant can explain this to you (maybe!). Therefore, if you are planning to use this type of trust in your multigenerational planning, you would use a GRUT since with a GRUT you can allocate the GST exemption to the trust when it is formed. Since with a GRUT the percentage paid to you is based on the value of assets each year, more of the assets wind up being paid back to your estate where they would be subject to the estate tax. Your estate ends up with a considerable portion of the appreciation in trust assets and your heirs get less. Thus, you pay a price to use a GRUT in multigenerational planning.

SALES TO DEFECTIVE GRANTOR TRUSTS (INTENTIONALLY DEFECTIVE TRUSTS)

Background on Intentionally Defective Trusts

The sale to an intentionally defective irrevocable trust (intentionally defective trust) is a complex, unproven, and aggressive estate tax planning technique that could potentially save your heirs huge amounts of estate tax. This technique involves a sale of assets to a trust that you form. The trust is prepared so that all income will be taxed to you for income tax purposes (the trust is a defective trust structured to be characterized as a grantor trust for income tax purposes). Despite this perhaps unusual income tax result, the trust is prepared so that the assets you give to the trust will in fact be removed from your estate (i.e., the gifts qualify as a completed gift for gift and estate tax purposes).

All items of income, gain, expense and deduction flow through to the grantor's personal return and are reported on his or her personal Form 1040. Since the trust is not recognized as a separate tax-paying entity for income tax purposes, when you sell assets to the trust, it is as if it was a sale to yourself and no gain or loss is recognized for income tax purposes.

Since the trust, while having some assets, won't have enough money to pay you for the assets, you take back a note. The trust is obligated to pay you the money over time, just as an installment sale or home mortgage obligates you to pay the bank. This must be an interest-bearing note, with interest payments at the prevailing interest rates. It will probably have a balloon payment due at the end.

If this transaction is properly structured, the note the trust owes you should be equal to the value of the asset you sold to the trust, and therefore there is no gift. The technique raises several gift, estate, generation-skipping, and income tax ramifications that you must review with an estate planning specialist.

Tax Consequences and Issues if You Use a Sale to a Defective Grantor Trust

The sale to the grantor trust must be done to avoid having the trust assets pulled back into your estate. The trust, however, is to be structured as a grantor trust for income purposes. Therefore, no gain or loss is recognized in any transaction between grantor and the trust, and the sale of the asset to the trust does not affect the basis of the assets transferred. So if the asset is sold, you would have the same income tax consequence as if the entire transaction had not occurred. If you should die during the term of the note, the note is included in your estate; however, the underlying asset is not included. Although your estate will pay the estate tax on the full value of the note, the underlying asset will not receive a step-up in basis. Therefore, unless the property had a significant total net return, the results of the sale are not as good as if the transaction had never occurred.

FAMILY LIMITED PARTNERSHIPS AND LIMITED LIABILITY COMPANIES

Choosing the Appropriate Entity

One of the hottest and most talked about estate planning techniques is the family limited partnership (FLP). Limited liability companies (LLCs), a popular new form for organizing business and investment activities, offer the same benefits as FLPs, as well as additional advantages.

How do you choose which entity is better, LLC or FLP? Consult with an estate and business lawyer in your state. The choice will generally be based on technical differences between your state's LLC and FLP laws. The differences between states can be important so don't assume that a generic answer will work.

Benefits from Using FLPs and LLCs

FLPs and LLCs can help you achieve the following benefits.

Asset Protection

Owning assets in an FLP/LLC can help you protect your money from creditors and claimants. First, using FLPs and LLCs can help prevent a domino effect.

EXAMPLE: You own two rental properties. If you are sued on one property, the claimant can reach all of your assets, including the second rental property, which had no problem. If each rental property is transferred to a separate LLC or FLP, then a lawsuit against one property cannot reach the other unaffected property. One property's loss cannot create a domino effect knocking down the others.

Second, the assets in the FLP or LLC also have a measure of protection because a claimant that successfully sues you cannot generally receive access to the cash or assets owned by the entity. What a successful creditor receives is a charging order or assignee interest in the entity. This entitles the creditor to receive whatever cash distributions are made, and nothing else. This limited result provides protection to the assets.

Controlling Assets

If you give assets to your heirs, you have no control over them, other than moral persuasion. If instead, you put the same assets in an FLP or LLC and you're the general partner of the FLP, or the manager of the LLC, you have substantial control over the assets.

Estate Planning

The control feature previously noted is just one of many estate planning benefits an FLP or LLC can provide. You can transfer assets to an FLP and gift ownership interests to your heirs as limited partners. You could still control the entire FLP by serving as the general partner, or the LLC by being the manager. Your heirs would have some of the value of the partnership assets transferred to their names. This would remove the value of what you have given them, plus any appreciation on those assets, from your estate, even though you still control it. These gifts are often made at discounted value for even more benefit. The discount planning technique is discussed in the following section. Using an FLP or LLC can also make it easier to give assets. For example, if you own a real estate property, to make gifts an attorney would have to prepare a deed to each person each year you make a gift. This process is expensive and cumbersome. Instead, if you transfer the real estate property to an FLP or LLC, you would simply complete a one-page assignment of FLP or LLC ownership to each person you make a gift to. It's simple, cheaper, and easier.

DISCOUNTS

Valuations and Estate Planning

It is important to properly value interests in real estate partnerships (general or limited), LLCs, and other types of business entities (such as C corporations, S corporations, trusts, etc.), and assets that you use for gifts or own at your death. A significant issue in determining the value of an interest in a business entity is whether and to what extent a reduction to reflect the interest's lack of control and its lack of marketability is applicable. These reductions are referred to as "discounts."

Minority Discount

The concept of a minority discount is that the sum of the parts is worth less than the whole. An undivided minority interest is worth less than the allocable share of the entire value of the entity as a result of the restrictions and limitations that affect the minority interest. The minority interest discount is designed to reflect that a member, shareholder, or partner who owns less than a majority of the voting interest in the entity has no meaningful control over the day-to-day and long-range managerial and policy decisions of the business. This inability to control the entity depresses the value of the interest so that a buyer would pay less to acquire it. The discount also reflects the interest holder's inability to obtain his or her pro rata share of the entity's net assets by forcing a liquidation.

Depending on each case's specific facts and circumstances, combined discounts in the range of 25 percent to 50 or more percent are not uncommon. To strengthen the argument for a discount, the documents for the FLP or LLC (i.e., the partnership agreement or the operating agreement) should include certain restrictions on the abilities of members (or anyone who obtains an interest in the LLC) to transfer their interest or liquidate the entity.

If the interest being valued is a limited partnership interest that does not have the power to be involved in management decisions, a minority interest discount is applicable.

In determining the appropriate discount for a minority interest, crucial factors are the rights possessed by the owner of the LLC membership interest. Courts examine the following rights of factors: the interest holder:

- Ability to share in the LLC's profits and losses.
- Ability to manage and control the LLC's assets.
- Ability to compel the payment of distributions.

- Authority to be paid salaries.
- Power to admit new members.
- Ability to withdraw from the LLC.
- Authority to dissolve the LLC.
- Power to institute lawsuits to resolve conflicts among the members.

An FLP or LLC partner or member may be prohibited from participating in management if the Operating Agreement vests management in a few selected individuals, who may or may not be members. A limited partnership interest is prohibited by statute from participating in the management of partnership operations. Similarly, holders of a relatively small interest in a closely held corporation do not have the power to control management policy. Thus the value of a membership interest in an LLC, shares of a closely held corporation, or of a limited partnership interest is commonly discounted. The rationale for the discount is that the perceived investment risk is greater where the investor cannot control the company's course of conduct.

You can claim both discounts for lack of marketability and for minority interest discounts. While the minority interest discount focuses on a member's ability to affect the profitable distribution of his or her own membership interests, the marketability discount is designed to reflect that there is no ready market for membership interests in a closely held FLP or LLC. The marketability discount also reflects that investors prefer investments that have access to a liquid secondary market and that can be easily converted into cash.

QUALIFIED PERSONAL RESIDENCE TRUSTS

What Is a QPRT and How Does It Work?

A qualified personal residence trust (QPRT) provides a mechanism to remove the value of your home or vacation home from your estate at a substantially discounted rate. With a QPRT, you, as grantor, transfer your residence to a trust, retaining a term interest (the right to live in the house for a specified number of years) and naming family members as remainder beneficiaries. QPRTs, similar to GRATs, GRUTs, and other estate planning techniques discussed earlier take advantage of the time value of money to dramatically reduce federal estate and gift taxation.

You transfer your residence (a principal residence, other qualifying residence, or a vacation home) to a trust and reserve the sole and exclusive right to use the residence for a specified term of years. On the expiration of the term of years, the residence is then distributed to other family members, typically your children. The residence, however, can be retained in yet a further trust for those family members at such time (i.e., when the term of the QPRT ends). The key benefits of the QPRT technique thus include the ability to leverage the use of your applicable exclusion as a result of the time value of money discount feature of the QPRT calculation. The QPRT technique also removes future appreciation from your estate (i.e. an increase in the value of the house after transferring it to the QPRT).

Several requirements must be met for a QPRT to obtain the desired tax benefits. The only assets that the QPRT can hold are a residence (defined in the following paragraph) and home insurance policies (and payments under such policies) and a modest amount of cash for upkeep.

The property contributed to the QPRT must be a qualified residence: a principal residence, vacation home, or even a fractional interest in a principal residence. A key concept is that the residence must be available for your use as a residence. Interests in a cooperative apartment can also qualify. The IRS has permitted interests in a cooperative apartment to qualify even where the cooperative board of directors refused to give permission to the grantor to make the transfer. The definition of vacation home provides that if the personal use of the property exceeds the greater of 14 days or 10 percent of the days the property is rented, it is classified as a residence. Any particular QPRT can only hold a single residence, used by the grantor, for the entire term of the QPRT. If the qualifying residence held by the QPRT is sold, another qualifying replacement residence must be acquired within two years. If the qualifying residence held by the QPRT is damaged or destroyed, it must be repaired or replaced within two years.

During the term of the QPRT, the trust agreement must prohibit the trustees from making income or principal distributions to any person other than the grantor. The only exception is that on termination trust distributions can be made to the remainder beneficiaries instead of to the grantor. Income earned by the QPRT must be distributed to the grantor not less frequently than annually. This distribution must be made mandatory by the QPRT agreement.

SUMMARY

This chapter has highlighted additional asset protection and sophisticated tax planning techniques. When your estate is large, or your assets, profession, or reputation create considerable liability exposure, a combination of the techniques highlighted in this chapter may be appropriate. The techniques should be selected to conform with your objectives, best address your unique asset/liability mix, and coordinate with your other planning steps.

18 OPERATING YOUR COMPREHENSIVE LIVING TRUST PROGRAM

YOUR COMPREHENSIVE LIVING TRUST PROGRAM PRESENTS SPECIAL OPERATIONAL ISSUES

If your estate or personal circumstances warrant using a Comprehensive Living Trust Program, you must take additional steps to coordinate your estate, business, and other planning. Otherwise, you cannot achieve the benefits of this program.

ANCILLARY ENTITIES FORMED AS PART OF YOUR COMPREHENSIVE LIVING TRUST PROGRAM

Once you have decided on your Comprehensive Plan, you will have to arrange to form each of the trusts, FLPs, LLCs, or other entities, generally with the help of a lawyer. For trusts, this means having a lawyer prepare a trust contract. For business entities, it will mean having a lawyer prepare a form to file with the appropriate county or state government agency. Once the entities are legally formed, depending on the circumstances any or all of the following may have to be addressed:

- Obtain a tax identification number.
- Open a bank and/or brokerage account.
- Transfer assets to the entity. For a GRAT/GRUT, CLUT/CLAT and other trusts this might mean some combination of stock, cash, real estate, or other assets, even FLPs or LLCs that own some combination of stock, cash, real estate, or other assets. Sample documents for transferring some of these are presented at the end of this chapter (see Forms 18.1 and 18.2).
- Complete gifts to children or other heirs of some portion of the entities involved. This will often require that you have an appraisal done to determine the value of the property being given. If any of the discounts discussed earlier will apply, you should have the amount of the

Form 18.1 Sample Assignment of Partnership Interests

Smith Family Partnership Assignment of Partnership Interests

The undersigned hereby assigns by gift to John Smith, Jr. Trust, an irrevocable trust, with a mailing address c/o Jane Smith, Trustee, who resides at 123 Main Street, Anytown, USA, and whose trust's federal tax identification number is 00-0000000 (the "Assignee"), a limited partnership interest in Smith Family Holdings, FLP, a Somestate limited partnership (as such term is defined in an Agreement of Partnership of Smith Family Holdings, FLP dated 3/4/06), and whose federal tax identification number is 11-2345678.

The percentage interest hereby assigned is Two Percent (2.00%) of the total interests in the partnership. The estimated value of this interest is $9,876.00.

ASSIGNOR/DONOR:

_____   Date: 5/6/07

Ida Smith, Grantor

Accepted by ASSIGNEE/DONEE:
John Smith, Jr., Trustee

By: _____
           Jane Smith, Co-Trustee

State of Somestate   )

                              :ss.:

County of County Name   )

On May 6, 2007 before me personally came, Ida Smith, to me known and known to me, by presentation of a driver's license of Somestate, to be the individual described in and who executed the foregoing instrument, and such grantor duly acknowledged to me that such grantor understood the meaning of the instrument and that such grantor executed the same for the purposes expressed therein.

_____

Notary Public

discounts confirmed in a written appraisal report as well. You will then have to complete documents to transfer the interests and confirm that the gift was made. This could include a gift letter in which you describe the assets you are giving, to whom they are being given, the value of the assets given, and that the transfer is a gift (and not a sale or some other arrangement).

ONGOING STEPS TO MAINTAIN YOUR COMPREHENSIVE LIVING TRUST PROGRAM

Once you've set up your Living Trust and the ancillary entities and documentation that comprise your Comprehensive Living Trust Program, your work is not done. You must take steps periodically, usually at least once per year, to maintain each entity, preserve the tax, legal, and other

Form 18.2 Sample Assignment of LLC Membership Interest

Smith Family Management, LLC Assignment of LLC Membership Interests

The undersigned hereby assigns by gift to Jonny Smith, II Trust, an irrevocable trust, with a mailing address c/o Joseph Smith, trustee, who resides at 456 Main Street, Someplace, USA, and whose trust's federal tax identification number is 22-4567890 (the "Assignee"), a membership interest in Smith Family Management, LLC, a Someplace limited liability company (as such term is defined in an Operating Agreement of Smith Family Management, LLC, dated 2/3/03), and whose federal tax identification number is 33-22222222.

The percentage interest hereby assigned is Five Percent (5.00%) of the total interests in the limited liability company. The estimated value of this interest is $9,990.

ASSIGNOR/DONOR:

_____   Date: 4/3/03
Joanne Smith, Grantor

Accepted by ASSIGNEE/DONEE:
Jonny Smith, II Trust

By: _____
        Joseph Smith, Co-Trustee

State of Someplace   )

                              :ss.:

County of Big County   )

On April 3, 2003, before me personally came, Joanne Smith, to me known and known to me, by presentation of a driver's license of Someplace, to be the individual described in and who executed the foregoing instrument, and such grantor duly acknowledged to me that such grantor understood the meaning of the instrument and that such grantor executed the same for the purposes expressed therein.

_____
Notary Public

benefits you are seeking, and keep your planning current. The following are some of the many steps:

- Verify that casualty and liability insurance is current and in the correct name. If you had real estate appraised before making gifts to your children, be sure that the property is insured for at least that value. If your insurance coverage has not been reviewed in many years, the amounts might be too low. You also have to be very careful to assure that the insurance limits are correct. If a FLP now owns your property, the FLP must be listed as the owner on the insurance policy.

- Monitor all financial transactions to be certain that the formalities of each entity are observed. If you have different properties or businesses owned by different LLCs, FLP, and trusts, you must be sure that income is deposited to the correct entity, expenses paid from the correct entity, and so forth. If you don't observe the formalities and independence of each entity, don't be surprised if the IRS or creditors also succeed in ignoring the formalities. This could jeopardize all your potential benefits.

- Often gifts are made every year to take advantage of the annual gift tax exclusion ($10,000 in 1999, indexed for inflation). Each year you will then have to revalue the property and again complete documents similar to the gift documents described earlier that you completed when the entity was initially formed and you made the first gift.

- You should always periodically review the status of your planning with your accountant and attorney. This is especially important given the

Form 18.3 Sample Written Consent

Smith Family Corporation
Unanimous Written Consent
Consent of All Shareholders and Directors to Transfer Stock

The undersigned, being all of the directors and shareholders of the Corporation, hereby take the following action:

RESOLVED, The Corporation acknowledges receiving notice from a shareholder, Joanne Smith, in the form of a Stock Power, requesting that certain Shares owned by such Shareholder, be transferred to Joanne Smith Revocable Living Trust.

RESOLVED, The officers of the Corporation are hereby directed to cancel the following stock certificates received from the above Shareholder:

Shareholder Name	Class of Stock	Number of Shares	Cert. No.
Joanne Smith	Common	100	34

and to issue the following stock certificates to the Shareholders listed for the shares indicated:

Shareholder Name	Class of Stock	Number of Shares	Cert. No.
Joanne Smith Revocable Living Trust	Common	100	34

RESOLVED, The officers of the Corporation are hereby authorized to take any actions necessary to effecting the above Resolutions.

Dated: April 3, 2003

_____

Joanne Smith, Shareholder

_____

Sam Smith, Shareholder and Director

_____

Jane Smith, Shareholder and Director

increased complexity that the Comprehensive Living Trust Program involves as contrasted with the Foundation Living Trust and the Family Tax Planning Living Trust.

- File annual tax returns. Many entities and trusts will require an annual income tax return. Don't overlook these. You may also have to file quarterly estimates for the entity, even if you never filed quarterly estimates for yourself personally. Certain state filings also may be required in addition to tax returns.

- If you have real estate or business assets, there may be other formalities to address such as written lease agreements for property rented, management agreements if you or an entity you own is managing your other business for a fee, and so forth. Salary, interest on loans and other payments will have to be made. Be sure to review these before December 31 each year with your accountant to be sure everything is in order while payments and changes may still be possible for that year.

- For corporations, FLPs, and LLCs, you may want to have all shareholders, partners, or members sign minutes of an annual meeting or perhaps a unanimous written consent. These will acknowledge and agree to many of the actions taken during the year. This can be especially helpful to prevent people from fighting in future years over a claim that they were not apprised of things that were done. It can also be important to confirm who the officers and directors of a corporation or LLC are, and so forth (see Form 18.3).

SUMMARY

This chapter has discussed some of the many steps you must take to coordinate each component of your Comprehensive Living Trust Program and how to operate the Comprehensive Program, once it is in place.

Part Six

ADDITIONAL ISSUES

19 LIVING TRUSTS FOR SPECIAL CIRCUMSTANCES AND ASSETS

The key point of the Complete Living Trusts Program is that a standard single document or approach does not work for everyone. You are unique and have your own goals, your own financial picture, and your own issues. The Complete Living Trusts Program endeavors to use a building block approach to help you develop the living trust program that works for you. This chapter highlights a few of the special steps you might want to consider in adapting the Complete Living Trusts Program to best fit your personal needs.

The benefits of the revocable living trust plan are best achieved if the documents are tailored for the particular circumstances.

SENIOR CITIZENS

The best protection for someone advancing in years is to fund, with significant investment assets, if not all their assets that are appropriate to transfer, a revocable living trust naming the senior and a bank or trust company as initial co-trustees. If you have a spouse or partner, he or she can be the successor trustee to serve with the bank or trust company if you become disabled. Consolidate all investment assets with the institution. In the event of disability, the institution and successor co-trustees will be in the best position to assist you. This approach will help you safeguard assets and your estate from attorneys or other professionals who seek to take advantage of your difficulties. It will assure an independent and professional management through the institution, while keeping a personal touch through the co-trustee named. Actually moving assets into the trust now, rather than waiting for an emergency is always the safest approach. This also avoids having to rely on a family member to use a durable power of attorney to transfer assets later. Consolidating assets into one institution will probably save you fees, may help you get a better investment return since your investment strategies will be better coordinated, and so forth.

PEOPLE WITH LIMITED SAFETY NET OF RELIABLE OTHERS

Will your two nieces in Detroit, whom you see only at Christmas time, really spend money to assure you the best medical care? Perhaps they would rather spend the least on you and preserve the maximum inheritance for themselves. If you don't have a close, reliable and almost guaranteed trust-worthy safety net of people to name as trustees, name an institution as a co-trustee. Importantly, be very clear in your trust document what you want. While your sister might spend money in the way she knew you wanted, no bank or trust company will deviate from the terms of the trust document. Therefore, if you want money spent to assure that you receive the finest medical care, even if it results in your distant family members receiving less, say so.

GAYS AND LESBIANS

Gays and lesbians may face disapproval or worse from family members of a disabled or deceased partner. The family may have been cooperative while your partner was alive, but animosities or problems may come to the sur-face when he or she isn't. A living trust, by avoiding the filing of a public document like a will, and perhaps by expediting the distribution of assets, may minimize the aggravation your deceased partner's family can cause. In the event of your partner's disability, a living trust may make it easier for you to retain control and involvement. If your partner signed a living trust naming you as successor trustee, a durable power of attorney naming you as agent, and a living will/health care proxy naming you as agent, you should be able to avoid a guardianship proceeding whereby a court would appoint someone to manage your disabled partner's affairs. Avoiding this could pre-vent a battle with your partner's family over who should make decisions, you or them.

State laws that "fill in" where wills are inadequate or nonexistent do not provide for distributions to nonmarried partners in the manner that they do for a spouse. The result is that a revocable trust (and will) although somewhat different, is even more important for nonmarried couples. These laws, called laws of "intestacy," determine who inherits your prop-erty if you die without a will. Although different from state to state, on the death of one spouse, the surviving spouse will generally inherit a substan-tial portion of the estate, even without a will. If there is no spouse, then other relations will inherit. If a nonmarried partner dies, no consideration of the partnership is made by state statute. Therefore, it is essential that advance planning be done.

This planning includes a properly drafted will and/or living trust pro-viding for distributions to the surviving partner, tax planning, properly planned ownership (title) to assets, and trusts. If these steps are not taken, the property will pass on death to the deceased partner's family members, and not the surviving partner. This could have devastating financial con-sequences to the surviving partner. It can also create substantial personal conflicts where the family members succeeding to the property did not ap-prove of the relationship.

IF YOU WANT TO MINIMIZE PUBLICITY

If a significant concern of yours is avoiding publicity for your estate, a revocable living trust can be part of the answer. When using a revocable living trust where confidentiality is important, be certain that the trust is not funded with assets likely to create publicity (e.g., stock in a closely held business where other shareholders' consents to transfer may be required), require a recording of a trust memorandum, and so forth. Most importantly, review with your attorney the idea of not using the typical pour-over will if publicity is a concern. This is because if there are any probate assets (it happens frequently that an asset or two are accidentally not transferred to the trust), your will would be probated. If the will is probated and it has a pour-over provision, anyone reading it will be informed about your trust. If you have a will with no pour-over (and the Safe-Keeper Will can function fine without it), you will avoid this problem.

To achieve greater confidentiality, consider completing gifts while alive to avoid any information becoming public at death. Consider the use of irrevocable trusts funded during life.

AVOIDING ANCILLARY PROBATE

Vacation homes and other tangible assets located in a state other than where you reside will create the need for ancillary probate. Consider the use of a revocable living trust to avoid this. In such instances, funding the trust with the assets involved today will often be preferable, rather than waiting for future actions (e.g., an agent acting under your durable power of attorney) or a pour-over will.

REAL ESTATE ASSETS

Real estate, such as a rental property or vacation home, is a common investment for millions of people. As a result, most living trust books and programs speak about their transfer to revocable living trusts. This is not always the best solution. If the property is a rental property, consider potential liability issues from rental real estate. A revocable living trust will provide no protection. Instead, review the use of an FLP or LLC as discussed in the Comprehensive Living Trust Plan with your attorney. These entities can hold real estate and not only avoid ancillary probate, but minimize liability risk too.

S CORPORATION STOCK

S corporations, despite the popularity of limited liability companies (LLCs) remain, and will continue to remain for many decades, the most common ownership structure for closely held businesses. This requires careful consideration in drafting, planning, and implementing revocable living trusts. As discussed earlier, if an irrevocable trust may own S corporation stock, special provisions have to be included to meet the S corporation tax rules. (See Chapter 16.) If you set up a trust and retain certain reversionary rights, the trust income is taxable fully to you. An example is the revocable living trust. All trusts, however, will not qualify to hold S corporation stock so you must exercise caution. Since a revocable living trust can qualify as an S corporation stockholder, there may still be an issue. This is because on your death the revocable living trust becomes irrevocable, and in many situations the trust agreement provides for the distribution of assets of the trust in further trust. The nature of these further trusts can be important to analyze.

INSTALLMENT NOTES

An installment note is an asset that is created when an asset (real estate, business, etc.) is sold, with payments to be made to the seller over time. These payments are evidenced by a note agreement and may be secured by a mortgage evidencing a lien on real estate, a Uniform Commercial Code filing evidencing a lien on equipment, and so forth. If an installment note is sold or transferred all the previously unrecognized gain (deferred gain) can be triggered. This will not occur on the transfer of the installment note to a revocable living trust.

RETIREMENT ASSETS

Don't transfer any retirement assets to your living trust. You could trigger all of the deferred income tax. There is also no reason to transfer retirement assets while you are alive to your trust since the assets in your retirement plan can avoid probate by your simply completing the beneficiary designation forms at your bank or brokerage firm. However, the situation is not always so simple. For many people, some portion or all of their retirement plan assets may have to be used to fund the applicable exclusion or bypass trust formed under their Family Tax Planning Living Trust. If this is not done, the estate tax benefits of your applicable exclusion (or your spouse's) could be lost.

There are several ways to integrate planning for your pension assets and your Family Tax Planning Living Trust. You could name the bypass trust formed under your Family Tax Planning Living Trust to be the recipient of IRA and qualified plan assets. Another alternative is to name your spouse as the primary beneficiary of the IRA plan and to have your trust prepared to provide that if your spouse disclaims (renounces; files papers in court stating that she does not want the inheritance provided) the interests in your IRA or qualified plan assets, these funds would then be distributed into the marital deduction trust or into a credit shelter trust under your will. These trusts, which would be included under your trust, would be drafted to receive the IRA or qualified plan assets as a result of a disclaimer. They should meet the minimum distribution requirements.

LIFE INSURANCE

If insurance on your life is owned by your revocable living trust, it will be included in your taxable estate. Where the policies are small enough that even when combined with the estate no tax would be due, your living trust may own your spouse's life insurance. There is no tax benefit in the sense of avoiding the estate tax, but in the event of her death, the assets would be paid to your trust where they could be managed. In other instances, you may name your bypass trust formed under your Family Tax Planning Living Trust as the beneficiary of your insurance. On your death then, your life insurance would be used to help you fund your bypass trust. These assets would then be available for your surviving spouse's benefit (as well as the benefit of other heirs if you wished) but they would not be taxable in her estate.

Carefully consider using an irrevocable life insurance trust to remove the asset from both spouses' estates, before having a revocable living trust own, or be named beneficiary for, life insurance.

SUMMARY

This chapter has highlighted some of the issues that arise when dealing with particular assets and circumstances and your Complete Living Trusts Program. Be certain to make the extra effort to determine that your plan and documents address all your own unique personal issues.

20 ADDITIONAL TAX ISSUES

TAX ISSUES AND LIVING TRUSTS GENERALLY

Most people believe, correctly, that living trusts don't pay income tax. However, this one simple result is often extrapolated to an assumption that there are no tax issues. As the discussions of S corporation stock, applicable exclusion amounts, generation-skipping transfer tax, and other tax problems in preceding chapters should have made clear, you may have to address many sophisticated tax issues in the context of living trust planning. This chapter will alert you to a few more of them.

INCOME TAX REPORTING FOR YOUR LIVING TRUST

During your lifetime, your revocable living trust is characterized as a grantor trust for federal income tax purposes. Therefore, all trust income is reported on your personal tax return, Form 1040. There are several ways you can handle this for tax reporting to the IRS. You can file a "skeleton" Form 1041, U.S. Income Tax Return for Estates and Trusts, with a statement attached saying that your trust is a grantor trust and all income and deductions are reported on your personal income tax return (Form 1040), and give the IRS your Social Security number. Another option is for you to issue, as trustee of your trust, tax reporting Form 1099 to your own name and Social Security number. You would also complete Form W-9, Request for Taxpayer Identification Number and Certification. File these with the IRS reporting each type of income and each item of gross proceeds paid to your living trust during the tax year, showing the trust as payor and showing yourself (in your capacity as grantor/owner of the trust) as the payee.

TAX ALLOCATION CLAUSE

Any properly drafted living trust and will should include a carefully planned allocation of estate and related taxes. If the allocation is not handled properly, the distribution of assets could be different than desired and the tax costs could be exacerbated. This is essential because taxes can constitute more than 50 percent of an estate. Your will and the revocable living trust should each include a clause that clearly establishes which sources of funds, assets, bequests, or distributions should bear the tax. This allocation should be analyzed under different scenarios (e.g., the size of the estate increases or decreases; certain beneficiaries predecease) to be certain that the allocation initially considered remains appropriate.

A revocable living trust formed and funded by the decedent will be nonprobate property. The coordination of the provisions of the living trust and the will can be significant for determining how taxes will be allocated between the probate assets and the nonprobate assets held by the revocable living trust (and otherwise). The increasing use of revocable living trusts presents complications to the estate planner attempting to plan for tax allocation. The will is typically a pour-over will into the trust. Consideration must be given to what assets will be subject to which instrument. Would the IRS or a court read the will and living trust as a coordinated plan, or as separate instruments?

The tax allocation clause of the will often includes language directing the executor to seek reimbursement from the Trustee of the Revocable Living Trust if necessary.

SAMPLE LANGUAGE FOR POUR-OVER WILL: If the assets subject to this Will are insufficient to pay all taxes, then the Executor shall seek payment from the revocable living trust that I formed during my lifetime. The Executor is authorized and directed to give to the Trustee of such Trust a certification of the amount of estate tax and the shortfall requiring recovery from said Trust. The Executor is directed to request such certification, and cooperate with the Trustee of said Trust so that overall estate taxes and expenses for all assets are minimized in a manner that causes the least deviation from my intended dispositive scheme.

When such an approach is used, the typical arrangement is for the Revocable Living Trust to contain language as follows:

SAMPLE LANGUAGE FOR REVOCABLE LIVING TRUST: Upon the death of the Grantor, there may not be sufficient cash or other liquid assets in Grantor's Probate Estate to pay debts, costs of estate administration, bequests, and income and/or death taxes payable by Grantor's Estate. In any of such events, the Trustee shall, from the assets of the Trust, either pay to Grantor's personal representative such amounts as are necessary therefor, or discharge such obligations directly as it may in its sole discretion determine best. The Trustee shall not seek to recover any expenses or taxes from any Beneficiary provided sufficient funds are available in the Trust and/or the Grantor's Estate to discharge such obligations.

Proper planning for the allocation of estate and related taxes requires the consideration of many matters.

EXAMPLE 1: Several $5,000 specific bequests are made. To simplify administration of the estate, the tax allocation clause specifically exempts these modest distributions. Thus, these bequests can be made quickly and with substantially less calculations and concerns.

EXAMPLE 2: A specific bequest of $350,000 is made. The remaining estate is approximately $6 million and is distributed to the decedent's nephews. The specific bequest may or may not bear a proportionate share of tax costs, depending on the testator's/grantor's wishes.

EXAMPLE 3: A specific bequest of $350,000 is made. The remaining estate is approximately $490,000 and is distributed to the decedent's only child. The specific bequest may or may not bear a proportionate share of tax costs, depending on the testator's/grantor's wishes. However, considering the relative size of the estate it is quite likely that the specific bequest would bear at least a pro rata portion of the tax cost.

Most people do not want to burden nominal or token cash legacies with a tax burden. However, since the beneficiary of a cash legacy will have cash to pay the tax, no hardship is created.

Most people want to avoid burdening the beneficiaries of personal property bequests with the tax cost attributable to those bequests. Further, if tax is allocated to such bequests, a true hardship can be created because those beneficiaries may not have adequate cash to pay the tax. Finally, if very valuable personal property is involved, special considerations may have to be made. For example, the large personal property bequests could be required to bear their proportionate share of tax, and cash bequests or other arrangements could be made.

The marital or QTIP trust included in your Family Tax Planning Living Trust should generally bear the tax attributable to it on your spouse's death.

In most situations, where property is intended to pass to a charity qualifying for the estate tax charitable contribution deduction, taxes should not be allocated against those assets. If taxes are paid from those assets, there will be a "spoiler" effect in that the payment will reduce the assets passing to the charity. This is because the estate tax charitable contribution is based on the assets actually made available for charitable uses after the payment of any taxes. If this occurs, it will reduce the charitable contribution deduction and hence increase the overall tax due, resulting in a circular calculation. As a result of this, the typical state estate tax apportionment statute includes a general provision to consider the availability of deductions resulting from distributions to certain beneficiaries.

GST tax, if any is incurred in your Multigenerational Living Trust, should generally be allocated against the assets creating the GST tax, and not simply against the residuary estate.

Closely held business interests, planned for as part of your Comprehensive Living Trust Program, that could benefit from estate tax deferral or exclusion rules, should generally bear the burden of the tax payments attributable to the business so deferred.

GIFT GIVING AND YOUR LIVING TRUST

Since trustees under revocable living trusts can make gifts, you may have two persons making gifts: your trustee under your living trust and your agent under your power of attorney. Coordinate the gift-giving powers under your durable power of attorney and the gift-giving powers under your revocable living trust.

SAMPLE PROVISION: Gifts made under this authority, to each donee in any calendar year, shall not exceed the maximum amount that is excluded as a taxable gift under Code Section 2503(b) and 2503(e), or any successor statute, effective as of the date of any gift. Although this amount is presently limited to $10,000 ($20,000 for gifts split with Grantor's spouse) and amounts paid for educational or medical expenses (as defined under Code Section 2503(e)), Grantor understands that this amount may be changed by legislation and or indexing following the execution of this Power of Attorney and Grantor intends to have the power herein limited or expanded as necessary to conform with the maximum amounts so permitted in the year of any gift.

In addition, should Grantor qualify to make a contribution to a Education Investment Account (IRA) under Code Section 530, gifts may be made to such accounts on behalf of any Authorized Donee without reduction of the amounts permitted to be given above.

The gift power, as indicated, should not be limited to a flat $10,000 since this amount will be indexed. You may also wish to permit an additional $500 gift to an Educational IRA.

TREATING YOUR LIVING TRUST AS PART OF YOUR ESTATE

Certain qualified revocable living trusts can be treated as part of your estate if your executor elects to do so. For this election to be effective, the trustee of the revocable living trust must join the election with the executor. This may provide your executor with an opportunity to obtain some income tax benefits: claim a charitable contribution deduction for amounts permanently set aside for charitable purposes without the amounts having been first paid; waive the active participation requirement for passive loss limitation rules; and qualify for amortization of reforestation expenditures. There is no estate tax cost to making this election because the trust assets are included in the descendent's gross estate in any event.

The successor trustee of a revocable living trust can join with the executor of your estate to elect to have the trust assets treated as part of your estate if your executor elects to do so.

SAMPLE CLAUSE:

Trustee Decision Making and Authority

• *Trustee Election Concerning Revocable Living Trust and Grantor's Estate.*

The Trustee of this Revocable living trust may join the executor of Grantor's estate to elect to include this Trust Estate, or any portion hereof if permissible under applicable tax law including but not limited to Code Sections 646 and 2652(b)(1), in Grantor's estate. This election may be made in the Trustee's discretion in order to:

claim a charitable contribution deduction for amounts permanently set aside for charitable purposes prior to such amounts having been first paid; waive the active participation requirement for passive loss limitation rules; qualify for amortization of reforestation expenditures; or obtain any other tax or other benefit.

The generation-skipping transfer tax (GSTT) should not apply to a revocable living trust so long as the preceding election is in place. This result appears to follow from the fact that the definitions of a taxable distribution and termination for GST purposes require a trust. If this special election is made, then the assets involved are not considered to be in a trust while the election is effective. If, however, the trustee of the revocable trust (now irrevocable as a result of the grantor's death) transfers assets to new trusts (e.g., trusts for grandchildren provided for under the revocable trust), the special election may be terminated and the GST tax issues triggered.

CAN LIVING TRUSTS BE USED FOR A SPECIAL INCREASE IN TAX BASIS?

The general rule is that property held at death receives a step-up in tax basis from the decedent's tax basis to the fair market value at the date of death. Assume that the decedent had rental property worth $250,000, which was purchased for $150,000 and on which $70,000 of depreciation was claimed. The decedent's tax basis was $80,000 [$150,000 – $70,000]. However, on death the assets tax basis is increased (stepped-up) to its fair market value of $250,000. If the heirs sell the property, they will not have any capital gains to recognize. This concept applies whether the asset is held in the decedent's name directly or in a revocable living trust of the decedent.

These simple rules have been applied with a "twist" in an endeavor to secure an even greater tax benefit through revocable living trusts when married couples are involved. The objective of this twist is to obtain a step-up in all of the couple's assets no matter which spouse dies first. Normally, as in the preceding paragraph, a step-up would only be realized on the assets owned by the decedent.

Here's how the twist works. Each spouse creates a revocable living trust to own, say, one-half of the assets of the estate. Each living trust gives the other spouse (i.e., the husband's living trust grants to the wife) a general power of appointment. A general power of appointment can be a right to appoint assets to anyone, including yourself, or creditors of yours, or your estate or creditors of your estate. Thus, the husband's revocable living trust would grant to the wife a right to appoint the assets in the husband's revocable living trust to herself. Assume that the wife dies first. Because the wife has a general power of appointment over the assets in the husband's revocable living trust, these assets are all included in her taxable estate when she dies. The assets in husband's estate are argued to receive a step-up in tax basis on wife's death, and pass to the husband as the surviving spouse. Since the husband is a spouse, the unlimited marital deduction prevents estate tax. There are, however, serious doubts as to the viability of this approach. Has the surviving spouse, the husband in this example, taken an interest qualifying for the marital deduction? It does not appear that he has since he has always owned the assets involved. Similarly, the laws governing powers of appointment require inclusion in the taxable estate, and hence grant a step-up in basis if acquired through the exercise or nonexercise of a power of appointment. How meaningful can the power of appointment be if the husband could revoke his living trust at any time prior to the wife's death?

MISCELLANEOUS TAX ISSUES AFFECTING LIVING TRUSTS

Tax Year

Trusts must generally file tax returns using the calendar year (i.e., January to December). An estate can choose a fiscal year (any twelve-month period, such as March to February). This gives an estate more flexibility than a trust, which can provide tax savings opportunities.

Passive Losses

Passive losses and other losses of trusts are subject to more severe restrictions than losses by estates.

Related Party Transactions

An estate is not subject to the restrictions on deducting losses and deductions on related party transactions. A trust is subject to these rules.

Exemption

Trusts get a smaller personal exemption than estates. The tax exemption allowed to an estate is $600 while most trusts will only qualify for a $100 exemption.

SUMMARY

This chapter has explored some of the many ancillary tax issues pertaining to the use of living trusts.

21 ADDITIONAL LEGAL ISSUES

WHAT LEVEL OF COMPETENCY IS REQUIRED FOR A GRANTOR TO FORM A REVOCABLE LIVING TRUST?

The levels of competency (capacity) for signing (executing) a will and a revocable living trust are different. The standard that some courts have accepted for a person to sign a will requires the person signing to be aware of his or her descendants (called "bounty") and the extent of his or her assets. Thus, where a disabled or infirm person is perhaps incapable of signing a contract but does have sufficient capacity to sign a will, a will and not a living trust should be used. Testamentary capacity is the capacity or awareness that you must have to legally sign a will. This requires that you know the extent of your property. If you know that your property has value, it does not matter if you don't know the full value. You must also know the "natural objects of your bounty" (e.g., your family). You must understand the nature of the disposition of your assets. This is a lower or easier standard to meet than the standard required to sign a trust. A very low degree of intelligence will suffice for testamentary capacity to validly sign a will. This is a lesser degree of mental capacity than is required to enter into a contract or to manage a business. The fact that a testator can manage a business is evidence of testamentary capacity. You can even be ignorant of the practical effect of your will if you at least know what it says, and the will is valid.

Signing a trust requires the same capacity that you must have to sign any contract or execute a conveyance (e.g., a deed). If you have sufficient mental capacity to transfer assets to another person as a gift or by sale, then you have sufficient capacity to form a revocable trust and transfer the property to the trust. The same concept can be stated this way: if you have the capacity to transfer assets outside a trust you have capacity to transfer the assets in trust. If you are under a disability (e.g., infancy or insanity), any trust you execute, as well as transfers to it, would be void or voidable.

A revocable living trust can be challenged on the basis of undue influence, mental incompetency, or lack of independent advice of counsel. Incompetency can be established, for example, by the testimony of several physicians and others treating the person whose capacity is in question. The key concept is that the grantor did not understand the nature and effect of her act in signing the trust. The key question is whether the grantor had sufficient reason to understand the nature and effect of the act of forming the trust. Factors to consider include the grantor's age and health. The conduct of the person can be telling. Did the person talk intelligently; were his directions plain; was his mind clear? The fact of feeble health alone is not determinative.

SPOUSAL RIGHT OF ELECTION

What Is a Spousal Right of Election?

A spousal right of election, particularly as a result of the increases in second and later marriages and the growing divorce rate, can be important in determining how any decedent's assets will ultimately be distributed. The laws of almost every state recognize that the surviving spouse should be entitled to some minimum portion of the deceased spouse's estate. The rationale for this is that state legislatures believe that it is in the public's interest to protect surviving spouses. While many states assure the surviving spouse at least one-third of the estate, subject to various conditions, limitations, and other requirements, not all do.

The spousal right of election laws of a particular state generally apply to any married person who dies domiciled in that state. Determining the state of domicile is essential since the laws differ considerably from state to state. Domicile is generally defined as a place of permanent residence to which you ultimately intend to return. The determination as to which state a person is domiciled is a facts-and-circumstances analysis.

Not every surviving spouse is entitled to the protection of this rule. A surviving spouse may be denied the right of election where the couple was living separate and apart in different homes, or where the couple had ceased to cohabit as husband and wife under circumstances that would give rise to a cause of action for divorce (or nullification of the marriage) from the decedent, prior to death. Mere separation does not defeat the right of election.

Even if the right is available, it is not always obvious what it will amount to. In some states, any transfer under which the decedent retained the possession or enjoyment of, or right to income from, the property, at the time of death, enables the surviving spouse to elect against that property. A revocable living trust is such an asset.

How Does a Revocable Living Trust Affect the Spousal Right of Election?

Generally, a revocable living trust should not impact this right. The logical theory behind this result is that courts have viewed revocable living trusts, because of the control by the grantor, as illusory. Therefore, they have subjected assets of the trust to elective share rights. Surprisingly, depending on state law, it may be possible that the use of a revocable living trust could affect this important right. In some states, the surviving spouse may not have the right to elect against assets in a revocable living trust. The determination of who (e.g., a revocable living trust) should own an asset can affect the extent to which a surviving spouse may be able to exercise a spousal right of election to obtain a portion of that asset.

What Is a Surviving Spouse Typically Entitled to?

A typical state spousal right of election law guarantees the surviving spouse a one-third share of the estate. Not only may the percentage vary from state to state, but the definitions of what is included in the estate will vary considerably. Prior gifts may be included in the calculation; there may be subtractions for assets owned by or given to the surviving spouse; and so forth. Assets held in different types of trusts may be included or excluded, depending on the trust and state law. For example, an interest in a trust created by the decedent spouse during his lifetime may be excluded from the calculation of the estate against which the election can be made. If a trust is set up for the surviving spouse under the Will, such as a marital or QTIP trust under the deceased spouse's will for the benefit of the surviving spouse, it may be only partially counted. Another common right-of-election issue is to what extent property held in trust for the benefit of the surviving spouse will be counted toward meeting her elective share (the amount the surviving spouse is entitled to). In many states, property in trust is only counted at 50 percent in value. In some states, a life estate (the surviving spouse is given the right to use property, such as a house, but doesn't own it) and interests held in a trust do not qualify as satisfying the surviving spouse's right of election at all.

EXAMPLE: Husband dies in 2002 leaving a $2 million estate. $500,000 are joint assets that pass to the deceased husband's child from a prior marriage. The probate estate consists of $1.5 million of securities. The will leaves $800,000 in a marital trust, a QTIP, for his surviving spouse. The remaining $700,000 assets are distributed to a bypass trust, protected from estate tax by the applicable exclusion amount. The surviving spouse and the husband's children from a prior marriage are all beneficiaries of the bypass trust. Under state law, the bypass trust is included in the calculation of the estate but does not count as an asset paid to the surviving spouse. Under a typical state statute, assets in a QTIP trust will count 50 percent as meeting the spousal right of election. If insurance is included in the estate for calculating the spousal right of election under state law, then the surviving spouse has a right of election against a $2 million estate. A one-third elective share is $666,666. The only bequest that counts toward satisfying the spousal right of election is the QTIP trust of $800,000. This only counts at a 50 percent rate, or as if the surviving spouse received $400,000. Thus, the surviving spouse would be entitled to an additional $266,666 [$666,666 – $400,000] if she elects against the estate.

To prevent an end run around the spousal right of election laws, many state laws permit the surviving spouse to obtain a percentage of assets given away just before death. For example, some states include any transfer made within two years of death of the decedent to the extent that the aggregate transfer to any one donee in either of the years exceeds $3,000. However, if the surviving spouse gave a written consent to the transfer, or joined in the transfer, the property transferred may not be reached.

Another complication in applying the spousal right of election rules is that they often permit the surviving spouse to inherit a specified percentage of the value of the decedent's estate. Thus, all assets must be valued. If real estate or closely held business interests are involved, this can be complex and can lead to arguments between the surviving spouse and the beneficiaries named to receive the property under the decedent's will.

Be Certain That the Surviving Spouse Did Not Waive the Right

> **NOTE:** Too often, people execute documents without understanding their importance. This is the exact reason why most state statutes require that the spouse executing be fully informed and represented by counsel. Carefully ascertain what was signed. Some states, Connecticut as an example, appear to provide that if a payment was made "in lieu of the statutory share" the election won't be available. This may be more difficult to ascertain if an executed waiver did not accompany the payment.

In many situations, when the testator's will is to provide the surviving spouse less than the amount of the statutory election, the surviving spouse will be requested to formally waive his or her right of election. This is done specifically to prevent the surviving spouse from using the election to upset the dispositions provided for under the testator's will. The method of assuring that the dispositive scheme will be respected is to have the spouse waive her right of election. The waiver may be wholly or partially effective. It may be completed prior to, or after, the marriage. To be effective, the waiver of the right of election must meet specified requirements under state law. The rules will vary from state to state, but might include the following.

The waiver must be in the form of a written contract or agreement signed by the spouse waiving the right. The waiver will be effective only if there is full disclosure. It would be unfair for a spouse to be able to effectively waive his or her rights under state law without knowing the assets involved. How can you agree to forgo what you don't know? The waiver must be both clear and certain. A waiver in a prenuptial agreement or divorce property settlement agreement can be effective.

When you are serving as an executor, if the surviving spouse exerts her right of election, be certain to confirm whether a waiver ever was signed. If so, the next step is to consult with the estate's attorney to determine if the waiver is effective. Also, if the surviving spouse is provided less under the will than the spousal right of election would provide, you should not distribute assets of the estate until the issue of whether the election will be asserted is resolved.

INVESTMENT DECISIONS AND THE PRUDENT INVESTOR RULE

There is a tendency, probably attributable to the many consumer books and products touting the "simplicity" of living trusts, to treat living trusts rather informally. This is a risky attitude. State law requirements governing how trust funds can be invested apply to revocable living trusts. Thus, successor trustees (those taking over in the event of the death or disability of the grantor) must pay particular attention to the trust investments.

Investment language has often been ignored as boilerplate. Since no trust can carry out the grantor's wishes without having a proper investment strategy to assure distributions to the grantor during disability (when successor trustees must take over) and to successor beneficiaries (i.e. those after the grantor's death) this is a terrible mistake. You need to discuss in reasonable detail your goals for a trust, how money should be invested and distributed (investment provisions and distribution provisions are integrally related), and then modify provisions to meet your needs, or custom draft provisions to address your concerns. These matters can add substantially to the complexity, time requirement, and cost of preparing a trust. Failing to do so, however, can be even more costly. It is imperative to analyze and coordinate investment and distribution provisions of your trust, and to be certain that they all reflect your goals for the trust.

State Law Affects Investment Standards

When considering how trust assets should be invested, you should consider the law applicable in your state. State laws governing investment of trust (and estate) assets are in transition and can vary widely. The modern trend appears to be the enactment of the Uniform Prudent Investor Act, or something similar. The Uniform Act was prepared by the National Conference of Commissioners on Uniform State Laws. The general rule is that a trustee investing and managing asset owes a duty to the beneficiaries of the trust to comply with the prudent investor rule as defined by your state's laws.

The prudent investor rule is a default rule that may be expanded, restricted, eliminated, or otherwise altered by express provisions of the trust instrument. Thus, reading state law in isolation is insufficient. You must interpret, as trustee, both state law and the trust agreement and how they interact. If you are contemplating establishing a trust, you should consider what aspects of your state's law you might want to modify in your trust agreement. Because the laws of so many states are changing, or may change in the near future, it is best to err on the side of addressing investment matters at length in your trust agreement.

The prudent investor rule, in its various forms in various states, is changing dramatically the view of how investments of trust, estate, and other assets should be made. The trend is to apply the standard of determining investment prudence to the portfolio as a whole, rather than to individual securities. Thus, investing in any particular type of security will, in states adopting this modern view, no longer be deemed imprudent. However, if the grantor prohibited investing in a particular type of security, such as derivatives or options, in the trust agreement, the trustee will still be bound to that restriction. This is why it is so important for grantors to assure that the trust reflects their wishes, and for trustees to study the trust agreement's investment provisions.

The trade-off between risk and return is a central consideration of the trustee's investments. No class or type of security is per se not permissible if it fits within the overall investment plan and is, as part of such plan, prudent. Assets will have to be diversified (modern portfolio theory) unless a specific reason not to is present. If you want a particular investment to be retained, such as a family business, you must state that you do and provide guidelines as to when it can be sold.

Delegation of Investment Management

Investment management can and should be delegated where the fiduciary does not have requisite skills. The revised rule results in trustees having to formulate a comprehensive investment plan for each trust based on the facts and circumstances affecting that trust, including expected distributions, inflation, and so forth. While these simple sounding goals make the important step toward conforming fiduciary investment standards to those of the general investment community, many thorny issues and problems must be addressed by grantors establishing trusts, beneficiaries of estates and trusts, trustees of trusts, executors of estates, attorneys, accountants and investment advisers advising all of the preceding. As this area of the law continues to evolve, you are best protected by consulting periodically with your trust and estate adviser to be certain you understand any pertinent changes.

Asset Allocation

Diversification of the trust's investments through asset allocation is an essential component in any thorough trust investment plan. Asset allocation can address many important estate planning goals, including:

- Minimizing the risk investment assets are exposed to, thus giving greater security to the estate.
- Improving total return on trust assets; thus, over the long term, maximizing income and capital gains and asset values.
- Providing direction and guidance to trustees where the trust document indicates the grantor's risk tolerance and investment philosophy.

What is asset allocation? It is the process of identifying the asset classes in which a particular investor will invest, and then allocating the investor's capital to those asset classes through an analysis of rates of return and risk tolerance. The basis of this is modern portfolio theory. The investor must provide his or her personal guidance to the financial planner or money manager as to "How much risk are you willing to endure to achieve the return you desire?"

Modern portfolio theory, in general terms, assumes that the investment markets are efficient. Therefore, deciding which asset categories to allocate investor capital is more critical than picking specific assets (e.g., stocks) within any particular category. Selecting asset categories with negative correlation (i.e., when one rises the other tends to fall) can minimize risk while achieving the desired level of return. The relationship of asset categories can be indicated by their correlation. A correlation of +1.0 indicates assets whose values move in perfect tandem. A correlation of −1.0 indicates assets whose values move in opposite directions. The technical term *covariance* is used to describe the relationship between asset categories. Covariance is a measure of the likelihood of the assets to move in the same direction and the momentum of their likely movements.

Studies have demonstrated that more than 90 percent of the risk of a portfolio can be explained by the allocation of assets. Where a portfolio is diversified among asset categories, approximately 90 percent of the risk can be viewed as market risk, while only 10 percent or less of the risk of that portfolio will be specific risk of a particular stock.

Through an analysis of the covariance of particular assets and the expected return of those assets, a portfolio can be constructed that theoretically minimizes the risk faced by the investor attempting to achieve any particular level of return. By optimizing this relationship, in theory, an investor could earn greater returns than on his or her present portfolio while reducing risk.

Finally, in identifying and investing in asset categories, the categories should reflect the diverse global economy and not merely U.S. equity markets.

Modern portfolio theory holds that with investments, the more mundane but statistically proven superior method of allocating assets and committing to long-range strategies is preferable to market manipulation, timing, and individual security picking. However, if you are setting up a trust and want the trustees to pursue a different approach, be certain to modify the boilerplate investment provisions to state your objectives.

Factors the Trustee Should Consider

What Investment Goals Does the Trust Indicate?

The trustee must invest and manage trust assets as a prudent investor would considering the purposes, terms, distribution requirements, and other circumstances of the trust. To do this, however, the trust should provide some clear directions. Many trusts do not, instead relying on general and vague provisions. To best assure that your beneficiaries are treated as you wish and that your other goals are carried out, you must provide some meaningful guidance to the trustees. Also, the guidance you provide should be flexible enough to enable the trustees to deal with circumstances that may be unforeseeable at the time you complete the trust. If your directives are too specific (e.g., "The trustee shall never sell the family business"), you may create far worse problems than imagined. If you wish that consideration be given to retaining the family business interests so long as any family members work in the business, or may work in the business within five years, indicate this in the trust agreement. This latter approach is more specific, provides clearer guidance, and most importantly, gives the trustee flexibility to sell the business if your real objective, family employment, is not being presently met and is unlikely to be met in the foreseeable future.

How Is the Trustee's Performance to Be Evaluated?

The trustee's investment performance will be evaluated in the context of the trust portfolio as a whole and as part of an overall investment strategy having risk and return objectives reasonably suited to the trust. The trustee is authorized to invest in any type of asset. No specific investment or course of action is inherently imprudent. The trustee is generally directed to take reasonable steps to ascertain facts and circumstances relevant to the investment and management of trust assets. The trustee is permitted to rely on statistical, financial, corporate, or other information as to investment decisions.

Can the Trustee Reconcile Prudent Investor Rule Diversification with Special Trust Objectives?

The trustee is required to diversify the investments of the trust unless it is reasonably determined that because of special circumstances this is not preferable. This creates a potentially difficult situation for many types of trusts. If a successor trustee takes over management of a revocable living trust because of the temporary disability of the grantor, should the successor trustee conform the trust investments so that they comply with the applicable prudent investor act? What if the grantor regains capacity and again takes over asset management?

Factors Affecting Trust Investments for Specific Trusts in the Complete Living Trusts Program

When determining how to invest trust assets, it is not as simple as taking into account the best asset mix to meet beneficiary investment needs as discussed earlier. The first step in all instances must be to thoroughly understand any requirements of the trust instrument. You must determine whether you have the expertise to properly analyze the will or specific trust for which you are to provide investment advice. For example, the trust may be vague with respect to distributions and simply provide for distribution in the absolute discretion of the trustee for the term of the trust (e.g., until the child/beneficiary reaches a specified age). It is becoming more common, however, for trusts to be more specialized and more narrowly drafted. One of the most common trends is the increasing use of total return trusts. These trusts recognize the conflict created by the majority of trusts that focus on distribution of income to a current income beneficiary. Such a concept implies a requirement to generate current cash income, rather than capital appreciation. Because total return (income consisting of dividend and interest as well as capital gains) is the modern investment goal, more trusts are being drafted in a manner that requires a distribution each year, typically in monthly installments in arrears, of a specified percentage, say 5 percent (5%) of trust principal as of January 1 of each year.

> The Trustee shall pay an amount equal to 6 percent (6%) of the net fair market value of the Trust assets valued as of the first day of each tax year of the Trust (except as otherwise provided herein). Said amount shall be paid in equal monthly installments on the last day of each month during such year.

Some trusts provide more guidance as to investment horizon by indicating objectives for trust distributions, and so forth. When the trust document provides a more specific or modern standard for investments and distributions, it is important to consider these parameters when you formulate an investment strategy. Many trusts for which you begin to provide investment advisory services may have been created many years ago before much attention was paid to investment provisions. In these instances, it is possible that the investment clauses may not adequately address the breadth and scope of investment opportunities.

COMMUNITY PROPERTY

Generally, all property acquired by a husband and wife during their marriage, while they are domiciled in one of the community property states belongs to each of the marriage partners, share and share alike. They share not only in the physical property acquired but also in the income from the property and their salaries, wages, and other compensation for services. At the same time, each may have separate property. They may also hold property between them in joint tenancy and generally may adjust between themselves their community and separate property (i.e., use a transmutation agreement). Couples can state prior to marriage via a prenuptial agreement that they will not be bound by the community property laws of their state of domicile.

Generally, community property assets retain that character even after the parties have moved to a non-community-property state, unless the parties themselves are able to adjust their rights between themselves. This is important when you are determining your actions with respect to the assets held. For example, your restructuring of title to any assets presently owned individually or in joint name could affect this characteristic. Therefore, consideration of the caveats (independent and specialized counsel) should be made before proceeding. In particular, in the event of a future divorce, the steps taken by either/both of you now with respect to the title to your assets could affect your retention of assets at such time.

Real estate, should you acquire ownership of any, will generally retain the form of ownership assigned to it. Real estate in a community property state acquired by either spouse while married may be treated as community property without regard to the domicile or residence of the spouses. It is the law of the situs of the real estate that determines whether the income therefrom is community property.

Property acquired before marriage retains the form of ownership it had when acquired—separate, joint, or other. Property acquired during the marriage by gift or inheritance by one of the parties retains the character in which it was acquired. Property purchased with community property is community property, and property purchased with separate property is separate property. Property purchased with commingled community and separate property, so that the two cannot be separated, is community property.

The implications of the preceding paragraphs is that it could be important to further analyze your assets to determine which, if any, could be subject to a community property status.

Community property is included in the estate of the first to die only to the extent of the decedent's interest, generally, half of its value and that half will be subject to probate. Transfers of community property between spouses qualify for the marital deduction.

A spouse's separate property consists of:

- Property owned by the spouse before marriage.
- Property acquired by the spouse during marriage by gift, devise, or descent.
- The recovery for personal injury sustained by the spouse during marriage, except the recovery for loss of earning ability during marriage.

Community property is the property, other than separate property, acquired by either spouse during the marriage. The presumption of holding community property exists if property was held by either spouse during or upon the dissolution of the marriage.

A spouse may record separate property in the county where he or she resides and where real estate is situated. A spouse has the sole management, control, and disposition of her or his separate property. Each spouse has the sole management, control, and disposition of the community property that he or she would have owned if unmarried. If mixed community property that is subject to the sole management, control, and disposition of one spouse with community property subject to the sole management, control, and disposition of the other spouse, then the combined or mixed community property is subject to the joint management, control and disposition of the spouses.

On the death of one spouse, all property belonging to the community estate of the husband and wife vests in the surviving spouse if there are no children of the deceased spouse or descendants of the children. If there is a child, as at present (or possibly children of the deceased spouse or descendants of these children), then the surviving spouse is entitled to one-half of the community property and the other one-half of the community property vests in the children or their descendants.

SUMMARY

This chapter has highlighted several of the complex legal issues that can affect your living trust. The best approach is one of caution. If a legal issue arises, consult with an attorney expert in the area. In most cases, you should address the issue as early on as possible.

INDEX